Sixth Workshop on Privacy in Natural Language Processing (PrivateNLP 2025)

Albuquerque, New Mexico, USA
4 May 2025

ISBN: 979-8-3313-1926-7

Printed from e-media with permission by:

Curran Associates, Inc.
57 Morehouse Lane
Red Hook, NY 12571

Some format issues inherent in the e-media version may also appear in this print version.

Association for Computational Linguistics
209 N. Eighth Street
Stroudsburg, Pennsylvania 18360

Phone: 1-570-476-8006
Fax: 1-570-476-0860

acl@aclweb.org

Additional copies of this publication are available from:

Curran Associates, Inc.
57 Morehouse Lane
Red Hook, NY 12571 USA
Phone: 845-758-0400
Fax: 845-758-2633
Email: curran@proceedings.com
Web: www.proceedings.com

PrivateNLP 2025

The Sixth Workshop on Privacy in Natural Language Processing

Proceedings of the Workshop

April 4, 2025

Introduction

Welcome to the Sixth Workshop on Privacy in Natural Language Processing. Co-located with NAACL 2025 in Albuquerque (NM), USA, the workshop is scheduled for April 4, 2025. To facilitate the participation of the global NLP community, we continue running the workshop in a hybrid format.

Privacy-preserving language data processing has become essential in the age of Large Language Models (LLMs) where access to vast amounts of data can provide gains over tuned algorithms. A large proportion of user-contributed data comes from natural language e.g., text transcriptions from voice assistants. It is therefore important to curate NLP datasets while preserving the privacy of the users whose data is collected, and train ML models that only retain non-identifying user data. The workshop brings together practitioners and researchers from academia and industry to discuss the challenges and approaches to designing, building, verifying, and testing privacy preserving systems in the context of Natural Language Processing.

Our agenda features a keynote speech, hybrid talk sessions both for long and short papers, and a poster session. This year we received 13 submissions. We accepted 9 submissions after a thorough peer-review. One accepted submissions has been withdrawn by the authors.

We would like to deeply thank to all the authors, committee members, keynote speaker, and participants to help us make this research community grow both in quantity and quality.

Workshop Chairs

Organizing Committee

Program Chairs

Ivan Habernal, Ruhr-University Bochum, Germany
Sepideh Ghanavati, University of Maine, United States
Vijayanta Jain, University of Maine, United States
Timour Igamberdiev, University of Vienna, Austria
Shomir Wilson, Pennsylvania State University, United States

Program Committee

Reviewers

Gergely Acs, Technical University of Budapest
Stefan Arnold, Friedrich-Alexander-Universität
Andrea Atzeni, Polytechnic Institute of Turin
Travis Breaux, Carnegie Mellon University
Christos Dimitrakakis, Université de Neuchâtel, University of Oslo and Chalmers University
Natasha Fernandes, Macquarie University
James Flemings, University of Southern California
Pierre Lison, Norwegian Computing Center
Christina Lohr, Universität Leipzig
Eugenio Martínez-Cámara, Universidad de Jaén
Stephen Meisenbacher, Technische Universität München
Isar Nejadgholi, National Research Council Canada and University of Ottawa
Sebastian Ochs, Technische Universität Darmstadt
Sai Teja Peddinti, Google
Lizhen Qu, Monash University
Afsaneh Razi, Drexel University
Peter Story, Clark University
David Sánchez, Universitat Rovira i Virgili
Ruyu Zhou, University of Notre Dame

Table of Contents

TUNI: A Textual Unimodal Detector for Identity Inference in CLIP Models

Songze Li[1,*,†], Ruoxi Cheng[1,*], Xiaojun Jia[2]

Abstract

The widespread usage of large-scale multimodal models like CLIP has heightened concerns about the leakage of PII. Existing methods for identity inference in CLIP models require querying the model with full PII, including textual descriptions of the person and corresponding images (e.g., the name and the face photo of the person). However, applying images may risk exposing personal information to target models, as the image might not have been previously encountered by the target model. Additionally, previous MIAs train shadow models to mimic the behaviors of the target model, which incurs high computational costs, especially for large CLIP models. To address these challenges, we propose a textual unimodal detector (TUNI) in CLIP models, a novel technique for identity inference that: 1) only utilizes text data to query the target model; and 2) eliminates the need for training shadow models. Extensive experiments of TUNI across various CLIP model architectures and datasets demonstrate its superior performance over baselines, albeit with only text data.

1 Introduction

Recent years have witnessed a rapid development of large-scale multimodal models, such as Contrastive Language–Image Pre-training (CLIP) (Radford et al., 2021). These models synthesize information across different modalities, particularly text and images, facilitating applications from automated image generation to sophisticated visual question answering systems. Despite their potential, these models pose significant privacy risks (Inan et al., 2021; Carlini et al., 2021; Leino and Fredrikson, 2020; Rigaki and Garcia, 2023; Helbling et al., 2023; Rahman et al., 2024; Rahman, 2023) as the vast datasets used for training often contain personally identifiable information (PII) (Schwartz and Solove, 2011; Abadi et al., 2016; Bonawitz et al., 2017), raising concerns (Xi et al., 2024) about PII leakage and misuse (Hu et al., 2023; Yin et al., 2021). Therefore, it is extremely important to develop tools to detect potential PII leakage from CLIP models. Specially, as the first step, we would like to address the identity inference problem, i.e., to determine if the PII of a particular person was used in training of a target CLIP model.

Traditional methods, like Membership Inference Attacks (MIAs) (Shokri et al., 2017), have focused on determining whether a specific data sample was used for model training. When applied to CLIP models, these approaches typically involve querying the model with both texts and images of the target individual (Ko et al., 2023), and exposing images of a person the CLIP model may have not seen in the training set brings new privacy leakage risk (He et al., 2022). Hence, it is desirable to have a detection mechanism for ID inference that *does not query the CLIP model with real images of the person* (see an example in Figure 1). Furthermore, traditional MIAs often rely on constructing shadow models that mimic the behaviors of the target model to obtain training data to construct attack models (Hu et al., 2022a), which demands extensive computational resources and is less feasible in environments with limited computational capabilities (Mattern et al., 2023; Hisamoto et al., 2020; Jagielski et al., 2024). Alternative methods for shadow models in MIAs, such as those based on cosine similarity (Ko et al., 2023) and self-influence functions (Cohen and Giryes, 2024), exhibit either lower accuracy or still necessitate substantial computational resources (Oh et al., 2023).

To address these limitations, we propose a textual unimodel detector (TUNI) for identity inference in CLIP models, which queries the target model with only text information during inference.

*Contributed equally to this work. [1]Southeast University, Nanjing China. [2]Nanyang Technological University, Singapore. †Corresponding authors: songzeli@seu.edu.cn.

Proceedings of the Sixth Workshop on Privacy in Natural Language Processing, pages 1–13
April 4, 2025

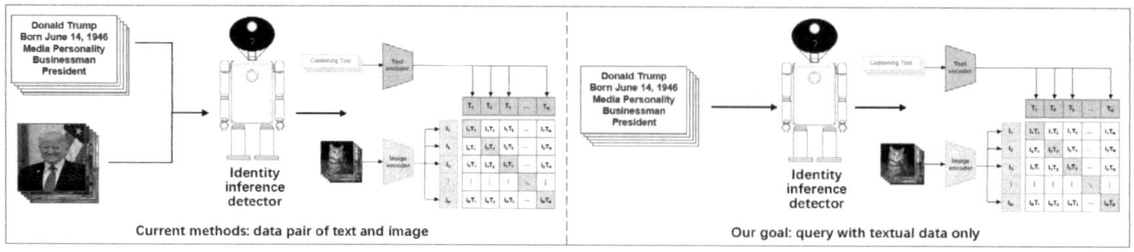

Figure 1: Current methods query LLMs with both text and image, while our goal is to conduct identity inference with only textual data.

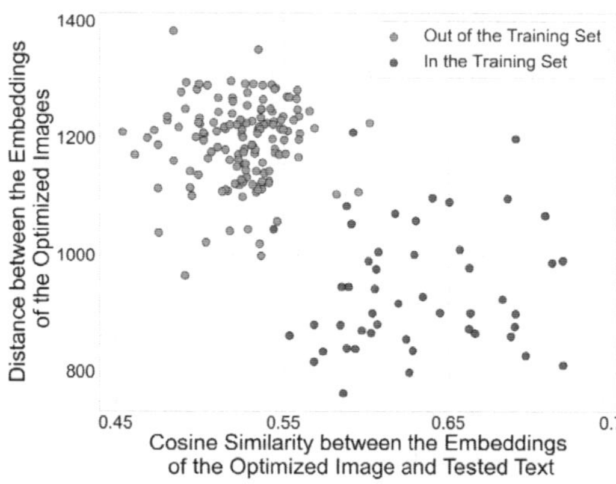

Figure 2: Features of textual descriptions extracted from the optimized images guided by a CLIP model with ResNet50x4 architecture, trained on a dataset where each person has 75 images. The cosine similarity between the embeddings of optimized image and the tested text, and the distance between the embeddings of the optimized images, can clearly distinguish between the samples within and outside the training dataset of the target CLIP model.

Specifically, we first propose a feature extractor, which maps a textual description to a feature vector through image optimization guided by the CLIP model; then, we randomly generate a large amount of textual gibberish, which we know do not match any textual descriptions in the training dataset. As shown in Figure 2, we make the key observation that the feature distributions of textual gibberish and member samples in the training set are well distinguishable.

Leveraging this property, we use the feature vectors of the generated textual gibberish to train multiple anomaly detectors to form an anomaly detection voting system. At test time, TUNI simply feeds the feature vector of the test text to the voting system, and determines that if the corresponding PII is included in the training set (abnormal) or not (normal). The training of the anomaly detector in TUNI costs only several hours with four NVIDIA GeForce RTX 3090 GPUs, avoiding training shadow models with the size of the CLIP model in traditional MIAs, which can cost over 18 days even with hundreds of advanced GPUs (Gu et al., 2022; Ko et al., 2023; Hu et al., 2022b).

Our contributions are summarized as follows:

- We propose a textual unimodal detector, dubbed *TUNI*, which is the first method to conduct identity inference in CLIP models with unimodal data, preventing risky exposure of images to the target model;
- We find that the feature distributions of texts that are in and out of the target CLIP model are well separated, and propose to adopt randomly generated text to train anomaly detectors for ID inference, avoiding the need for computationally intensive shadow models in traditional MIAs.
- Extensive experiments conducted across six kinds of CLIP models have indicated that the proposed TUNI achieves better performance than current methods for identity inference, even when using only textual data.

2 Related Work

2.1 Privacy Leakage in CLIP Models

CLIP model exemplifies modern multimodal innovation by integrating an image encoder and a text encoder into its architecture (Radford et al., 2021). These encoders transform inputs into a shared embedding space, enabling effective measurement of semantic similarity (Ramesh et al., 2022). Despite the significant advances and expansive applicability of CLIP models, the vast and diverse datasets utilized for training such models could potentially include sensitive information, raising concerns about privacy leakage (Hu et al., 2022b). Various inference attacks, including model stealing (Dziedzic et al., 2022; Liu et al., 2022; Wu et al., 2022), knowledge stealing (Liang et al., 2022), data stealing (He and Zhang, 2021), and membership inference attacks (Liu et al., 2021; Ko et al., 2023), have been developed for CLIP, exposing potential vulnerability in privacy leakage. These privacy concerns underscore the necessity for developing robust defense mechanisms to safeguard sensitive information in CLIP models (Golatkar et al., 2022; Jia et al., 2023; Huang et al., 2023).

2.2 Personally Identifiable Information and Leakage Issues

Personally Identifiable Information (PII) is defined as any data that can either independently or when combined with other information, identify an individual. Training Large Language Models (LLMs) often utilizes publicly accessible datasets, which may inadvertently contain PII. This elevates the risk of data breaches that could compromise individual privacy and entail severe legal and reputational consequences for the deploying entities (Lukas et al., 2023; Abadi et al., 2016; Bonawitz et al., 2017; Rahman et al., 2020; Shamshad et al., 2023). Various attacks have been developed to reveal PII from LLMs. A method is proposed in (Panda et al., 2024) to steal private information from LLMs via crafting specific queries to GPT-4 that can reveal sensitive data by appending a secret suffix to the generated text; Zhang et al. introduced the ETHICIST method for targeted training data extraction, through loss smoothed soft prompting and calibrated confidence estimation, significantly improving extraction performance on public benchmarks (Zhang et al., 2023); Carlini et al. also studied training data extraction from LLMs, emphasizing the predictive capability of attacks given a prefix (Carlini et al., 2021); ProPILE, proposed in (Kim et al., 2024), probes privacy leakage in LLMs, by assessing the leakage risk of PII included in the publicly available Pile dataset; Inan et al. investigated the risks associated with membership inference attacks using a Reddit dataset, further emphasizing the persistent threat of PII leakage in various data environments (Inan et al., 2021).

2.3 Current Identity Inference Methods and Their Limitations

Identity inference, critical in privacy preserving data analysis, has garnered significant attention across domains, such as genomic data (Erlich et al., 2018), location-based spatial queries (Kalnis et al., 2007), person re-identification scenarios (Karaman and Bagdanov, 2012), computer-mediated communication (Motahari et al., 2009)and face recognition (Zhou and Lam, 2018; Prince et al., 2011; Sanderson and Lovell, 2009). Membership Inference Attacks (MIAs), which determine if specific data points were in a model's training dataset, can be used to perform identity inference. Traditional MIAs often require constructing shadow models to mimic the target model's behavior, posing computational efficiency challenges for large models (Truex et al., 2019; Ye et al., 2022; Meeus et al., 2023; Xue et al., 2023).

While identity inference has been mainly performed on unimodal models, it is recently extended to CLIP models. Identity Detection Inference Attack (IDIA) (Hintersdorf et al., 2022) does not need shadow models; it involves providing real photos of the tested individual and 1000 prompt templates including the real name to choose from. The attacker generates multiple queries by substituting the <NAME> placeholder and analyzes the model's responses to calculate an attack score based on correct predictions. If the correct name is predicted for a threshold number of templates, the individual is inferred to be in the training data. Cosine Similarity Attacks (CSA) (Ko et al., 2023) uses cosine similarity (CS) between image and text features to infer membership, as CLIP is trained to maximize CS for training samples. Based on CSA, Weak Supervision Attack (WSA) uses a new weak supervision MIA framework with unilateral non-member information for enhancement. Both IDIA and WSA avoid the high costs associated with shadow models, but require querying the target model with real images the model may have never seen, raising new privacy concerns.

3 Methodology

3.1 Problem Setup and Threat Model

Consider a CLIP model M trained on a dataset D_{train}. Each sample $s_i = (t_i, x_i)$ in D_{train} records the personally identifiable information (PII) of an individual person, and consists of a textual description t_i (e.g., name of the person) and a corresponding image x_i (e.g., face photo of the person). For distinct indices $i \neq j$, it is possible that $t_i = t_j$ and $x_i \neq x_j$, indicating that multiple non-identical images of the same person may exist.

A detector would like to probe potential leakage of a person's PII through the target CLIP model M, via conducting an identity inference task against

M, to determine if any PII samples of this person were included in the training set D_{train}.

Detector's Goal. For a person with textual description t, a detector would like to determine whether there exits a PII sample $(t_i, x_i) \in D_{\text{train}}$, such that $t_i = t$.

Note that rather than detecting for a particular text-image pair (t, x), our goal is to detect existence of *any* (one or more) pair with a textual description of t. This is because that multiple images of the same person can be used for training, and any one of these images may lead to potential PII leakage.

Detector's Knowledge and Capability. The detector can query M and observe the output, including extracted image and text embeddings as well as their matching score, but does not know the model architecture of M, the parameter values, or the training algorithms. For the target textual description t, depending on the application scenarios, the detector may or may not have actual images corresponding to t. *Nevertheless, in the case where the detector knows corresponding images, due to privacy concerns, it cannot include them in the queries to* M. The detector cannot modify M or access its internal state.

3.2 TUNI: Textual Unimodal Detector for ID Inference

We design a textual unimodal detector for ID inference (TUNI), to determine whether the PII of a person is in the training set of the target CLIP model M, with the restriction that only the textual description of the person can be exposed to M. Firstly, for a textual description t, we develop a feature extractor to map t to a feature vector, through image optimization guided by the CLIP model. Then, we make the key observation that *textual gibberish like "D2;l-NOXRT"—random combinations of numbers and symbols clearly do not match any textual descriptions in the training set*, and hence the detector can generate large amount of textual gibberish that are known out of D_{train}. Using feature vectors extracted from these textual gibberish, the detector can train multiple anomaly detectors to form an anomaly detection voting system. Finally, during the inference phase, the features of the target textual description are fed into the system, and the inference result is determined through voting. Additionally, when the actual images of the textual description is available to the detector, they can be leverage to perform clustering on the feature vectors of the test samples to further enhance detection performance. An overview of the proposed TUNI framework is shown in Figure 3.

Algorithm 1: CLIP-guided Feature Extraction

Input: Target CLIP model M, textual description t
Output: Mean optimized cosine similarity S, standard deviation of optimized image embeddings D

$n \leftarrow$ number of epochs
$m \leftarrow$ number of optimization iterations per epoch
$\mathcal{S} \leftarrow \emptyset$, $\mathcal{V} \leftarrow \emptyset$
$v_t \leftarrow M(t)$ ▷ Obtain text embedding from M
for $i = 1$ **to** n **do**
  $x_0 \leftarrow$ Rand() ▷ Randomly generate an initial image
  for $j = 0$ **to** $m - 1$ **do**
    $v_{x_j} \leftarrow M(x_j)$ ▷ Obtain image embedding from M
    $x_{j+1} \leftarrow \arg\max_{x_j} \frac{v_t \cdot v_{x_j}}{\|v_t\| \|v_{x_j}\|}$ ▷ Update image to maximize cosine similarity
  end for
  $S_i \leftarrow \frac{v_t \cdot v_{x_m}}{\|v_t\| \|v_{x_m}\|}$ ▷ Optimized similarity for epoch i
  $\mathcal{S} \leftarrow \mathcal{S} \cup \{S_i\}$, $\mathcal{V} \leftarrow \mathcal{V} \cup \{v_{x_m}\}$
end for
$S \leftarrow \frac{1}{n} \sum_{S_i \in \mathcal{S}} S_i$
$\bar{v} \leftarrow \frac{1}{n} \sum_{v \in \mathcal{V}} v$
$D \leftarrow \sqrt{\frac{1}{n} \sum_{v \in \mathcal{V}} \|v - \bar{v}\|^2}$
return S, D

Feature Extraction through CLIP-guided Image Optimization. The feature extraction for a textual description t involves iterative optimization of an image x, to maximize the correlation between the embeddings of t and x out of the target CLIP model. The extraction process, described in Algorithm 1, iterates for n epochs; and within each epoch, an image is optimized for m iterations, to maximize the cosine similarity between its embedding of the CLIP model and that of the target textual description. The average optimized cosine similarity S and standard deviation of the optimized image embeddings D are extracted as the features of t from model M.

Generation of Textual Gibberish. TUNI starts the detection process with generating a set of ℓ gibberish strings $\mathcal{G} = \{g_1, g_2, \ldots, g_\ell\}$, which are random combinations of digits and symbols with certain length. As these gibberish texts are randomly generated at the inference time, with overwhelming probability that they did not appear in

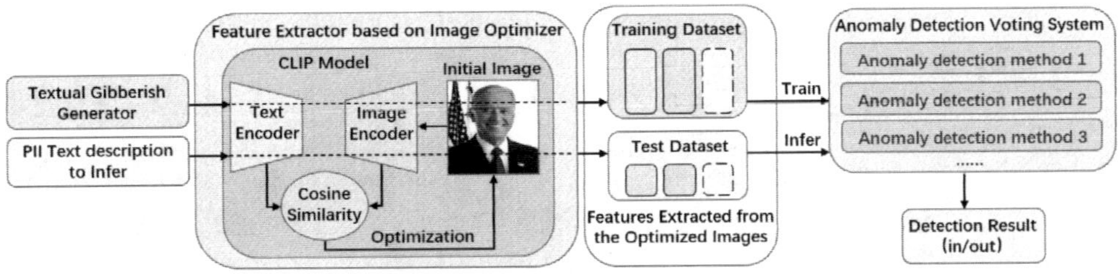

Figure 3: Overview of TUNI.

the training set. Applying the proposed feature extraction algorithm on $\mathcal{G}$, we obtain ℓ feature vectors $\mathcal{F} = \{f_1, f_2, \ldots, f_\ell\}$ of the gibberish texts.

Training Anomaly Detectors. Motivated by the observations in Figure 2 that the feature vectors of the texts that are in and out of the training set of M are well separated, we propose to train an anomaly detector using $\mathcal{F}$, such that texts out of D_{train} are considered "normal", and the problem of ID inference on textual description t is converted to anomaly detection on the feature vector of t. More specifically, t is detected to be in D_{train}, if its feature vector is detected "abnormal" by the trained anomaly detector. Specifically in TUNI, we train several anomaly detection models on $\mathcal{F}$, such as Isolation Forest, LocalOutlierFactor (Cheng et al., 2019) and AutoEncoder (Chandola et al., 2009). These models constitute an anomaly detection voting system that will be used for ID inference on the test textual descriptions.

Textual ID Inference through Voting. For each textual description t in the test set, TUNI first extracts its feature vector f using Algorithm 1, and then feeds f to each of the obtained anomaly detectors to cast a vote on whether t is an anomaly. When the total number of votes exceeds a predefined detetion threshold N, t is determined as an anomaly, i.e., PII with textual description t is used to train the CLIP model M; otherwise, t is considered normal and no PII with t is leaked through training of M.

Enhancement with Real Images. At inference time, if real images of the test texts are available at the detector (e.g., photos of a person), they can be used to extract an additional feature measuring the average distance between the embeddings of real images and those of optimized images using the CLIP model, using which the feature vectors of the test texts can be clustered into two partitions with one in D_{train} and another one out of D_{train}. This adds an additional vote for each test text to the above described anomaly detection voting system, potentially facilitating the detection accuracy.

Specifically, for each test text t, the detector is equipped with a set of c real images $\{x^1_{\text{real}}, x^2_{\text{real}}, \ldots, x^c_{\text{real}}\}$. Similar to the feature extraction process in Algorithm 1, over k epochs with independent initializations, k optimized images $\{x^1_{\text{opt}}, x^2_{\text{opt}}, \ldots, x^k_{\text{opt}}\}$ for t are obtained under the guidance of the CLIP model. Then, we apply a pretrained feature extraction model F (e.g., DeepFace (Taigman et al., 2014) for face images) to the real and optimized images to obtain real embeddings $\{v^1_{\text{real}}, v^2_{\text{real}}, \ldots, v^c_{\text{real}}\}$ and optimized embeddings $\{v^1_{\text{opt}}, v^2_{\text{opt}}, \ldots, v^k_{\text{opt}}\}$. Finally, we compute average pair-wise ℓ_2 distance between real and optimized embeddings, denoted by R, over $c \cdot k$ pairs, and use R as an additional feature of the text t.

For a batch of B test texts $(t_1, t_2, \ldots, t_B)$, we start with extracting their features $((S_1, D_1, R_1), (S_2, D_2, R_2), \ldots, (S_B, D_B, R_B))$. Feeding the first two features S_i and D_i into the trained anomaly detection system, each text t_i obtains an anomaly score as the number of anomaly detectors who believe that it is abnormal. Additional, the K-means algorithm with $K = 2$ is performed on the feature vectors $\{(S_i, D_i, R_i)\}_{i=1}^{B}$ to partition them into a "normal" cluster and an "abnormal" cluster, adding another vote on the anomaly score of each test instance. Then, the ID inference of each text is performed by comparing its total number of received votes and a detection threshold N'.

4 Evaluations

We evaluate the performance of TUNI, for the task of ID inference from the name of a person, with the corresponding image being the face photo of the person.

4.1 Setup

Our experiments leverage datasets and target CLIP models from (Hintersdorf et al., 2022).

Table 1: Performance comparison with baseline methods across different CLIP models. Δ indicates the improvement of TUNI.

Architecture	Number of photos per person in training set	Method	Precision	Δ	Recall	Δ	Accuracy	Δ
ResNet-50	1	WSA	0.6653 ± 0.0032	0.1979	0.2925 ± 0.0045	0.6896	0.6675 ± 0.0037	0.2497
		IDIA	0.6922 ± 0.0023	0.1712	0.4032 ± 0.0027	0.5789	0.6836 ± 0.0034	0.2336
		TUNI	**0.8634 ± 0.0031**	-	**0.9821 ± 0.0042**	-	**0.9172 ± 0.0028**	-
	75	WSA	0.6625 ± 0.0018	0.2017	0.2867 ± 0.0061	0.6968	0.6710 ± 0.0043	0.2322
		IDIA	0.6901 ± 0.0024	0.1741	0.3998 ± 0.0049	0.5837	0.6907 ± 0.0075	0.2125
		TUNI	**0.8642 ± 0.0057**	-	**0.9835 ± 0.0019**	-	**0.9032 ± 0.0033**	-
ResNet-50x4	1	WSA	0.6712 ± 0.0029	0.1901	0.2912 ± 0.0048	0.6835	0.6808 ± 0.0031	0.2547
		IDIA	0.6625 ± 0.0036	0.1963	0.3980 ± 0.0031	0.5267	0.6957 ± 0.0029	0.2398
		TUNI	**0.8613 ± 0.0033**	-	**0.9747 ± 0.0013**	-	**0.9355 ± 0.0038**	-
	75	WSA	0.6724 ± 0.0022	0.1988	0.2935 ± 0.0054	0.6981	0.6685 ± 0.0047	0.2777
		IDIA	0.7085 ± 0.0021	0.1627	0.3904 ± 0.0018	0.6012	0.7167 ± 0.0035	0.2295
		TUNI	**0.8712 ± 0.0043**	-	**0.9916 ± 0.0037**	-	**0.9462 ± 0.0029**	-
ViT-B/32	1	WSA	0.6323 ± 0.0064	0.0268	0.2964 ± 0.0052	0.3421	0.6812 ± 0.0045	0.0025
		IDIA	0.6783 ± 0.0047	0.0308	0.3746 ± 0.0033	0.2639	0.6772 ± 0.0041	0.0065
		TUNI	**0.7091 ± 0.0056**	-	**0.6385 ± 0.0062**	-	**0.6837 ± 0.0044**	-
	75	WSA	0.7045 ± 0.0075	0.0137	0.2806 ± 0.0048	0.3566	0.6895 ± 0.0052	0.0052
		IDIA	0.6890 ± 0.0051	0.0292	0.3811 ± 0.0063	0.2561	0.6927 ± 0.0045	0.0020
		TUNI	**0.7182 ± 0.0068**	-	**0.6372 ± 0.0046**	-	**0.6947 ± 0.0078**	-

Dataset Construction. The datasets for training and ID inference are constructed from three datasets: LAION-5B (Schuhmann et al., 2022), Conceptual Captions 3M (CC3M) (Changpinyo et al., 2021), and FaceScrub (Kemelmacher-Shlizerman et al., 2016). Specifically, 200 celebrities—100 for training and 100 for validation, with their face photos accompanied by labels containing their names are selected from the FaceScrub dataset; then these data samples are augmented by additional photos of the selected celebrities found in LAION-5B, such that each person has multiple photos; finally these augmented data points are mixed with the CC3M dataset to form the training set of the CLIP model. By doing this, we have the ground truth on which people are in the training set and which are not. In our experiments, we construct two datasets, one with a single photo for each person, and another with 75 photos for each person. Samples of this dataset are shown in Figure 4 and a more detailed description is given in appendix.

Models. Our analysis involves ID inference from six pre-trained target CLIP models, categorized into ResNet-50, ResNet-50x4, and ViT-B/32 architectures. The ResNet-50 and ResNet-50x4 models are based on the ResNet architecture (He et al., 2016; Theckedath and Sedamkar, 2020); and ViT-B/32 models employ the Vision Transformer architecture (Chen et al., 2021). DeepFace (Serengil and Ozpinar, 2020) is used for facial feature extraction for enhancement with real images.

Evaluation Metrics. TUNI's effectiveness is assessed using Precision, Recall, and Accuracy metrics, measuring anomaly prediction accuracy, correct anomaly identification, and overall prediction correctness, respectively.

Baselines. Current ID inference detection methods for CLIP models typically require detector to query target model with corresponding real images. Most MIAs involve training shadow models and related methods like shadow encoders (Liu et al., 2021), which can be particularly costly for large-scale multimodal models. We empirically compare the performance of TUNI with the following SOTA inference methods, which both avoid using shadow models, but still require submitting both text and image to the target CLIP model for inference.

- **Identity Inference Attack (IDIA) (Hintersdorf et al., 2022)** detects with a list of 1000 names to choose from and 30 real photos for a tested person. In IDIA, the attacker (detector) selects candidate names as prompt templates, and predicts names for each image and prompt. Once the correct name is predicted, it's inferred that the target individual is in training dataset. We compare IDIA using 3 photos for each test sample with TUNI using only text.

- **Weakly Supervised Attack (WSA) (Ko et al., 2023)** uses cosine similarity between image and text features to infer membership, and adds a weak supervision MIA framework

Figure 4: Samples from the dataset for training CLIP models.

based on non-member data generated after the release of the target model.

All experiments are performed using four NVIDIA GeForce RTX 3090 GPUs. Each experiment is repeated for 10 times, and the average values and the standard deviations are reported.

4.2 Results

On training anomaly detectors, we randomly generated $\ell = 50$ textual gibberish (some of them are shown in Table 3).

The image optimization was performed for $n = 100$ epochs; and in each epoch, $m = 1000$ Gradient Descent (GD) iterations with a learning rate of 0.02. Four anomaly detection models, i.e., LocalOutlierFactor (Cheng et al., 2019), IsolationForest (Liu et al., 2008), OneClassSVM (Li et al., 2003; Khan and Madden, 2014), and AutoEncoder (Chen et al., 2018) were trained, and $N = 3$ was chosen as the detection threshold.

As shown in Table 1, TUNI, even with only text information, consistently outperforms WSA and IDIA in all metrics by a large margin, across all model architectures and datasets, demonstrating its superior performance.

We also evaluate the effect of providing the TUNI detector with an real photo of the inferred person. In this case, the embedding distances between the real and optimized images of the test samples are used to perform a 2-means clustering, adding another vote to the inference result. We accordingly raise the detection threshold N' to 4. As illustrated in Table 2, the given photo helps to improve the performance of TUNI across all tested CLIP models. While recalls in some ResNet models experience minor declines attributed to the raised threshold, all remain above 94%. Conversely, the ViT-B models exhibit an almost 11% increase in recall. A lower detection threshold aids recall enhancement but may concurrently lead to declines in other metrics.

4.3 Ablation Study

We further explore the impacts of different system parameters on the detection accuracy.

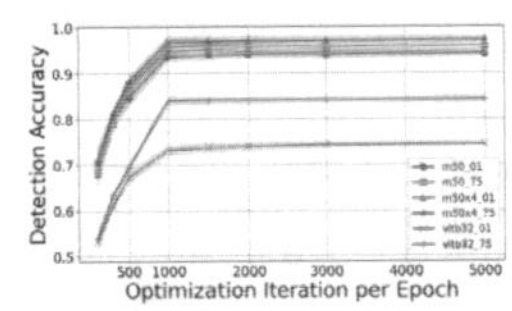

Figure 5: Detection accuracy for different numbers of optimization iterations per epoch.

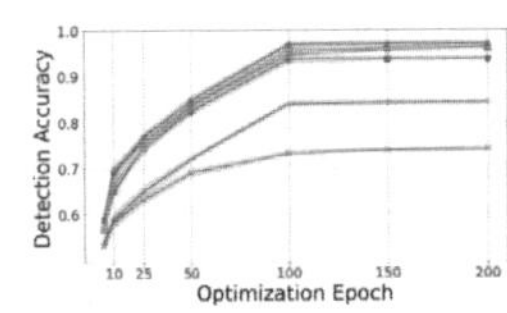

Figure 6: Detection accuracy for different numbers of epochs.

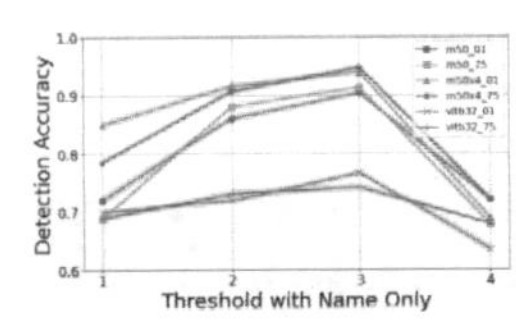

Figure 7: Detection accuracy with name only.

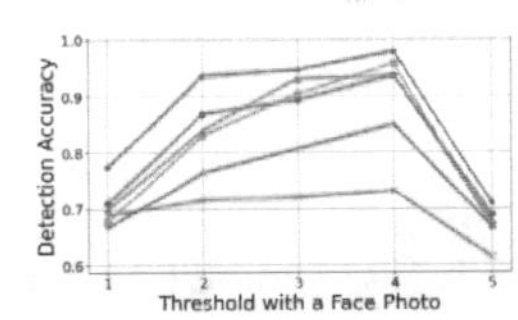

Figure 8: Detection accuracy with a face photo.

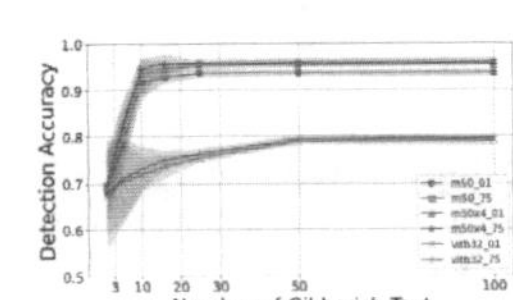

Figure 9: Detection accuracy for different numbers of gibberish.

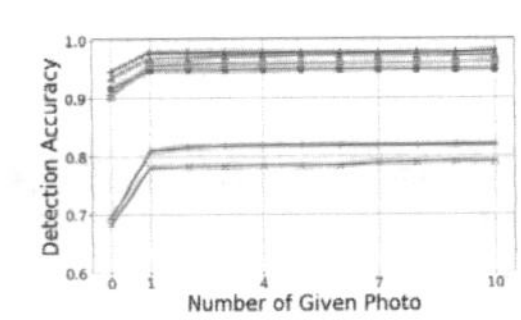

Figure 10: Detection accuracy for different number of real photos.

Optimization parameters. Figure 5 and 6 show that during feature extraction, optimizing for $n = 100$ epochs, each with $m = 1,000$ iterations, offers the optimal performance. Additional epochs and optimization iterations, while incurring additional computational cost, do not significantly improve the detection accuracy.

Table 2: Detection performance with a given photo during inference. Δ indicates performance improvement.

Architecture	Number of photos per person in training set	TUNI	Precision	Δ	Recall	Δ	Accuracy	Δ
ResNet-50	1	Text only	0.8634 ± 0.0031	0.1019	**0.9821 ± 0.0042**	-0.0396	0.9172 ± 0.0028	0.0303
		With 1 photo	**0.9653 ± 0.0032**	-	0.9425 ± 0.0057	-	**0.9475 ± 0.0041**	-
	75	Text only	0.8642 ± 0.0057	0.1183	**0.9835 ± 0.0019**	-0.0188	0.9032 ± 0.0033	0.0538
		With 1 photo	**0.9825 ± 0.0031**	-	0.9467 ± 0.0024	-	**0.9570 ± 0.0038**	-
ResNet-50x4	1	Text only	0.8613 ± 0.0033	0.1290	**0.9747 ± 0.0013**	-0.0183	0.9355 ± 0.0038	0.0317
		With 1 photo	**0.9923 ± 0.0011**	-	0.9564 ± 0.0044	-	**0.9672 ± 0.0028**	-
	75	Text only	0.8712 ± 0.0043	0.0912	0.9916 ± 0.0037	0.0019	0.9462 ± 0.0029	0.0323
		With 1 photo	**0.9624 ± 0.0042**	-	**0.9935 ± 0.0029**	-	**0.9785 ± 0.0037**	-
ViT-B/32	1	Text only	0.7091 ± 0.0056	0.1432	0.6385 ± 0.0062	0.1084	0.6837 ± 0.0044	0.0975
		With 1 photo	**0.8523 ± 0.0038**	-	**0.7469 ± 0.0078**	-	**0.7812 ± 0.0031**	-
	75	Text only	0.7182 ± 0.0068	0.1353	0.6372 ± 0.0046	0.1086	0.6947 ± 0.0078	0.1148
		With 1 photo	**0.8535 ± 0.0042**	-	**0.7458 ± 0.0039**	-	**0.8095 ± 0.0063**	-

Table 3: Samples of randomly generated gibberish.

<table>
<tr><td>±7IKXb2Y</td><td>FR!pnI<5xS</td><td>euiT_;yw/</td></tr>
<tr><td>je|%5(s=G_</td><td>?Ŵ<E{Dvmz</td><td>hqf- =j<q5</td></tr>
<tr><td>#lEZ0yrZ5ig</td><td>’2_:6[jiOa</td><td>X*|<tFx|4/</td></tr>
<tr><td>Fa<Z*Oike[</td><td>\93W4̃>x5u</td><td>?=&QplxC-c</td></tr>
</table>

Table 4: Covert gibberish that seem to be real names.

Karinix	Zylogene	Glycogenyx
Zylotrax	Vexilith	Dynatrix
Exodynix	Novylith	Glycosyne
Xenolynx	Rynexis	Delphylith

Detection threshold. Figure 7 and 8 show that the system attains higher accuracy, when it adopts a threshold of three votes for considering an input as an anomaly with text only, and four votes with an added detection model using an additional given photo. Setting a high threshold may result in failing to detect an anomaly, while setting a low one may lead to identifying a normal one as anomaly.

Number of textual gibberish. As shown in Figure 9, for different target models, the detection accuracies initially improve as the number of gibberish texts increases, and converge after using more than 50 gibberish strings.

Number of real photos. As shown in Figure 10, integrating real photos can enhance the detection accuracy; however, the improvements of using more than 1 photo are rather marginal.

5 Defense and Covert Gibberish Generation

In real-world scenarios, target models being detected may deploy defense mechanisms to recognize anomalous inputs like gibberish and provide misleading outputs, causing TUNI to misjudge inclusion of PII.

To generate more covert gibberish data, we can create strings resembling normal text, with a few characters replaced by syllables from another language. For instance, the detector can craft query texts, by randomly combining English names with syllables from Arabic medical terminology. One way to do this is to start by prompting LLMs like GPT-3.5-turbo to create lists of common initial and final syllables in English words. These syllable lists are then extracted and refined to ensure diversity and eliminate duplicates. Next, the refined syllable combinations are randomly paired to create pseudo-English names, such as “Karinix”, “Zylogene”, “Glycogenyx”, and “Renotyl”. It’s crucial to verify the novelty of these names by checking against a database of real names to avoid collision. Then by prompting the LLM to generate strings using the refined syllable combinations, covert gibberish strings resembling real names are produced (some examples are given in Table 4).

6 Conclusion

In this paper, we propose TUNI, the first method to conduct identity inference without exposing acutal images to target CLIP models. TUNI turns inference problem into anomaly detection, through randomly generating textual gibberish that are known to be out of training set, and exploting them to train anomaly detectors. Furthermore, the incorporation of real images is shown to enhance detection performance. Through evaluations across various CLIP model architectures and datasets, we demonstrate the consistent superiority of TUNI over baselines.

7 Limitations

Due to constraints resources, we conducted experiments using the name of the individual as textual descriptions. This approach may not fully encapsulate the complexities and nuances of real-world PII leakage including addresses, phone numbers, and other sensitive information.

8 Ethics and Social Impact

The development of TUNI highlights crucial ethical considerations in identity inference using multimodal models like CLIP. By enabling identity inference with only textual data, TUNI reduces the risks associated with exposing PII through images. This approach not only helps protect individual privacy but also minimizes the potential for misuse in harmful applications. As such technologies evolve, it is essential for researchers to adhere to ethical guidelines and promote transparency, ensuring that advancements in AI prioritize user privacy and foster responsible usage in society.

9 Potential Risks

TUNI aims to bolster privacy by aiding in identity inference and safeguarding personal identifiable information within AI systems. While mindful of the risk of misuse, TUNI should adhere to data regulations and be employed only with explicit consent from involved data subjects, promoting privacy and security in AI practices.

References

Martin Abadi, Andy Chu, Ian Goodfellow, H Brendan McMahan, Ilya Mironov, Kunal Talwar, and Li Zhang. 2016. Deep learning with differential privacy. In *Proceedings of the 2016 ACM SIGSAC conference on computer and communications security*, pages 308–318.

Keith Bonawitz, Vladimir Ivanov, Ben Kreuter, Antonio Marcedone, H Brendan McMahan, Sarvar Patel, Daniel Ramage, Aaron Segal, and Karn Seth. 2017. Practical secure aggregation for privacy-preserving machine learning. In *proceedings of the 2017 ACM SIGSAC Conference on Computer and Communications Security*, pages 1175–1191.

Nicholas Carlini, Florian Tramer, Eric Wallace, Matthew Jagielski, Ariel Herbert-Voss, Katherine Lee, Adam Roberts, Tom Brown, Dawn Song, Ulfar Erlingsson, et al. 2021. Extracting training data from large language models. In *30th USENIX Security Symposium (USENIX Security 21)*, pages 2633–2650.

Varun Chandola, Arindam Banerjee, and Vipin Kumar. 2009. Anomaly detection: A survey. *ACM computing surveys (CSUR)*, 41(3):1–58.

Soravit Changpinyo, Piyush Sharma, Nan Ding, and Radu Soricut. 2021. Conceptual 12m: Pushing web-scale image-text pre-training to recognize long-tail visual concepts. In *Proceedings of the IEEE/CVF conference on computer vision and pattern recognition*, pages 3558–3568.

Xiangning Chen, Cho-Jui Hsieh, and Boqing Gong. 2021. When vision transformers outperform resnets without pre-training or strong data augmentations. *arXiv preprint arXiv:2106.01548*.

Zhaomin Chen, Chai Kiat Yeo, Bu Sung Lee, and Chiew Tong Lau. 2018. Autoencoder-based network anomaly detection. In *2018 Wireless telecommunications symposium (WTS)*, pages 1–5. IEEE.

Zhangyu Cheng, Chengming Zou, and Jianwei Dong. 2019. Outlier detection using isolation forest and local outlier factor. In *Proceedings of the conference on research in adaptive and convergent systems*, pages 161–168.

Gilad Cohen and Raja Giryes. 2024. Membership inference attack using self influence functions. In *Proceedings of the IEEE/CVF Winter Conference on Applications of Computer Vision*, pages 4892–4901.

Adam Dziedzic, Haonan Duan, Muhammad Ahmad Kaleem, Nikita Dhawan, Jonas Guan, Yannis Cattan, Franziska Boenisch, and Nicolas Papernot. 2022. Dataset inference for self-supervised models. *Advances in Neural Information Processing Systems*, 35:12058–12070.

Yaniv Erlich, Tal Shor, Itsik Pe'er, and Shai Carmi. 2018. Identity inference of genomic data using long-range familial searches. *Science*, 362(6415):690–694.

Aditya Golatkar, Alessandro Achille, Yu-Xiang Wang, Aaron Roth, Michael Kearns, and Stefano Soatto. 2022. Mixed differential privacy in computer vision. In *Proceedings of the IEEE/CVF Conference on Computer Vision and Pattern Recognition*, pages 8376–8386.

Jiaxi Gu, Xiaojun Meng, Guansong Lu, Lu Hou, Niu Minzhe, Xiaodan Liang, Lewei Yao, Runhui Huang, Wei Zhang, Xin Jiang, et al. 2022. Wukong: A 100 million large-scale chinese cross-modal pre-training benchmark. *Advances in Neural Information Processing Systems*, 35:26418–26431.

Kaiming He, Xiangyu Zhang, Shaoqing Ren, and Jian Sun. 2016. Deep residual learning for image recognition. In *Proceedings of the IEEE conference on computer vision and pattern recognition*, pages 770–778.

Xinlei He, Zheng Li, Weilin Xu, Cory Cornelius, and Yang Zhang. 2022. Membership-doctor: Comprehensive assessment of membership inference against machine learning models. *arXiv preprint arXiv:2208.10445*.

Xinlei He and Yang Zhang. 2021. Quantifying and mitigating privacy risks of contrastive learning. In *Proceedings of the 2021 ACM SIGSAC Conference on Computer and Communications Security*, CCS '21, page 845–863, New York, NY, USA. Association for Computing Machinery.

Alec Helbling, Mansi Phute, Matthew Hull, and Duen Horng Chau. 2023. Llm self defense: By self examination, llms know they are being tricked. *arXiv preprint arXiv:2308.07308*.

Daniel Hintersdorf, Lukas Struppek, Maximilian Brack, et al. 2022. Does clip know my face? *arXiv preprint arXiv:2209.07341*.

Sorami Hisamoto, Matt Post, and Kevin Duh. 2020. Membership inference attacks on sequence-to-sequence models: Is my data in your machine translation system? *Transactions of the Association for Computational Linguistics*, 8:49–63.

Hongsheng Hu, Zoran Salcic, Lichao Sun, Gillian Dobbie, Philip S Yu, and Xuyun Zhang. 2022a. Membership inference attacks on machine learning: A survey. *ACM Computing Surveys (CSUR)*, 54(11s):1–37.

Li Hu, Anli Yan, Hongyang Yan, Jin Li, Teng Huang, Yingying Zhang, Changyu Dong, and Chunsheng Yang. 2023. Defenses to membership inference attacks: A survey. *ACM Computing Surveys*, 56(4):1–34.

Pingyi Hu, Zihan Wang, Ruoxi Sun, Hu Wang, and Minhui Xue. 2022b. M^4i: Multi-modal models membership inference. *Advances in Neural Information Processing Systems*, 35:1867–1882.

Alyssa Huang, Peihan Liu, Ryumei Nakada, Linjun Zhang, and Wanrong Zhang. 2023. Safeguarding data in multimodal ai: A differentially private approach to clip training. *arXiv preprint arXiv:2306.08173*.

Huseyin A Inan, Osman Ramadan, Lukas Wutschitz, Daniel Jones, Victor Rühle, James Withers, and Robert Sim. 2021. Training data leakage analysis in language models. *arXiv preprint arXiv:2101.05405*.

Matthew Jagielski, Milad Nasr, Katherine Lee, Christopher A Choquette-Choo, Nicholas Carlini, and Florian Tramer. 2024. Students parrot their teachers: Membership inference on model distillation. *Advances in Neural Information Processing Systems*, 36.

Jinyuan Jia, Hongbin Liu, and Neil Zhenqiang Gong. 2023. 10 security and privacy problems in large foundation models. In *AI Embedded Assurance for Cyber Systems*, pages 139–159. Springer.

Panos Kalnis, Gabriel Ghinita, Kyriakos Mouratidis, and Dimitris Papadias. 2007. Preventing location-based identity inference in anonymous spatial queries. *IEEE transactions on knowledge and data engineering*, 19(12):1719–1733.

Svebor Karaman and Andrew D Bagdanov. 2012. Identity inference: generalizing person re-identification scenarios. In *Computer Vision–ECCV 2012. Workshops and Demonstrations: Florence, Italy, October 7-13, 2012, Proceedings, Part I 12*, pages 443–452. Springer.

Ira Kemelmacher-Shlizerman, Steven M Seitz, Daniel Miller, and Evan Brossard. 2016. The megaface benchmark: 1 million faces for recognition at scale. In *Proceedings of the IEEE conference on computer vision and pattern recognition*, pages 4873–4882.

Shehroz S Khan and Michael G Madden. 2014. One-class classification: taxonomy of study and review of techniques. *The Knowledge Engineering Review*, 29(3):345–374.

Seonghyeon Kim, Sooyeon Yun, Hwanil Lee, et al. 2024. Propile: Probing privacy leakage in large language models. In *Advances in Neural Information Processing Systems*, volume 36.

Minseon Ko, Minseok Jin, Chen Wang, et al. 2023. Practical membership inference attacks against large-scale multi-modal models: A pilot study. In *Proceedings of the IEEE/CVF International Conference on Computer Vision*, pages 4871–4881.

Klas Leino and Matt Fredrikson. 2020. Stolen memories: Leveraging model memorization for calibrated {White-Box} membership inference. In *29th USENIX security symposium (USENIX Security 20)*, pages 1605–1622.

Kun-Lun Li, Hou-Kuan Huang, Sheng-Feng Tian, and Wei Xu. 2003. Improving one-class svm for anomaly detection. In *Proceedings of the 2003 international conference on machine learning and cybernetics (IEEE Cat. No. 03EX693)*, volume 5, pages 3077–3081. IEEE.

Siyuan Liang, Aishan Liu, Jiawei Liang, Longkang Li, Yang Bai, and Xiaochun Cao. 2022. Imitated detectors: Stealing knowledge of black-box object detectors. In *Proceedings of the 30th ACM International Conference on Multimedia*, pages 4839–4847.

Fei Tony Liu, Kai Ming Ting, and Zhi-Hua Zhou. 2008. Isolation forest. In *2008 eighth ieee international conference on data mining*, pages 413–422. IEEE.

Hongbin Liu, Jinyuan Jia, Wenjie Qu, and Neil Zhenqiang Gong. 2021. Encodermi: Membership inference against pre-trained encoders in contrastive learning. In *Proceedings of the 2021 ACM SIGSAC Conference on Computer and Communications Security*, pages 2081–2095.

Yupei Liu, Jinyuan Jia, Hongbin Liu, and Neil Zhenqiang Gong. 2022. Stolenencoder: stealing pre-trained encoders in self-supervised learning. In *Proceedings of the 2022 ACM SIGSAC Conference on Computer and Communications Security*, pages 2115–2128.

Nils Lukas, Ahmed Salem, Robert Sim, Shruti Tople, Lukas Wutschitz, and Santiago Zanella-Béguelin. 2023. Analyzing leakage of personally identifiable information in language models. In *2023 IEEE Symposium on Security and Privacy (SP)*, pages 346–363. IEEE.

Justus Mattern, Fatemehsadat Mireshghallah, Zhijing Jin, Bernhard Schölkopf, Mrinmaya Sachan, and Taylor Berg-Kirkpatrick. 2023. Membership inference attacks against language models via neighbourhood comparison. *arXiv preprint arXiv:2305.18462*.

Matthieu Meeus, Shubham Jain, Marek Rei, and Yves-Alexandre de Montjoye. 2023. Did the neurons read your book? document-level membership inference for large language models. *arXiv preprint arXiv:2310.15007*.

Sara Motahari, Sotirios Ziavras, Richard P Schuler, and Quentin Jones. 2009. Identity inference as a privacy risk in computer-mediated communication. In *2009 42nd Hawaii International Conference on System Sciences*, pages 1–10. IEEE.

Myung Gyo Oh, Leo Hyun Park, Jaeuk Kim, Jaewoo Park, and Taekyoung Kwon. 2023. Membership inference attacks with token-level deduplication on korean language models. *IEEE Access*, 11:10207–10217.

Ashwinee Panda, Christopher A Choquette-Choo, Zhengming Zhang, Yaoqing Yang, and Prateek Mittal. 2024. Teach llms to phish: Stealing private information from language models. *arXiv preprint arXiv:2403.00871*.

Simon Prince, Peng Li, Yun Fu, Umar Mohammed, and James Elder. 2011. Probabilistic models for inference about identity. *IEEE transactions on pattern analysis and machine intelligence*, 34(1):144–157.

Alec Radford, Jong Wook Kim, Chris Hallacy, Aditya Ramesh, Gabriel Goh, Sandhini Agarwal, Girish Sastry, Amanda Askell, Pamela Mishkin, Jack Clark, et al. 2021. Learning transferable visual models from natural language supervision. In *International conference on machine learning*, pages 8748–8763. PMLR.

Md Abdur Rahman. 2023. A survey on security and privacy of multimodal llms-connected healthcare perspective. In *2023 IEEE Globecom Workshops (GC Wkshps)*, pages 1807–1812. IEEE.

Md Abdur Rahman, Lamyaa Alqahtani, Amna Albooq, and Alaa Ainousah. 2024. A survey on security and privacy of large multimodal deep learning models: Teaching and learning perspective. In *2024 21st Learning and Technology Conference (L&T)*, pages 13–18. IEEE.

Tahleen Rahman, Mario Fritz, Michael Backes, and Yang Zhang. 2020. Everything about you: A multimodal approach towards friendship inference in online social networks. *arXiv preprint arXiv:2003.00996*.

Aditya Ramesh, Prafulla Dhariwal, Alex Nichol, Casey Chu, and Mark Chen. 2022. Hierarchical text-conditional image generation with clip latents. *arXiv preprint arXiv:2204.06125*, 1(2):3.

Maria Rigaki and Sebastian Garcia. 2023. A survey of privacy attacks in machine learning. *ACM Computing Surveys*, 56(4):1–34.

Conrad Sanderson and Brian C Lovell. 2009. Multi-region probabilistic histograms for robust and scalable identity inference. In *Advances in biometrics: Third international conference, ICB 2009, alghero, italy, june 2-5, 2009. Proceedings 3*, pages 199–208. Springer.

Christoph Schuhmann, Romain Beaumont, Richard Vencu, Cade Gordon, Ross Wightman, Mehdi Cherti, Theo Coombes, Aarush Katta, Clayton Mullis, Mitchell Wortsman, et al. 2022. Laion-5b: An open large-scale dataset for training next generation image-text models. *Advances in Neural Information Processing Systems*, 35:25278–25294.

Christoph Schuhmann, Richard Vencu, Romain Beaumont, Robert Kaczmarczyk, Clayton Mullis, Aarush Katta, Theo Coombes, Jenia Jitsev, and Aran Komatsuzaki. 2021. Laion-400m: Open dataset of clip-filtered 400 million image-text pairs. *arXiv preprint arXiv:2111.02114*.

Paul M Schwartz and Daniel J Solove. 2011. The pii problem: Privacy and a new concept of personally identifiable information. *NYUL rev.*, 86:1814.

Sefik Ilkin Serengil and Alper Ozpinar. 2020. Lightface: A hybrid deep face recognition framework. In *2020 Innovations in Intelligent Systems and Applications Conference (ASYU)*, pages 23–27. IEEE.

Fahad Shamshad, Muzammal Naseer, and Karthik Nandakumar. 2023. Clip2protect: Protecting facial privacy using text-guided makeup via adversarial latent search. In *Proceedings of the IEEE/CVF Conference on Computer Vision and Pattern Recognition*, pages 20595–20605.

Reza Shokri, Marco Stronati, Congzheng Song, and Vitaly Shmatikov. 2017. Membership inference attacks against machine learning models. In *2017 IEEE symposium on security and privacy (SP)*, pages 3–18. IEEE.

Yaniv Taigman, Ming Yang, Marc'Aurelio Ranzato, and Lior Wolf. 2014. Deepface: Closing the gap to human-level performance in face verification. In *Proceedings of the IEEE conference on computer vision and pattern recognition*, pages 1701–1708.

Dhananjay Theckedath and RR Sedamkar. 2020. Detecting affect states using vgg16, resnet50 and seresnet50 networks. *SN Computer Science*, 1(2):79.

Stacey Truex, Ling Liu, Mehmet Emre Gursoy, Lei Yu, and Wenqi Wei. 2019. Demystifying membership inference attacks in machine learning as a service. *IEEE transactions on services computing*, 14(6):2073–2089.

Yixin Wu, Rui Wen, Michael Backes, Ning Yu, and Yang Zhang. 2022. Model stealing attacks against vision-language models.

Zhaohan Xi, Tianyu Du, Changjiang Li, Ren Pang, Shouling Ji, Jinghui Chen, Fenglong Ma, and Ting Wang. 2024. Defending pre-trained language models as few-shot learners against backdoor attacks. *Advances in Neural Information Processing Systems*, 36.

Mingfu Xue, Chengxiang Yuan, Can He, Yinghao Wu, Zhiyu Wu, Yushu Zhang, Zhe Liu, and Weiqiang Liu. 2023. Use the spear as a shield: An adversarial example based privacy-preserving technique against membership inference attacks. *IEEE Transactions on Emerging Topics in Computing*, 11(1):153–169.

Jiayuan Ye, Aadyaa Maddi, Sasi Kumar Murakonda, Vincent Bindschaedler, and Reza Shokri. 2022. Enhanced membership inference attacks against machine learning models. In *Proceedings of the 2022 ACM SIGSAC Conference on Computer and Communications Security*, pages 3093–3106.

Yu Yin, Ke Chen, Lidan Shou, and Gang Chen. 2021. Defending privacy against more knowledgeable membership inference attackers. In *Proceedings of the 27th ACM SIGKDD Conference on Knowledge Discovery & Data Mining*, pages 2026–2036.

Zhexin Zhang, Jiaxin Wen, and Minlie Huang. 2023. ETHICIST: Targeted training data extraction through loss smoothed soft prompting and calibrated confidence estimation. In *Proceedings of the 61st Annual Meeting of the Association for Computational Linguistics (Volume 1: Long Papers)*, pages 12674–12687, Toronto, Canada. Association for Computational Linguistics.

Huiling Zhou and Kin-Man Lam. 2018. Age-invariant face recognition based on identity inference from appearance age. *Pattern recognition*, 76:191–202.

A Dataset Description

We utilized the datasets from previous work (Hintersdorf et al., 2022).

LAION-400M (Schuhmann et al., 2021), comprising 400 million image-text pairs, primarily employed for pre-training the CLIP model, offering a wide array of visual content and textual descriptions to facilitate the model's learning of relationships between images and text, including direct associations between specific individuals and images. In the experiment, this dataset is used to analyze the frequency of individuals appearing within it to identify individuals with lower frequencies of appearance, thereby avoiding the use of those individuals that appear very frequently to prevent skewing the experimental results. A threshold is set to only use individuals with fewer than 300 appearances for the experiments to ensure that the experimental results would not be dominated by individuals with very high occurrence frequencies, thus ensuring the accuracy and reliability of the experimental outcomes.

LAION-5B (Schuhmann et al., 2022), containing over 5.8 billion pairs and LAION-400M is its subset. In the experiment, LAION-5B is used to expand the CC3M dataset, enriching and increasing the sample size and diversity of the dataset. LAION-5B is used to find similar pairs to those in the FaceScrub dataset for each of the 530 celebrities. After confirming the presence of these celebrities' names in the captions of the found images, these image-text pairs were added to the CC3M dataset for training the target CLIP models.

Conceptual Captions 3M (CC3M) (Changpinyo et al., 2021), consisting of 2.8 million image-text pairs, anonymizes image captions by replacing named entities (e.g., celebrity names) with their hypernyms (e.g., "actor"). This dataset was also employed for pre-training the CLIP model. However, in this experiment, researchers analyzed the dataset using facial recognition technology to determine if specific celebrity images were present, and selectively added image-text pairs for model training adversarial attacks. As the named entities in CC3M dataset are anonymized in image captions, i.e., specific celebrity names replaced with their hypernyms like "actor," after confirming the presence or absence of specific celebrity images in the CC3M dataset, controlled additions of image-text pairs were made to the CC3M dataset.

FaceScrub (Kemelmacher-Shlizerman et al., 2016), containing images of 530 celebrities, was used to ascertain whether the identities one intends to infer are part of the training data. Celebrities were chosen due to the wide availability of their images in the public domain, minimizing privacy concerns associated with using their images.

To accurately calculate evaluation metrics, it was necessary to analyze which individuals were already part of the dataset and which were not. For the LAION-5B dataset, names of the 530 celebrities from the FaceScrub dataset were searched within all captions, and corresponding image-text pairs were saved, which were then added to the CC3M dataset. This was done to train the CLIP model and evaluate the effectiveness of IDIA under controlled conditions. In the experiments with the CC3M dataset, a total of 200 individuals were used, with 100 added to the dataset for model training and the remaining 100 held out for model validation. The selection of data in this process was balanced in terms of gender, with an equal distribution of male and female individuals to enhance the persuasiveness of the results. We construct two datasets for training the CLIP models of three architectures relatively, one with a single photo for each person, and another with 75 photos for each person. Samples of the datasets are shown in Figure 4.

TAROT: Task-Oriented Authorship Obfuscation Using Policy Optimization Methods

Gabriel Loiseau[1,2] Damien Sileo[2] Damien Riquet[1] Maxime Meyer[1] Marc Tommasi[2]
[1]Hornetsecurity, Hem, France
[2]Univ. Lille, Inria, CNRS, Centrale Lille, UMR 9189 - CRIStAL, F-59000 Lille, France
gabriel.loiseau@inria.fr

Abstract

Authorship obfuscation aims to disguise the identity of an author within a text by altering the writing style, vocabulary, syntax, and other linguistic features associated with the text author. This alteration needs to balance privacy and utility. While strong obfuscation techniques can effectively hide the author's identity, they often degrade the quality and usefulness of the text for its intended purpose. Conversely, maintaining high utility tends to provide insufficient privacy, making it easier for an adversary to de-anonymize the author. Thus, achieving an optimal trade-off between these two conflicting objectives is crucial. In this paper, we propose TAROT: **T**ask-Oriented **A**utho**r**ship **O**bfuscation Using Policy Op**t**imization, a new unsupervised authorship obfuscation method whose goal is to optimize the privacy-utility trade-off by regenerating the entire text considering its downstream utility. Our approach leverages policy optimization as a fine-tuning paradigm over small language models in order to rewrite texts by preserving author identity and downstream task utility. We show that our approach largely reduces the accuracy of attackers while preserving utility. We make our code and models publicly available.[1]

1 Introduction

Text is a primary medium for storing user data, training machine learning models, and interacting with large language models (LLMs) during inference. However, it also poses significant privacy risks, as sensitive or personal information contained within text can be exposed or misused. Text anonymization is a vital technique to address these concerns by removing or obfuscating personal information. This process protects individual privacy while ensuring that machine learning models can still derive meaningful insights and patterns from anonymized data, preserving its utility.

[1]https://github.com/hornetsecurity/tarot

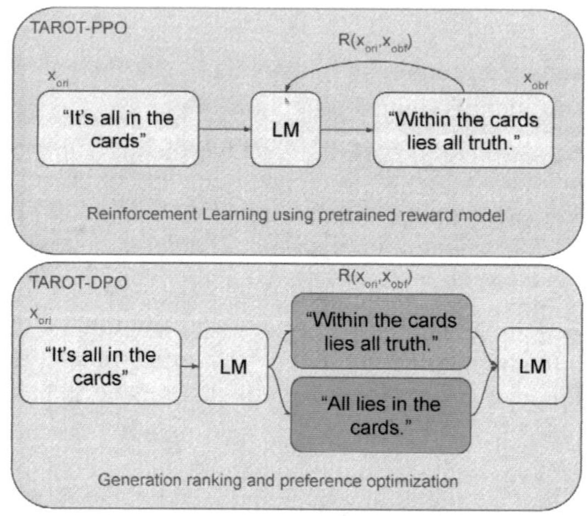

Figure 1: Illustration of the two versions of TAROT: We generate obfuscation candidates and optimize the best policy using reinforcement learning and preference optimization.

Currently, most work done on text anonymization focuses on redacting sensitive entities in a given document (Lison et al., 2021). This is sufficient for texts where the only private aspects are named entities, such as medical reports, court cases, or biographies. But it is inadequate for removing the author's writing style, or the weak signals that can be used as hints for identification, which is, for example, the case for blog articles or emails. Redacting entities in text while keeping stylometric features linked to a specific individual would eventually result in a leak of information. Indeed, the writing style is a strong indicator of a person's identity (Mosteller and Wallace, 1963). Previous work on authorship attribution highlights the large amount of information that can be extracted from seemingly anonymized texts and the ease of identification of authors, especially for long documents (Fabien et al., 2020).

To solve this issue, authorship obfuscation (AO) aims to hide the author's identity by replacing some part of the text associated with authorship indicators. Modifying the original text can impact its usability

Proceedings of the Sixth Workshop on Privacy in Natural Language Processing, pages 14–31
April 4, 2025 ©2025 Association for Computational Linguistics

for specific tasks (i.e. utility), and therefore badly affects the downstream performances and text comprehension of machine learning models. The enforcement of privacy creates a trade-off between privacy and utility, where keeping the original text preserves the unchanged utility of the text, while not defending against attribution attacks. On the other hand, obfuscating the entire text guarantees privacy, but leads to unusable text in practice. Previous approaches design their obfuscation by maximizing the preserved text content. They limit the modifications to small and targeted edits in order to preserve text meaning and keep textual content as close as possible to the original. While this strategy is necessary to maintain the exact content and ensure that we convey the exact same message (before publishing the text online for example), those approaches often lead to insufficient modification in the text, especially against realistic attack scenarios (Zhai et al., 2022).

To address these limitations, we reframe the AO problem into an adversarial problem between two adversaries (e.g. machine learning models): one attacker model whose goal is to reveal the identity of a given author from written texts, and one utility model that aims to perform a given task using authors' data. The goal is to provide a modified version of the original text such that the utility model can accurately perform its task while preventing the attacker from identifying the author, making the obfuscation task-oriented. This perspective is more angled towards data users who need to privately perform utility tasks on the data, where some degree of content alteration may be acceptable if it enhances privacy. The notion of task-oriented obfuscation/anonymization also takes its origin in the law. As stated by GDPR (European Parliament and Council of the European Union, 2016), the collection and processing of personal information (including written texts) must be specified for a given usage.

In order to learn this privacy-utility trade-off, we use the combination of supervised fine-tuning (SFT) and policy optimization (PO) to guide a generative model into generating privacy- and utility-preserving outputs. Our model learns to rewrite the text while removing potential authorship signals, and preserving the text utility for a downstream task. This rewriting goal is further validated by the conclusion of Weitzenboeck et al. (2022) which showed how difficult it is to comply with GDPR requirements concerning text anonymization without changing the entire text.

We fine-tune a text simplification model for AO using a customized reward model. We design an unsupervised reward model for PO using two pretrained sentence embedding models. The utility reward penalizes the fact that the General Text Embeddings (Li et al., 2023) of the anonymized sentence is too far removed from that of the original sentence. The author rewards does the opposite on the embedding built by the Universal Authorship Representation model from Rivera-Soto et al. (2021). Our final models are trained in an open-world setting where the number of authors is not defined, the same goes for the end utility for our model to work on a multi-task setting. We also provide experimentation on three different datasets, movie reviews, blog articles and scholar documents. We show that TAROT can be used on multiple datasets targeting different tasks while protecting authorship.

In summary, we list the main contributions as follows:

- We design a new framework for task-oriented AO by leveraging PO algorithms to maximize the end usage of data. The objective is to help reduce the traditional constraints associated with utility preservation in the literature (strict content preservation and semantic quality) by looking for a downstream classification task to achieve with the anonymized data.
- Starting from this framework, we propose TAROT, a task-oriented generation model aiming to obfuscate text without any prior knowledge of the author (making it unsupervised, and usable on any dataset, even if the authors are not clearly indicated) while maximizing the utility for a variety of tasks. We release two versions of TAROT from two different fine-tuning PO algorithms: TAROT-PPO and TAROT-DPO.
- We further evaluate TAROT on three datasets associated with different classification tasks, using different authorship attackers and downstream usage scenarios.

2 Related Work

Authorship Obfuscation Obfuscation techniques can be regrouped into two categories, depending on their implementation. Generic methods, on one hand, are methods that were not explicitly designed for AO, but show interesting performance. These methods include machine translation (Altakrori et al., 2022; Keswani et al., 2016), paraphrasing (Krishna et al., 2023), or synonym replacements (Potthast et al., 2016).

More recently, advanced techniques were built explicitly for AO, often relying on a trained attacker performing authorship attribution attacks on the obfuscated text. Then, they perform accurate adversarial text edits from the attacker knowledge on authors in order to obtain a privatized output. Mutant-X (Mahmood et al., 2019), is a genetic algorithm that utilizes GloVE (Pennington et al., 2014) word embeddings selected from an SVM or Random Forest attacker to replace words in a document with similar ones.

Jamdec (Fisher et al., 2024) is an unsupervised approach for obfuscating the writing style of text while preserving semantics. It uses embedding-based and likelihood-based methods, rather than attacker-based methods, to extract keywords, then generates multiple text variations using Constrained Diverse Beam Search on GPT2-XL (1.61B parameters). Finally, the candidates are filtered using Natural Language Inference (NLI) and Corpus of Linguistic Acceptability (CoLA) metrics to ensure coherence, content preservation, and grammatical correctness.

Recently, ALISON (Xing et al., 2024) employs a lightweight multilayer perceptron classifier using part-of-speech sequences to guide obfuscation, and leverages a BERT pre-trained language model to generate replacement sequences. By ranking and replacing important part-of-speech n-grams, ALISON obfuscates text uniformly, reducing classifier confidence.

Related studies share a common approach to evaluating privacy: they measure it through the performance of authorship attribution classifiers against obfuscated texts. Zhai et al. (2022) push forward this evaluation framework by introducing adversarial attackers that can resist obfuscation techniques. For measuring utility, the standard is to treat AO as a reference-less natural language generation problem, and to rely on standard metrics used for similar tasks such as machine translation and summarization (Altakrori et al., 2022).

Reinforcement Learning In NLP, reinforcement learning (RL) is often used to capture small signals over word or sentence embedding. For example, Mosallanezhad et al. (2019) proposes a text representation anonymization approach that employs deep reinforcement learning to detect and modify text embeddings to maintain a good privacy-utility trade-off.

With the development of Reinforcement Learning from Human Feedback (RLHF) as a LLM fine-tuning paradigm, RL techniques have been leveraged to improve language models with scalar metrics by optimizing rewards from (human) feedback. It has emerged as a prominent tool for tackling undesirable behaviors such as toxicity, social biases, and offensive language (Ouyang et al., 2022). This is accomplished by implementing PO algorithms to optimize a language model (LM) by associating a reward with each generation, derived from a trained reward model.

Very recently, Liu et al. (2024) introduced an authorship style transfer method using PO. They optimize style transfer generation using style similarity reward models. Authorship style transfer is similar to AO in the way those task's goal is to change within a text the author writing style. However, style transfer assumes a distinct target style to achieve, whereas AO assumes a lack of distinct style. Fisher et al. (2024) also showed the ineffectiveness of style transfer for AO. To the best of our knowledge, our work is the first one applying PO algorithms on AO.

Private Synthetic Text Generation Our work lies at the frontier between private text editing and synthetic text generation. Creating private synthetic data often relies on established frameworks such as differential privacy (Dwork, 2006). In contrast to these approaches, we focus on the implementation of a single text-to-text transformation specifically designed for authorship obfuscation, rather than on the generation of new textual data derived from potentially multiple sources (Mattern et al., 2022a).

Differential privacy traditionally targets noise addition in documents to produce useful and private text representations (Feyisetan et al., 2019; Fernandes et al., 2019). Applying differential privacy to document rewriting primarily serves to mitigate membership inference attacks, addressing a distinct threat model compared to the authorship attribution attacks targeted by our approach. While these techniques exhibit emergent capabilities for masking authorship signals (Igamberdiev and Habernal, 2023; Weggenmann et al., 2022; Utpala et al., 2023), they typically do so at a substantial cost to text utility, both at the task-level and the syntactic-level (Mattern et al., 2022b). This approach introduces unnecessary noise to semantic content not relevant to authorship identification, often degrading the overall coherence and readability of the text. In contrast, our obfuscation methodology implements targeted modifications to stylometric features while maintaining the overall integrity of the source text.

3 Methodology

3.1 Problem Formulation

Let x_{ori} represent the original document authored by a specific author $a \in \mathcal{A}$. $\mathcal{A}$ denoting a predetermined set of authors. The objective of authorship obfuscation is to generate a new document, denoted as x_{obf}, which cannot be attributed to the original author a. To assess the effectiveness of obfuscation, we employ a classification model, denoted as $f_{attr}(\cdot)$ (i.e. an authorship attribution model), which has been trained to distinguish documents based on their respective authors within $\mathcal{A}$. The goal of authorship obfuscation is to design an obfuscation method $O(\cdot)$, such that $f_{attr}(O(x_{\text{ori}})) \neq f_{attr}(x_{\text{ori}})$.

In addition, a successful obfuscation algorithm would not only trick an attacker into predicting the wrong author, but also preserve the document utility for downstream usage. In this paper, instead of mainly measuring this utility change though various semantic or content preservation metrics (i.e. METEOR score, BERT score, etc.) we highlight the selection of a prior task $\mathcal{T}$ in order to evaluate obfuscation with respect to $\mathcal{T}$. We denote as $f_{\mathcal{T}}(\cdot)$ the classification model used for a utility task. An ideal $O(\cdot)$ would preserve the original label $f_{\mathcal{T}}(O(x_{\text{ori}})) = f_{\mathcal{T}}(x_{\text{ori}})$.

Note that $\mathcal{T}$ is likely not known when we train the obfuscation model, underscoring the necessity for a versatile obfuscation strategy. This task-agnostic approach prevents the obfuscation model from learning to transform the text specifically to fit the label of $\mathcal{T}$, which would compromise its generality across different tasks.

3.2 Framework Overview

Our task-oriented framework can be decomposed in two steps. First, we initialize our generation model from a SFT baseline, this will first guide our LM to generate modified versions of the input text instead of proceeding text copy. Second, we apply a PO algorithm to fine-tune our SFT model. We experiment with two different PO algorithms, Proximal Policy Optimization (Schulman et al., 2017) and Direct Preference Optimization (Rafailov et al., 2023) (see Figure 1). We optimize our SFT generations using a reward model composed of both privacy and content preservation components.

3.3 SFT Initialization

First, we use a fine-tuned LM to initiate our text generation task. We employ the *Keep It Simple*[2] simplification model (Laban et al., 2021) as an SFT baseline. This model is a fine-tuned version of `GPT2-medium` on the Newsela[3] dataset for text simplification. The utilization of a simplification model encourages a reduction in the amount of information conveyed by a sentence, thereby affording the opportunity to eliminate author-specific features[4]. To our knowledge, this is the first time that a simplification model has been used for AO. Moreover, our framework is broadly compatible with any autoregressive LM, and can be adapted with larger architectures and other generation tasks.

3.4 Policy Optimization Algorithms

We use two different PO algorithms to optimize generations of our SFT baseline. The Proximal Policy Optimization (PPO) (Schulman et al., 2017) algorithm is a policy gradient method whose goal is to optimize a policy with respect to continuous rewards. In our case, a policy is a generation strategy, i.e. a final LM. Initialized from the SFT policy, we sample completions y given prompts x and the reward model parametrized by ϕ produces a score $r_\phi(x,y)$ based on these completions. The reward score $r_\phi(x, y)$ is then combined with a Kullback–Leibler (KL) penalty to ensure the policy does not deviate too much from the SFT policy (leading to unusable generations). Specifically, the reward of the RL problem is:

$$R(x,y) = r_\phi(x,y) - \beta \mathbb{D}_{\text{KL}} \left[\pi_\theta(y \mid x) \,||\, \pi_{\text{SFT}}(y \mid x) \right]$$

where β is a parameter controlling the strength of the KL penalty, θ the parameters of RL policy π_θ, and r_ϕ the reward model with parameters ϕ. Then, PPO is used to maximize the following objective:

$$\max_{\pi_\theta} \mathbb{E}_{x \sim \mathcal{D}_{\text{SFT}}, y \sim \pi_\theta(y|x)} R(x,y)$$

where $\mathcal{D}_{\text{SFT}}$ is the prompts in the SFT dataset.

Rafailov et al. (2023) later introduced the Direct Preference Optimization (DPO) algorithm, which

[2]`https://hf.co/philippelaban/keep_it_simple`

[3]`https://newsela.com/`

[4]Our preliminary experiments revealed that using a simplification model outperformed comparable models of similar size for copy, paraphrasing, back-translation, and summarization, delivering superior privacy and utility.

Dataset	Authors	Texts	Avg. Texts / Author (std)	Avg. Words / Text (std)	Avg. Tokens / Text (std)	Avg. Chars / Text (std)
IMDb	10	10000	$1000(\pm 0)$	$364(\pm 209)$	$393(\pm 228)$	$1869(\pm 1077)$
	20	20000	$1000(\pm 0)$	$345(\pm 209)$	$371(\pm 225)$	$1767(\pm 1081)$
BAC	10	23534	$2353(\pm 639)$	$118(\pm 195)$	$120(\pm 236)$	$524(\pm 1027)$
	20	39379	$1969(\pm 599)$	$118(\pm 175)$	$123(\pm 214)$	$529(\pm 921)$
AMT	10	196	$20(\pm 2)$	$497(\pm 14)$	$592(\pm 41)$	$2956(\pm 194)$
	20	362	$18(\pm 2)$	$502(\pm 102)$	$590(\pm 38)$	$2956(\pm 207)$

Table 1: Dataset statistics

implicitly optimizes the same objective as PPO. DPO directly optimizes the model by a straightforward contrastive loss, boosting the reward of the preferred generation y_c and penalizing the one of the non-preferred generation y_r from a prompt x. DPO is a RL-free approach which has the following loss:

$$-\log\sigma\left(\beta\log\frac{\pi_\theta(y_c\,|\,x)}{\pi_{\text{SFT}}(y_c\,|\,x)}-\beta\log\frac{\pi_\theta(y_r\,|\,x)}{\pi_{\text{SFT}}(y_r\,|\,x)}\right)$$

where σ is the sigmoid function, and β the scaling parameter. In this study, we lack access to a preference dataset for DPO fine-tuning. Consequently, following the methodology of Rafailov et al. (2023), we generate this dataset by sampling responses from the same SFT dataset, and we rank those preferences using the same reward model (see Appendix A.3). This is justified as it is not possible to obtain a preference dataset from human feedback in the AO setting.

4 Experimental Setup

In this section, we describe the datasets involved for training and evaluation of our resulting models, and present our custom reward targeting the open-world authorship verification and multi-task text embeddings to learn this AO task. We then evaluate the resulting obfuscation against text edition and rewriting baselines.

4.1 Datasets

Training We use a separate dataset to train our PO models. We fine-tune our base simplification model on the Yelp reviews dataset[5] (Zhang et al., 2015) composed of reviews from Yelp. The dataset is extracted from the Yelp Dataset Challenge 2015. This dataset is employed in an unsupervised way, to ensure we train our models on a large number of authors.

Evaluation To evaluate our obfuscation models, we use three different datasets. (i) IMDb62[6], is a subset of the IMDb Authorship Attribution dataset initially presented by Seroussi et al. (2014). It consists of 62 authors with 1,000 texts per author taken from IMDb movie reviews. The utility task associated with this dataset is the review sentiment. For this, we map the movie rating between 0 and 10 associated with each review to a sentiment between *positive* and *negative*. A positive review occurs when the review rating is strictly larger than 5. (ii) The Blog Authorship Corpus[7] dataset (Schler et al., 2006) consists of aggregated blog posts from 19,320 bloggers gathered from blogger.com. We pick the list of 13 topics present in the dataset as the utility task. (iii) The Extended-Brennan-Greenstadt[8] dataset (Brennan et al., 2012) is composed of short paragraphs about scholar subjects gathered from 42 different authors from Amazon Mechanical Turk. The utility task of this dataset is indicated by the "background" column, as a binary classification problem.

For all datasets, we create two subsets containing the texts from 10 and 20 authors. For the Blog Authorship Corpus, we select the authors with the highest number of texts. We select the 10 (resp. 20) first authors listed in IMDb62 and Extended-Brennan-Greenstadt. We report summary statistics of each dataset in Table 1 and refer to every dataset as IMDb, BAC, and AMT followed by the number of considered authors. In summary, IMDb has rather long texts, numerous texts per author with a large associated standard deviation. BAC texts are shorter, with a higher number of texts per author compared to IMDb. Finally, for the AMT dataset, the texts are the longest with few variations, and the number of texts per author is the smallest.

[5] https://hf.co/datasets/yelp_review_full

[6] https://hf.co/datasets/tasksource/imdb62

[7] https://u.cs.biu.ac.il/~koppel/BlogCorpus.htm

[8] https://hf.co/datasets/tasksource/Drexel-AMT

4.2 Reward Models

To perform PO, we build a reward model from two different rewards components targeting respectively text semantics and text authorship, aiming to disentangle privacy and utility to control the trade-off.

For utility, we use a pretrained General Text Embeddings (GTE) (Li et al., 2023) to represent the reward as a cosine similarity between GTE before and after obfuscation[9]. Denote as $\mathrm{GTE}(x)$ the embedding vector of size 1024, our utility reward is defined as:

$$R_{util} = \mathrm{cossim}(\mathrm{GTE}(x_{ori}), \mathrm{GTE}(x_{obf}))$$

For the privacy reward, we use the Learning Universal Authorship Representations model (LUAR), from Rivera-Soto et al. (2021). LUAR's goal is to transform a given text into a 512 dimensions embedding, such that representations of texts by the same author are closer, according to cosine similarity, than those by other authors.

Denote as $\mathrm{LUAR}(x)$ the embedding vector given by the LUAR model, our privacy reward is defined as:

$$R_{priv} = 1 - \mathrm{cossim}(\mathrm{LUAR}(x_{ori}), \mathrm{LUAR}(x_{obf}))$$

where cossim denotes the cosine similarity.

We obtain our final reward by summing the two previous rewards $R = R_{util} + R_{priv}$. All implementation details are listed in Appendix A.1.

4.3 Evaluation

Privacy Metrics The goal for obfuscation is to change the text in order to reduce as much as possible the attacker accuracy. We employ authorship attribution as an evaluation attacker to simulate an attack scenario when the attacker has already access to some sample data of targeted authors to train an attacker classifier. This is a stronger scenario than directly using the reward model as evaluation, since it only assumes one-to-one comparison between texts. For each evaluation dataset, we train a DeBERTa-v3 (He et al., 2021) model as an authorship attribution classifier. We split each evaluation dataset in 80%, 10% 10% for training, validation and testing.We measure the accuracy of the attacker model on each test set.

Utility Metrics We evaluate the utility loss when performing obfuscation similarly to the privacy classifier. For each downstream task dataset, we train a DeBERTa model to quantify utility preservation after text obfuscation. In addition, we also measure the impact on content preservation and soundness (see Appendix B).

Baselines We use the following baselines:

Original Text We measure the performance of utility / privacy classifiers when evaluated on original data, the goal of AO would be to decrease the performance of privacy classifiers without decreasing too much the accuracy of utility classifiers.

Synonyms As a baseline, we perform a naive text edition using synonyms. We use GPTZzzs[10] to process original texts, it employs a dictionary of synonyms to replace a given proportion of words with their counterparts. The goal of this baseline is to evaluate the attacker behavior when very small edits are made in the original text.

ALISON We use ALISON, a recent state-of-the-art text edition AO model leveraging small replacements using a pretrained BERT model. Replacements spans are computed using a threshold on the explanations of an adversarial authorship attribution classifier trained on each evaluation dataset. We train this classifier on each training and validation set before evaluation.

GPT-3.5 Lastly, we include a comparison with GPT3.5 (`gpt-3.5-turbo`) (Ouyang et al., 2022) as a text generation baseline. We use a simple text obfuscation prompt to capture zero-shot capabilities of GPT-3.5 to perform AO. The prompt used can be found in Appendix A.2.

4.4 Realistic Attackers

So far, the considered privacy evaluation adopts the perspective of an attacker who does not have any knowledge about the obfuscation algorithm used. In a more realistic setting, the attacker can likely identify and reproduce the AO model, and perform more advanced attacks by creating adversarial threat models. Following Zhai et al. (2022), we also evaluate our obfuscation models against two enhanced authorship attribution attackers, better suited to simulate real-world attack scenarios. We list the different attackers and their specific aspects based on adversarial training:

[9] We use the `gte-large-en-v1.5` from `sentence-transformers` `https://hf.co/Alibaba-NLP/gte-large-en-v1.5`

[10] `https://github.com/Declipsonator/GPTZzzs`

Method	IMDb				BAC				AMT			
	10 Authors		20 Authors		10 Authors		20 Authors		10 Authors		20 Authors	
	Util. ↑	Attr. ↓	Util. ↑	Attr. ↓	Util. ↑	Attr. ↓	Util. ↑	Attr. ↓	Util. ↑	Attr. ↓	Util. ↑	Attr. ↓
Original	73.51	99.78	79.46	99.80	46.73	61.05	53.80	61.14	100	70.37	86.11	42.86
Synonyms	70.38	94.52	76.60	96.08	46.24	59.06	51.20	58.18	91.67	64.81	86.11	36.90
ALISON	61.88	89.59	**65.72**	91.02	**40.70**	40.67	41.00	39.22	**91.67**	70.37	73.33	35.84
GPT-3.5	63.33	66.67	47.37	35.00	37.20	42.73	**44.74**	31.27	60.00	44.44	61.11	31.14
SFT	**64.51**	62.50	39.47	80.00	40.41	32.44	40.10	28.28	90.00	26.85	**75.00**	21.23
TAROT-PPO	63.54	88.89	47.37	71.67	35.38	29.14	42.30	33.62	90.00	35.19	72.22	17.86
TAROT-DPO	57.14	**34.74**	60.72	**17.34**	24.57	**23.97**	28.39	**16.42**	86.67	**22.22**	64.18	**16.67**

Table 2: Evaluation results (Util: classifier accuracy on utility labels, Attr: authorship attribution accuracy) Best values are **bolded**.

- *Mix of original and obfuscated texts:* The attacker knows which AO algorithm was used and leverages this knowledge to create a new attribution model. This model is trained on a combination of original source texts and obfuscated texts generated by the known AO algorithm. We use a 50/50 distribution between original and obfuscated data to train this attacker.
- *Only obfuscated texts:* While the attacker is also aware of the AO algorithm, they train their authorship attribution classifier exclusively on the obfuscated samples. Zhai et al. (2022) demonstrated that this attack setting achieves the highest performance against text edition obfuscations.

For each attack scenario, we train a new authorship attribution classifier using the same parameters (see Appendix A.4 for hyperparameters) and compare the accuracy change from the original attacker.

4.5 Training new utility models with obfuscated texts

We experiment with a second use case to evaluate the downstream utility of obfuscated texts. We use the obfuscated texts of each method as a new training set for our utility classifier. This is useful to evaluate each method capability to generate useful training data that can be further used to train a new classifier on the same utility task.

5 Results

Downstream Effectiveness In Table 2, we present the accuracy change of privacy and utility classifiers. We observe that both SFT, PPO and DPO reduce the attacker accuracy compared to text edition methods (Synonyms and ALISON). PO helps to learn a good privacy-utility trade-off by largely improving the privacy of obfuscated texts compared to baselines, while preserving similar utility. We observe that DPO consistently outperforms the PPO algorithm on privacy preservation, while using the same base reward model. DPO is also the best-performing privacy preservation over all baselines, with a notable drop of 82,46% on IMDB-20. Note that the utility decrease is larger for the BAC dataset, which could be explained by the number of short texts contained in the dataset, whose edits affect a lot more the end utility. TAROT-DPO also outperforms GPT-3.5 by providing more utility and less attribution on IMDB-20, AMT-10 and AMT-20. The effectiveness of TAROT-PPO lays in its utility preservation capabilities. While not being as private, the utility drop is reduced on nearly each dataset compared to TAROT-DPO.

Adversarial Attackers Figure 2 highlights the accuracy of adversarial threat models on the IMDb-10 dataset. This attack strategy is effective against text edition approaches (Synonyms and ALISON) as shown by the accuracy gain compared to the base attack only trained on original texts. However, text generation methods (GPT-3.5, SFT, TAROT-PPO and TAROT-DPO) show resistance to adversarial threat models, and only GPT-3.5 and TAROT-DPO are susceptible to the attacker trained on a mix of original and obfuscated texts. This encourages the path of generation methods as promising obfuscators. Note that this is the first obfuscation approach that is shown to be resistant to threat models.[11]

Utility Preservation After Retraining Figure 3 presents the accuracy of a new utility classifier once trained with obfuscated texts. We observe

[11]Zhai et al. (2022) did not include generation models in their study of AO evaluation.

Method	Output
Original	I loved the whole story even though it was a tad corny at times . I think great acting and the content of the story kept it going.
Synonyms	I loved the quite whole story very even though it was a tad corny at times. I imagine too outstanding playing and the contents of the story kept it sledding.
ALISON	I thoroughly enjoyed the entire story even it did have a tad corny at times. I believe the great acting and the story's content were the main reasons to keep it going.
GPT-3.5	The entirety of the narrative was quite delightful, despite occasional moments of cheesiness. I believe the stellar performances and the substance of the storyline sustained its momentum.
SFT	I loved the whole story. It had many good parts and the writing was excellent. I think great acting and the subject matter of the story kept it going.
TAROT-PPO	I loved the whole thing. It was a good story and well-written. It also kept me going at times. I think great acting and the content of the story kept me going.
TAROT-DPO	I love the whole story. It's full of action, personality and humour. It keeps me going, though, and the content keeps me going.

Table 3: Obfuscation example from the IMDb dataset.

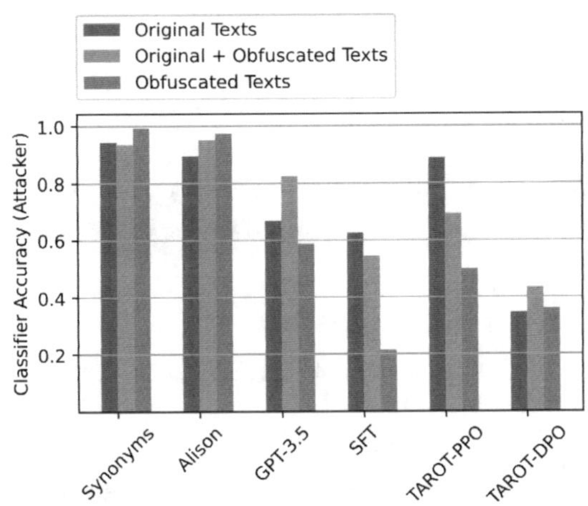

Figure 2: Authorship adversarial training accuracy results on IMDB-10 (lower is better). Generation models are resistant to adversarial training, compared to text edition methods.

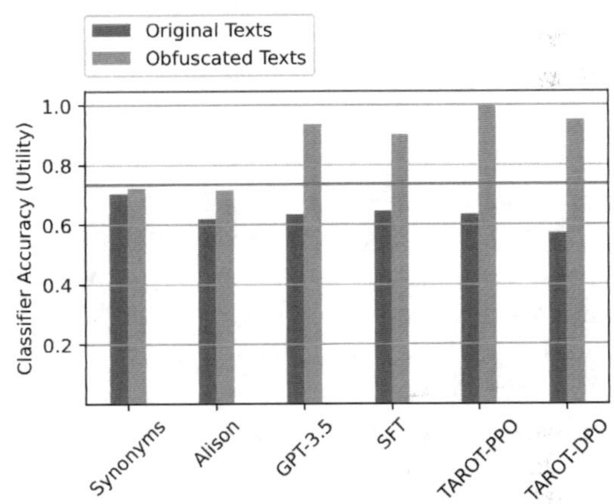

Figure 3: Utility classifier accuracy once trained on IMDB-10 obfuscated texts (higher is better). The red line indicates the classifier accuracy when trained and evaluated on original data. The overall utility always increases after training on obfuscated texts, this is key to compensate the utility drop of generation methods.

that the drop in accuracy caused by obfuscation can be compensated by training a new classifier, with an accuracy increase for all methods. Moreover, generation methods are even better candidates for training data, as the final accuracy is higher than the original classifier accuracy. TAROT-PPO and TAROT-DPO are the best-performing approaches on this dataset. This highlights the possibility of creating obfuscation methods that are both preserving privacy and keeping utility for training purposes.

Qualitative Analysis We show an obfuscation example in Table 3 for each method. The base Synonyms obfuscation results in awkward phrasing and less natural language, compromising readability. ALISON maintains coherence and clarity with slight formalization ("thoroughly enjoyed" instead of "loved"). GPT-3.5 significantly rephrases the text using sophisticated language. SFT simplifies and shortens the text, retaining clarity but reducing stylistic nuances. TAROT-PPO simplifies further, introducing some repetition, which makes the text less formal but still clear. TAROT-DPO alters the content more significantly, introducing new themes and repetition that can distract from the original meaning. The application of PO assists the text simplification SFT model in making additional modifications to the text. Although these changes in some cases alter the text's meaning, they preserve its overall utility. Appendix F provides more obfuscation examples from proposed and baseline methods.

Ablation Study As a complement, we perform an ablation study of each component of our reward model in Appendix D. It confirms the importance of using a combination of both privacy and utility rewards to learn this trade-off for obfuscation, especially for PPO.

6 Conclusion

We introduced a novel authorship obfuscation framework that focuses on optimizing the privacy-utility trade-off for a specific downstream data usage. We fine-tuned a text simplification model using two policy optimization algorithms to obfuscate the authorship of a given text, while preserving utility for multiple tasks. Our end-models are tuned using two sentence embedding rewards, one for content preservation and one for privacy, resulting in an unsupervised approach made for the open-world authorship setting. The results obtained help to improve the privacy from state-of-the-art AO methods, while preserving task utility. Our findings suggest that editing approaches are not suitable for privacy, especially against realistic attack settings. Additionally, we show that generated texts can be used to retrain utility classifiers and increase their performances, while limiting the accuracy of more advanced attackers. Ultimately, the performance of obfuscation methods largely varies depending on the downstream task choice, as does the resulting privacy-utility trade-off, highlighting the importance of selecting an appropriate model based on the specific requirements of the intended application. This calls for more research to design robust evaluation benchmarks for obfuscation systems, to assess and catch failure cases that can map to different real-world scenarios.

7 Limitations

The use of LM as text generators for obfuscation is not without risks, LM are known for their hallucination capabilities, so even if the downstream task is not affected, there is still a possibility that the trained LM generated plausible but false text from the original text. As we did not study the content preservation of resulting texts, we do not emphasize the risk of spread of misinformation or harm that can be generated by our fine-tuned LM.

Another limitation of our approach is that we rely on very small language models (380M parameters for `GPT2-medium`, our SFT baseline), which benefits from limited memory usage but suffers from a restricted context size for generation. As a result, our method tends to reduce the text length, especially for longer texts. This limitation could be mitigated by increasing the size of the SFT model.

Finally, these methods can be limited when applied to short texts, as the replacements create significant changes that directly affect the utility task.

8 Ethical Considerations

In this work, we present authorship obfuscation methods that are intended for beneficial purposes (learning insights from data while preserving privacy). But we recognize that this task presents some risks of misuse. It can facilitate harmful activities such as posting misinformation, spam, or harmful content, without accountability because of obfuscation. Moreover, these techniques might infringe on intellectual property rights by obscuring the authorship of creative works, depriving creators of their deserved credit. We strongly encourage users to carefully consider these potential dangers before employing such methods.

References

Malik Altakrori, Thomas Scialom, Benjamin C. M. Fung, and Jackie Chi Kit Cheung. 2022. A multifaceted framework to evaluate evasion, content preservation, and misattribution in authorship obfuscation techniques. In *Proceedings of the 2022 Conference on Empirical Methods in Natural Language Processing*, pages 2391–2406, Abu Dhabi, United Arab Emirates. Association for Computational Linguistics.

Michael Brennan, Sadia Afroz, and Rachel Greenstadt. 2012. Adversarial stylometry: Circumventing authorship recognition to preserve privacy and anonymity. *ACM Trans. Inf. Syst. Secur.*, 15(3).

Cynthia Dwork. 2006. Differential privacy. In *Automata, Languages and Programming*, pages 1–12, Berlin, Heidelberg. Springer Berlin Heidelberg.

European Parliament and Council of the European Union. 2016. General data protection regulation (GDPR).

Maël Fabien, Esau Villatoro-Tello, Petr Motlicek, and Shantipriya Parida. 2020. BertAA : BERT fine-tuning for authorship attribution. In *Proceedings of the 17th International Conference on Natural Language Processing (ICON)*, pages 127–137, Indian Institute of Technology Patna, Patna, India. NLP Association of India (NLPAI).

Natasha Fernandes, Mark Dras, and Annabelle McIver. 2019. Generalised differential privacy for text document processing. In *Principles of Security and Trust*, pages 123–148, Cham. Springer International Publishing.

Oluwaseyi Feyisetan, Tom Diethe, and Thomas Drake. 2019. Leveraging hierarchical representations for preserving privacy and utility in text. In *2019 IEEE International Conference on Data Mining (ICDM)*, pages 210–219. IEEE.

Jillian Fisher, Ximing Lu, Jaehun Jung, Liwei Jiang, Zaid Harchaoui, and Yejin Choi. 2024. Jamdec: Unsupervised authorship obfuscation using constrained decoding over small language models. *arXiv preprint arXiv:2402.08761*.

Pengcheng He, Xiaodong Liu, Jianfeng Gao, and Weizhu Chen. 2021. Deberta: Decoding-enhanced bert with disentangled attention. In *International Conference on Learning Representations*.

Timour Igamberdiev and Ivan Habernal. 2023. DP-BART for privatized text rewriting under local differential privacy. In *Findings of the Association for Computational Linguistics: ACL 2023*, pages 13914–13934, Toronto, Canada. Association for Computational Linguistics.

Yashwant Keswani, Harsh Trivedi, Parth Mehta, and Prasenjit Majumder. 2016. Author masking through translation. In *Working Notes of CLEF 2016 - Conference and Labs of the Evaluation forum, Évora, Portugal, 5-8 September, 2016*, volume 1609 of *CEUR Workshop Proceedings*, pages 890–894. CEUR-WS.org.

Kalpesh Krishna, Yixiao Song, Marzena Karpinska, John Wieting, and Mohit Iyyer. 2023. Paraphrasing evades detectors of ai-generated text, but retrieval is an effective defense. *arXiv preprint arXiv:2303.13408*.

Philippe Laban, Tobias Schnabel, Paul Bennett, and Marti A. Hearst. 2021. Keep it simple: Unsupervised simplification of multi-paragraph text. In *Proceedings of the 59th Annual Meeting of the Association for Computational Linguistics and the 11th International Joint Conference on Natural Language Processing (Volume 1: Long Papers)*, pages 6365–6378, Online. Association for Computational Linguistics.

Zehan Li, Xin Zhang, Yanzhao Zhang, Dingkun Long, Pengjun Xie, and Meishan Zhang. 2023. Towards general text embeddings with multi-stage contrastive learning.

Pierre Lison, Ildikó Pilán, David Sanchez, Montserrat Batet, and Lilja Øvrelid. 2021. Anonymisation models for text data: State of the art, challenges and future directions. In *Proceedings of the 59th Annual Meeting of the Association for Computational Linguistics and the 11th International Joint Conference on Natural Language Processing (Volume 1: Long Papers)*, pages 4188–4203, Online. Association for Computational Linguistics.

Shuai Liu, Shantanu Agarwal, and Jonathan May. 2024. Authorship style transfer with policy optimization.

Asad Mahmood, Faizan Ahmad, Zubair Shafiq, Padmini Srinivasan, and Fareed Zaffar. 2019. A girl has no name: Automated authorship obfuscation using mutant-x. *Proceedings on Privacy Enhancing Technologies*, 2019(4):54–71.

Justus Mattern, Zhijing Jin, Benjamin Weggenmann, Bernhard Schoelkopf, and Mrinmaya Sachan. 2022a. Differentially private language models for secure data sharing. In *Proceedings of the 2022 Conference on Empirical Methods in Natural Language Processing*, pages 4860–4873, Abu Dhabi, United Arab Emirates. Association for Computational Linguistics.

Justus Mattern, Benjamin Weggenmann, and Florian Kerschbaum. 2022b. The limits of word level differential privacy. In *Findings of the Association for Computational Linguistics: NAACL 2022*, pages 867–881, Seattle, United States. Association for Computational Linguistics.

Ahmadreza Mosallanezhad, Ghazaleh Beigi, and Huan Liu. 2019. Deep reinforcement learning-based text anonymization against private-attribute inference. In *Proceedings of the 2019 Conference on Empirical Methods in Natural Language Processing and the 9th International Joint Conference on Natural Language Processing (EMNLP-IJCNLP)*, pages 2360–2369, Hong Kong, China. Association for Computational Linguistics.

Frederick Mosteller and David L. Wallace. 1963. Inference in an authorship problem. *Journal of the American Statistical Association*, 58(302):275–309.

Long Ouyang, Jeff Wu, Xu Jiang, Diogo Almeida, Carroll L. Wainwright, Pamela Mishkin, Chong Zhang, Sandhini Agarwal, Katarina Slama, Alex Ray, John Schulman, Jacob Hilton, Fraser Kelton, Luke Miller, Maddie Simens, Amanda Askell, Peter Welinder, Paul Christiano, Jan Leike, and Ryan Lowe. 2022. Training language models to follow instructions with human feedback.

Jeffrey Pennington, Richard Socher, and Christopher Manning. 2014. GloVe: Global vectors for word representation. In *Proceedings of the 2014 Conference on Empirical Methods in Natural Language Processing (EMNLP)*, pages 1532–1543, Doha, Qatar. Association for Computational Linguistics.

Martin Potthast, Matthias Hagen, and Benno Stein. 2016. Author obfuscation: Attacking the state of the art in authorship verification. In *Conference and Labs of the Evaluation Forum*.

Rafael Rafailov, Archit Sharma, Eric Mitchell, Stefano Ermon, Christopher D. Manning, and Chelsea Finn. 2023. Direct preference optimization: Your language model is secretly a reward model.

Rafael A. Rivera-Soto, Olivia Elizabeth Miano, Juanita Ordonez, Barry Y. Chen, Aleem Khan, Marcus Bishop, and Nicholas Andrews. 2021. Learning universal authorship representations. In *Proceedings of the 2021 Conference on Empirical Methods in Natural Language Processing*, pages 913–919, Online and Punta Cana, Dominican Republic. Association for Computational Linguistics.

Jonathan Schler, Moshe Koppel, Shlomo Engelson Argamon, and James W. Pennebaker. 2006. Effects of age and gender on blogging. In *AAAI Spring Symposium: Computational Approaches to Analyzing Weblogs*.

John Schulman, Filip Wolski, Prafulla Dhariwal, Alec Radford, and Oleg Klimov. 2017. Proximal policy optimization algorithms.

Yanir Seroussi, Ingrid Zukerman, and Fabian Bohnert. 2014. Authorship attribution with topic models. *Computational Linguistics*, 40(2):269–310.

Saiteja Utpala, Sara Hooker, and Pin-Yu Chen. 2023. Locally differentially private document generation using zero shot prompting. In *Findings of the Association for Computational Linguistics: EMNLP 2023*, pages 8442–8457, Singapore. Association for Computational Linguistics.

Benjamin Weggenmann, Valentin Rublack, Michael Andrejczuk, Justus Mattern, and Florian Kerschbaum. 2022. Dp-vae: Human-readable text anonymization for online reviews with differentially private variational autoencoders. In *Proceedings of the ACM Web Conference 2022*, WWW '22, page 721–731, New York, NY, USA. Association for Computing Machinery.

Emily M Weitzenboeck, Pierre Lison, Malgorzata Cyndecka, and Malcolm Langford. 2022. The GDPR and unstructured data: is anonymization possible? *International Data Privacy Law*, 12(3):184–206.

Eric Xing, Saranya Venkatraman, Thai Le, and Dongwon Lee. 2024. Alison: Fast and effective stylometric authorship obfuscation. In *AAAI*.

Wanyue Zhai, Jonathan Rusert, Zubair Shafiq, and Padmini Srinivasan. 2022. Adversarial authorship attribution for deobfuscation. In *Proceedings of the 60th Annual Meeting of the Association for Computational Linguistics (Volume 1: Long Papers)*, pages 7372–7384, Dublin, Ireland. Association for Computational Linguistics.

Xiang Zhang, Junbo Zhao, and Yann LeCun. 2015. Character-level convolutional networks for text classification. In *Advances in Neural Information Processing Systems*, volume 28. Curran Associates, Inc.

A Experimentation Details

A.1 Hardware and code

We conducted all experiments with Nvidia A30 GPU card with 24GB memory and Intel Xeon Gold 5320 CPU. The main libraries used include `Pytorch` 2.2.2, Huggingface `transformers` 4.39.3, `datasets` 2.19.0, `tokenizers` 0.15.2, `trl` 0.8.6, `evaluate` 0.4.1 and `sentence-transformers` 3.0.0. Due to memory constraints, models are loaded with `float16` mixed precision.

Training time for PPO ranges from 15-20 hours, while time for DPO ranges from 6-12 hours. Evaluation time ranges approximately from 19-32 hours.

A.2 GPT-3.5 prompt

In our study, we compare with zero-shot prompting using GPT-3.5, a model with approximately 175 billion parameters. We obfuscate each text on a paragraph level, where the entire text is obfuscated as a unit. We use the following prompt to generate obfuscated texts: *"Rewrite the following paragraph so that the author's style is obfuscated."*

A.3 DPO training

While both PPO and DPO algorithms methods aim to optimize a model's performance based on a reward function, they differ in their approach to policy optimization. PPO uses a surrogate objective function that approximates the true objective function, while DPO directly optimizes the likelihood of generating a response chosen from a preference dataset over another response. This preference dataset is typically collected by having human annotators compare pairs of responses generated by a model and indicate which one is preferred. However, this protocol is impractical for authorship obfuscation because it is difficult to evaluate with human annotations. Therefore, we apply an initial preprocessing step to generate the preference dataset before DPO fine-tuning. We generate preference pairs from SFT outputs, and rank these preferences using the same reward model as PPO. Algorithm 1 outlines our method for creating this preference dataset for DPO. Preliminary experiments showed that removing samples with closely similar authorship rewards accelerates training convergence. So we specify filtering thresholds ϵ_{priv} and ϵ_{util}. After testing multiple values, we set $\epsilon_{priv} = 0.10$ and $\epsilon_{util} = 0.05$

Algorithm 1 Preference Dataset Generation

Require: SFT dataset $\mathcal{D}$, privacy threshold ϵ_{priv}, utility threshold ϵ_{util}
prompts = []
chosen = []
rejected = []
for prompt $\in \mathcal{D}$ **do**
left, right = generations from the SFT model
$R_{util-left}$, $R_{priv-left}$ = privacy and utility rewards from the left obfuscation candidate
$R_{util-right}$, $R_{priv-right}$ = privacy and utility rewards from the right obfuscation candidate
if $||R_{priv-right}$ - $R_{priv-left}|| > \epsilon_{priv}$ and $||R_{util-right}$ - $R_{util-left}|| < \epsilon_{util}$ **then**
if $R_{priv-right} > R_{priv-left}$ **then**
prompt.append(prompt)
chosen.append(right)
reject.append(left)
else
prompt.append(prompt)
chosen.append(left)
reject.append(right)
return prompts, chosen, rejected

A.4 Hyperparameters

Table 4 and Table 5 present hyperparameters used for PO algorithms and evaluation classifiers. Due to limited time and computational resources, we are unable to conduct an exhaustive search across all hyperparameters. Instead, we report the best-performing hyperparameters we identified.

	TAROT-PPO	TAROT-DPO
learning rate	1.47e-5	2.96e-5
batch size	16	32
# epochs	3	3
KL coef / beta	0.2	0.1
top p	1.0	1.0
temperature	1.0	1.0

Table 4: Training hyperparameters for PO algorithms.

	DeBERTa (Privacy)	DeBERTa (Utility)
learning rate	2e-5	2e-5
batch size	8	8
# epochs	3	3

Table 5: Training hyperparameters for evaluation models.

A.5 Baseline implementation details

Synonyms We use GPTZzzs to process original texts, it employs a dictionary of synonyms to replace a given proportion of words with their counterparts. The goal of this baseline is to evaluate the attacker behavior when very small edits are made in the original text. We use the `FinNLP` synonym list and ask the algorithm to change up to 90% of words, and 80% of adjectives.

ALISON We use the author's code implementation of ALISON, we use the largest edition parameters ($L = 250$ and $c = 1$) to edit the final text as much as possible.

GPT3.5 We use the `gpt-3.5-turbo` API endpoint from OpenAI to compute obfuscation, with default temperature, max_tokens and top_p.

B Content preservation and soundness study

We also study the impact on content preservation when obfuscating the text with generation models, including TAROT. Table 6 presents multiple content preservation metrics on the IMDB-10 dataset. Naturally, text edition methods obtain the best content preservation scores, compared to generation methods. In contrast, generation methods are superior in terms of linguistic acceptability (CoLA), since they generate the complete text as a whole. TAROT-DPO outperforms other methods on this metric.

C Complete Evaluation Results

Figure 4 presents the complete evaluation results of adversarial training on all datasets.

Figure 5 presents the complete utility evaluation after retraining on each dataset. The findings presented for IMDb-10 persist for IMDB-20 and AMT-20. We observe a smaller change in utility over the AMT-10 dataset due to the high base accuracy of the original classifier (1.0). However, this result does not hold for the BAC-10 and BAC-20 datasets, which is due to the lack of utility preserved after obfuscation. The blog authorship corpus dataset consists mainly of short texts, making it challenging for rewriting methods to transform the text without significantly affecting utility. This issue persists even after retraining the classifier on the obfuscated data.

	Rouge-1	Rouge-2	Rouge-L	BLEU	METEOR	BERT Score	CoLA
Original	-	-	-	-	-	-	69.31
Synonyms	83.86	68.61	83.68	64.64	92.41	94.61	30.20
ALISON	98.24	97.08	98.19	67.48	97.61	99.01	43.88
GPT-3.5	38.13	11.90	29.15	6.81	33.61	81.81	73.82
SFT	55.69	34.04	43.20	24.06	41.13	85.58	66.66
TAROT-PPO	51.33	29.36	38.67	20.77	37.93	84.50	74.46
TAROT-DPO	42.52	17.27	29.14	10.77	30.04	80.56	81.10

Table 6: Content preservation scores on the IMDB-10 dataset.

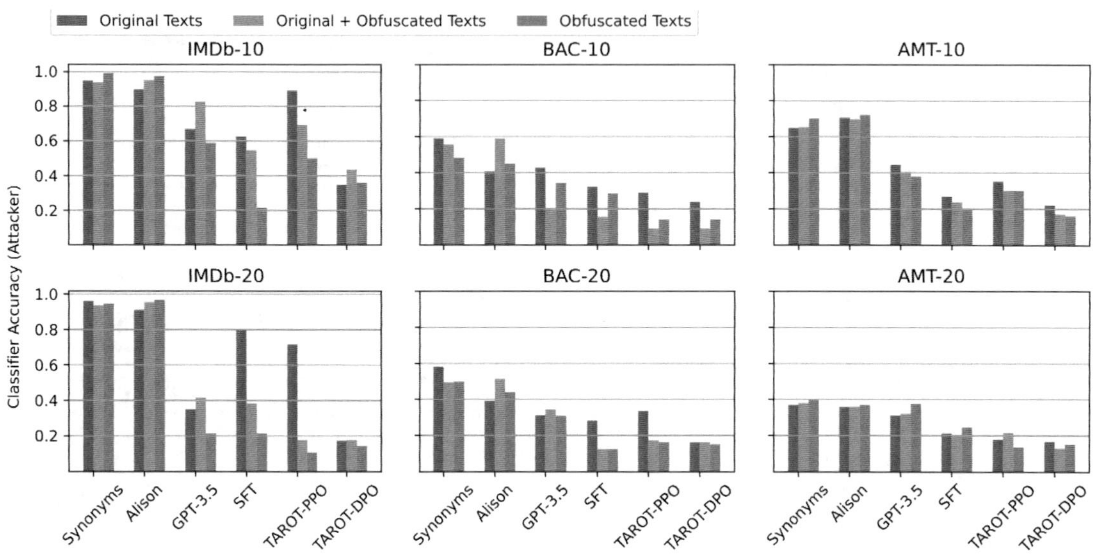

Figure 4: Adversarial training accuracy results (lower is better).

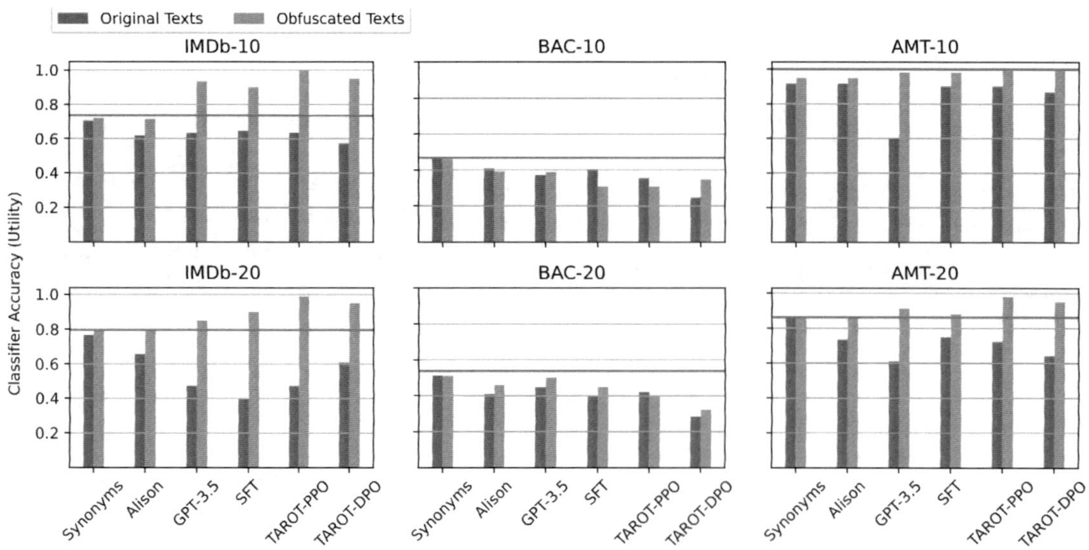

Figure 5: Utility classifier accuracy once trained on obfuscated texts (higher is better). The red line indicates the classifier accuracy when trained and evaluated on original data.

D Reward model ablation study

We perform a reward model ablation study to evaluate the importance of each reward component. Table 7 presents the reward value after training on different setups. We observe that the utility preservation and privacy components are both necessary to balance the privacy-utility trade-off. When we remove the LUAR-based reward, it leads to better GTE similarity at the expense of privacy. Similarly, removing the GTE reward leads to better privacy scores at the expense of utility. In practice, removing the privacy reward leads to models that try to copy the original text. While removing the utility reward leads to very short text, with only few words.

Method	TAROT-PPO		TAROT-DPO	
	LUAR	GTE	LUAR	GTE
No privacy	0.975	0.993	0.983	0.977
No utility	0.403	0.421	0.706	0.633
No ablation	0.931	0.825	0.915	0.738

Table 7: Reward model values when removing one component. A high LUAR value indicates low privacy, and a high GTE value high utility.

E Scientific Artifacts

We list in this section the licenses used in this paper:

Models DeBERTa-v3 (MIT) Keep It Simple (apache-2.0) LUAR (apache-2.0) GTE (apache-2.0)

Software GPTZzzs (GPL-3.0) ALISON (MIT) GPT-3.5 (Terms of use[12]) Pytorch (BSD-3) Huggingface `transformers`, `transformers`, `datasets`, `trl`, `evaluate` and `sentence-transformers` (apache-2.0)

[12]`https://openai.com/policies`

F Additional Obfuscation Examples

Dataset: IMDB	
Method	Output
Original	Walter Matthau was great as an aging man who lives to hang out in Central Park and tell outrageous lies. He strikes up a relationship with a man whom he drives nuts with his outlandish yarns. Matthau tries a con on several people trying to help them and himself out, but they all backfire . This film had a story that had me riveted to my chair. The entire production was filmed in Central Park, the scenery was beautiful, with many shots of the surrounding buildings. Wonderful movie - 5 stars.
Synonyms	Walter Matthau was really great as an aging man who lives to fall out in Central Park and evidence outrageous lies. He strikes up a relationship with a man whom he drives nuts with his outlandish yarns. Matthau tries a con on several people trying to assist them and himself out, but they all backfire. This film had a story that had me riveted to my chairman. The very full production was filmed in Central Park, the scenery was too beautiful, with extremely many shots of the surrounding buildings. Wonderful movie - 5 stars.
ALISON	Walter Matthau was great as an aging man to hang out in central park and tell outrageous lies. he strikes up a relationship with a man whom he drives nuts with his outlandish yarns.˙Matthau tries a con on several people trying to help them and himself out, but they all backfire. this film had a story that had me riveted to my chair. the entire production vet vet in central park, the scenery was beautiful, with many shots of the surrounding buildings. wonderful movie - 5 stars.
GPT-3.5	In portraying a mature chap who thrives on loitering in the heart of Central Park, Walter Matthau delivered an exceptional performance filled with fanciful fables. His character forms a peculiar bond with an individual who becomes perturbed by his fantastical tales. Matthau embarks on a series of deceits aimed at aiding both himself and others, all of which result in unfortunate outcomes. This cinematic masterpiece captivated me, ensuring I remained glued to my seat throughout. The entirety of the picture was shot within the confines of Central Park, showcasing its exquisite landscapes and featuring numerous glimpses of the adjacent edifices. A delightful piece of cinema - a resounding five-star rating.
SFT	Walter Matthau was wonderful as an aging man who lives in Central Park. He's a regular at the bar where he tells outrageous stories and tells wild stories. He strikes up a good relationship with a man whom he drives nuts with: his yarns. This film is shot in Central Park, with the backdrop of a long-running feud between Matthau and his friends. Wonderful movie.
TAROT-PPO	Walter Matthau was a joy to watch as an aging man who lives out in Central Park. He regularly tells wild stories about how he used to drive around town and tell wild lies. But he strikes up a good relationship with one person who wants to help him out and himself. This film has a lot going for it, with lovely scenery and lots of action. Wonderful film - 5 stars.
TAROT-DPO	Walter Matthau is one of those people who can never quite find the right balance between being a good friend and being funny. Though he lives in Central Park, he spends a lot of time telling his friends outrageous stories. This time, though, the relationship is quite straightforward. He strikes up a few conversations with people trying to help them get ahead of the game and, at the same time, he strikes up a relationship with a man who drives him nuts.

Dataset: BAC	
Method	Output
Original	Is anyone else gonna actually blog? It would be helpful you know!
Synonyms	Is anyone else gonna really blog? It would be very helpful you know!
ALISON	Is anyone else gonna actually blog? It would be helpful you know
GPT-3.5	Does the inclination exist for any additional individuals to engage in the act of blogging? Such contributions would undoubtedly prove advantageous, do you not concur?
SFT	Any other person writing about something like this? It would be helpful to know what other people are saying about the matter.
TAROT-PPO	Any other person blogging about something? it would be helpful to know who else is going to actually blog?
TAROT-DPO	Any other person on the list of potential bloggers? it would be helpful to know what they write about.

Dataset: AMT	
Method	Output
Original	The interplay between ""new"" and ""old"" ideas, methods, and forms in gothic literature gave it the intrinsic contradictory nature it retains today. The definition of ""gothic"" can never seemed to be agreed upon, the story within a gothic novel still seems to lost track of itself occasionally, the conflict between the emotional effect of terror, and the desire for a logical explanation (science and reason gradually began to replace the supernatural as the driving force behind the horrific) all remain. Neither the ancient nor the modern can be removed from the gothic without sacrificing something essential to the genre. [...]
Synonyms	The interplay between ""new"" and ""old"" ideas, methods, and forms in Gothic lit gave it the intrinsical contradictory nature it retains today. The definition of ""Gothic"" can never seemed to be agreed upon, the story within a Gothic refreshing relieve seems to missed cartroad of itself occasionally, the conflict between the emotional gist of terror, and the want for a logical account (science and intellect gradually began to replace the occult as the impulsive thrust behind the horrific) all remain. Neither the antediluvian nor the very modern can be removed from the Gothic without sacrificing something essential to the genre.
ALISON	The interplay between ""new"" and ""old"" ideas, methods, and forms in gothic literature gave it the intrinsic contradictory nature it retains today. The definition of ""gothic"" can never seemed to gothic gothic upon, the story within a gothic novel still seems to lost track of itself occasionally, the conflict between the emotional effect of terror, and the desire for a logical explanation (science and reason gradually began to replace the supernatural as the driving force behind the horrific) all remain. neither the ancient nor the modern can neither neither from the gothic without sacrificing something essential to the genre.
GPT-3.5	The perplexing interplay betwixt the ""novel"" and the ""antique"" concepulations, methodologies, and configurations in Gothic penmanship hath imbued it with a most incongruous essence that endures unto this day. The elucidation of ""Gothic"" hath forever eluded consensus, the narrative ensconced within a Gothic tome oft doth meander astray, the discord betwixt the emotive impact of dread, and the craving for a reasoned explication (where science and rationale inexorably supplanted the otherworldly as the impelling impetus behind the macabre) doth persevereth. Ne'er can the hoary nor the contemporaneous be excised from the Gothic sans forfeiting somewhat indispensable to the genre.
SFT	The interplay between new and old ideas is what gives gothic fiction its unique character. Methods and forms of storytelling, such as novel characters and their relationship to nature, give it a contradictory nature. The definition of gothic, however, cannot be agreed upon, the story within a gothic novel still seems to lack logic and reason, with terror still guiding the characters' actions and choices (science and reason gradually replaced the supernatural as the driving force, not just emotions).
TAROT-PPO	the interplay between ""new"" and ""old"" ideas, methods, and forms in gothic literature gave it the intrinsic contradictory nature it still retains today. the definition of ""gothic"" is never clearly agreed upon, the story within a gothic novel still seems to lack a logical foundation, and the desire for a logical explanation often clashes with the character's emotions and mental state. both the ancient and the modern are incompatible with the genre.
TAROT-DPO	But the two ideas are not linked by a common underlying logic. The definition of ""gothic"" can never seem to agree with reality. It can only seem to be full of contradictions and inconsistencies, with ideas such as new and old, new and old, about which there is never a clear line between right and wrong.

Dataset: BAC	
Method	Output
Original	New F-Zero title GBA bound - F-Zero: Falcon Densetsu News for Game Boy Advance at GameSpot yeah out this week to but overseas based on the anime btw which unfortunately is bad
Synonyms	New F-Zero claim GBA bound - F-Zero: Falcon Densetsu News for Game Boy Advance at GameSpot yeah out this week to but abroad based on the anime btw which regrettably is bad
ALISON	New F-Zero title GBA bound - F-Zero: Falcon Densetsu news for game boy advance at GameSpot yeah out this week to but overseas based on the anime btw which unfortunately is bad
GPT-3.5	A brand-new installment in the F-Zero franchise is set to debut on the Game Boy Advance, known as F-Zero: Falcon Densetsu. The release is anticipated this week, with availability limited to specific regions tied to its anime adaptation, which has been critically panned.
SFT	New title is GBA, a reference to falcon - a news service for game boy advance for the past three years. Yeah, out this week, though, overseas based on the anime btw which is just rubbish.
TAROT-PPO	New F-Zero title is a straight up rip-off of GBA. It features falcon news for the game boy advance, which again is crap online. Out this week, though, the anime btw are obviously not very good.
TAROT-DPO	An updated F-Zero title, this time with GBA, the title of a news show that the game boy advance on is. Yeah, out this week to news shows like F-Zero but overseas based on the anime, which is bad.

Dataset: AMT	
Method	Output
Original	Organisms would have the abilities to move, eat, hunt, and think. These functions would be optimized by genetic algorithms. To create this simulation, there were several steps. The first was to decide upon a programming language. The C++ programming language was chosen for its versatility and large pool of tutorial resources. The next step involved writing pseudo-code, or planning out the program itself. The actual program was broken into several functions. The first function, a global function that provided access to all other parts of the program, generated an arbitrary number of environments and filled them with a random number of food items that had a varying energy level based on the environment.
Synonyms	Organisms would get the abilities to go, eat, hunting, and think. These functions would be optimized by genetical algorithms. To make this simulation, thither were several steps. The 1st was to decide upon a programing speech. The C++ programing speech was elect for its versatility and really big kitty of tutorial resources. The next stair mired penning pseudo-code, or preparation out the programme itself. The factual program was crushed into several functions. The really first function, a worldwide function that provided approach to all other parts of the program, generated an arbitrary number of environments and filled them with a random figure of food items that had a variable vigor raze based on the environs.
ALISON	Organisms would have the abilities to move, eat, hunt, and think. these functions would be optimized by genetic algorithms. To create this simulation, there were several steps. The first was to decide upon a programming language. The C++ programming language for its versatility and large pool of tutorial resources. The next step involved writing pseudo-code, or planning out the program itself. The actual program planning planning into several functions. The first function, a global function that provided access to all other parts of the program, generated an arbitrary number of environments and filled them with a random number of food items that had a varying energy level based on the environment.
GPT-3.5	Living beings posses a range of functionalities, such as mobility, sustenance consumption, predatory behaviors, and cognitive processes, that are fine-tuned through complex genetic algorithms. To initiate the simulation, several procedural stages were undertaken. Initially, a choice was made regarding the selection of a programming language. Eventually, the decision was made to utilize the versatile and well-documented C++ language for its wide range of resources. Subsequently, the process involved the formulation of pseudo-code, a strategic blueprint for the development of the program. The program itself was compartmentalized into multiple functions. The primary function, acting as a global facilitator, was designed to generate artificial environments and populate them with random assortments of food items possessing varying energy levels depending upon the environment.
SFT	These organisms would have the ability to move, eat, hunt and think. These functions would be better optimized by genetic algorithms. These algorithms would be able to predict what environment a given creature would encounter next, and so on, generating different environments for each task. To create this simulation, programming language was used. Programming languages are usually designed to allow flexible programming of tasks for different stages in a person's life, like diet and training. These environments are then tested out in a variety of ways, like hunting or training. Tucking these algorithms into the program also meant creating more environment specific.
TAROT-PPO	These organisms would have the ability to move, eat, hunt and think. these functions would be optimized by genetic algorithms. These functions would be triggered by training programs that specifically targeted specific traits, such as hunger and thirst. To create this simulation, these would include programming languages for different types of environments, such as languages for animals and plants. These training programs would be tested against real-world situations and filled with different food types.
TAROT-DPO	These organisms are capable of thinking and eating. They can move and hunt, and they have even been observed to think about their environment. These functions, which would normally be optimized by a computer, are now well-suited for creating life on the planet. To train these organisms to perform these functions, for example, is to have a programming language that can be easily adapted to new situations. To put together a simulation of a particular environment, it would need to provide for training a range of animals, from which to choose. These kinds of simulations, which are relatively simple, would be ideal for training mental processes.

Dataset: IMDB	
Method	Output
Original	Funny romance / comedy with some well written lines for everybody . I especially enjoyed the give and take between Tony Randall and the Rock . Doris Day is soooooo cute ; I had a major crush on her during my junior high years . I liked Lynde's character , but I prefer his more sarcastic roles . 3 stars .
Synonyms	Funny latin / comedy with some swell written lines for everybody . I especially enjoyed the dedicate and take 'tween Tony Randall and the Rock . Doris Day is soooooo very cute ; I had a major smash on her during my junior so high years . I liked Lynde's character , but I favour his more sarcastic roles . 3 stars
ALISON	Funny romance / comedy with some well written lines for everybody. I especially enjoyed the give and take between Tony Randall and the rock. Doris Day is soooooo cute; I had a major crush on her during my junior high years. I liked Lynde's character, but I prefer his more sarcastic roles. 3 stars
GPT-3.5	A delightful tale of amusement and affection with a sprinkling of finely crafted dialogue that will appeal to all. The banter shared between the one called Tony Randall and the individual known as the Rock was particularly engaging. Doris Day exuded a charm that was utterly endearing; during my formative years, a deep infatuation for her blossomed. The portrayal by Lynde was rather enjoyable, though I find myself partial to his portrayals imbued with a sense of sarcasm. A rating of three stars is the verdict bestowed upon this film.
SFT	Funny romance / comedy with some funny lines. I loved the give-and-take between Tony Randall and the Rock, which was great to watch as I got older. Doris Day is soooooo cute ; she's always been this way, and I like her more in my junior high years. 3 stars.
TAROT-PPO	Funny romance / comedy with some well-written lines for everybody. I really enjoyed the give-and-take between Tony Randall and Doris Day. I loved her personality and her reaction to situations. They're both cute, but not as smart as Tony Randall. 3 stars.
TAROT-DPO	Funny romance. It's a good combination of comedy and give-and-take. There's always something interesting to say in front of the camera, or in front of the audience, about how they feel about someone else. Doris Day is soo cute, and soo funny. She's very much like me at my younger years, when I played sport. 3 stars."

Table 8: Additional qualitative examples for each obfuscation method.

Balancing Privacy and Utility in Personal LLM Writing Tasks: An Automated Pipeline for Evaluating Anonymizations

Stefan Pasch[1], Min Chul Cha[2]
[1]Division of Social Science & AI, Hankuk University of Foreign Studies, Seoul, Republic of Korea
[2]Division of Media Communication, Hankuk University of Foreign Studies, Seoul, Republic of Korea
(Corresponding Author)
stefan.pasch@outlook.com, minchulcha@hufs.ac.kr

Abstract

Large language models (LLMs) are widely used for personalized tasks involving sensitive information, raising privacy concerns. While anonymization techniques exist, their impact on response quality remains underexplored. This paper introduces a fully automated evaluation framework to assess anonymization strategies in LLM-generated responses. We generate synthetic prompts for three personal tasks—personal introductions, cover letters, and email writing—and apply anonymization techniques that preserve fluency while enabling entity backmapping. We test three anonymization strategies: simple masking, adding context to masked entities, and pseudonymization. Results show minimal response quality loss (roughly 1 point on a 10-point scale) while achieving 97%-99% entity masking. Responses generated with Llama 3.3:70b perform best with simple entity masking, while GPT-4o benefits from contextual cues. This study provides a framework and empirical insights into balancing privacy protection and response quality in LLM applications.

1 Introduction

The intersection of AI governance and data protection has garnered significant attention from academia (Yermilov et al., 2023; Staab et al. 2023), industry, (AWS, 2023; Azure, 2024) and regulatory bodies (European Data Protection Supervisor, 2025). As large language models (LLMs) become widely adopted, concerns regarding privacy risks in user interactions have increased. Particularly, the substantial costs of hosting LLMs, along with restricted access to certain proprietary models, pose significant challenges for individuals and small enterprises seeking to deploy LLMs locally. As a result, many rely on external LLM services, increasing privacy risks (Mao et al., 2024). Moreover, LLMs are frequently used in tasks that involve sensitive personal or corporate information, such as their names, company information, or location information. This raises critical questions about how anonymization strategies impact both privacy protection and response quality in these real-world use cases.

Existing research has primarily focused on privacy protection from adversarial attacks, such as attribute inference and re-identification risks (Staab et al., 2023; Chen et al., 2023). Approaches like differential privacy (Igamberdiev and Habernal, 2023) and prompt obfuscation (Sun et al, 2024) have been explored to mitigate these risks. However, these methods often concentrate on preventing external inference attacks rather than evaluating the direct trade-offs between anonymization and response quality in personal tasks.

While some studies have examined the utility of anonymized text, they often primarily focus on traditional NLP benchmarks like text classification or summarization (Yermilov et al., 2023; Riabi et al., 2024). However, the impact of anonymization on personalized, user-driven tasks, where coherence and contextual relevance are crucial, remains underexplored. Moreover, existing anonymization methods can degrade response quality, limiting real-world usability. Many privacy-enhancing techniques also rewrite entire user inputs, making it harder to retain original context and provide users with responses that align with their initial prompts.

In practice, however, many users engage large language models (LLMs) for tasks that involve

Proceedings of the Sixth Workshop on Privacy in Natural Language Processing, pages 32–41
April 4, 2025

sensitive personal or corporate information, such as drafting personal introductions, job applications, or emails. This raises concerns about how anonymization techniques affect the quality of LLM-generated responses in these personalized contexts, as there may be a trade-off between AI governance practices and response quality (Pasch, 2025).

In this paper, we analyze the effect of different anonymization techniques on personalized tasks and their impact on response quality. We introduce an automated end-to-end workflow to evaluate LLM-generated responses, encompassing the following steps:

1. **Creation of Synthetic Personal Prompts**: We generate prompts using LLMs for three writing tasks involving personal information: personal introductions, cover letters, and emails.
2. **Entity Identification**: Utilizing a BERT-based Named Entity Recognition (NER) model, we identify entities within these generated prompts.
3. **Anonymization Strategies**: We employ various anonymization techniques, enriching the initial entities using a local guardrail model to either provide context or substitute them with comparable pseudonyms.
4. **LLM Response Generation**: The anonymized prompts are input into LLMs to generate responses, simulating behavior in an unprotected environment.
5. **De-Anonymization**: We replace the masked entities in the responses with their original values.
6. **Evaluation**: We assess response quality using the LLM-as-a-Judge method and evaluate privacy by examining entity matches and LLM inference capabilities.

Our findings indicate that anonymization only slightly impacts response quality, with most settings showing a decrease of less than one point on a ten-point scale after de-anonymization. Notably, 97% to 99% of entities are effectively anonymized, demonstrating significant privacy enhancements. For responses generated by the Llama 3.3:70b model, a straightforward anonymization and de-anonymization approach outperforms more complex methods involving contextualization or pseudonymization. Conversely, for GPT-4o-generated responses, adding context further improves response quality.

This study contributes to the literature on LLM privacy in two major ways:

- Providing an end-to-end framework to evaluate anonymization strategies for personal writing tasks with LLMs.
- Assessing the effectiveness of various anonymization techniques in both privacy and response quality in personal writing tasks.

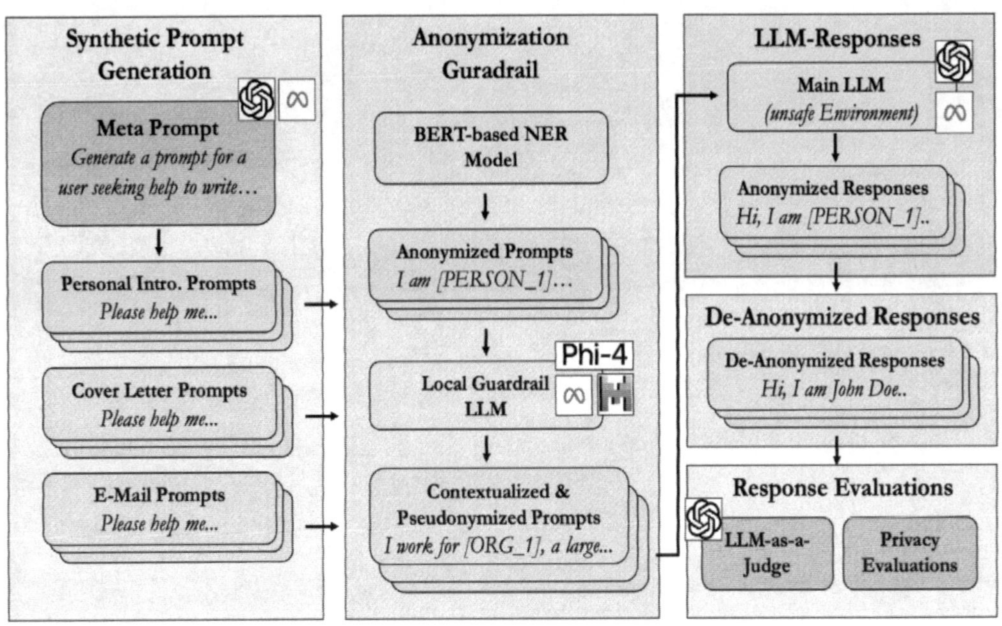

Figure 1. Overview of end-to-end anonymization and de-anonymization workflow

2 Methodology

Our approach presents a fully automated end-to-end workflow for evaluating anonymization strategies in LLM-based interactions, as depicted in Figure 1. Moreover, Figure 2 illustrates the different anonymization strategies. The pipeline spans synthetic prompt generation, guardrail-based anonymization, response generation, de-anonymization, and evaluation, ensuring a systematic assessment of privacy protection and response quality. To achieve this, we leverage two main categories of models:

Main LLM Models (Response Generation): These models are responsible for generating responses to user prompts. They reflect how proprietary AI systems process user inputs in real-world applications. We experiment with two state-of-the-art LLMs to evaluate the effects of anonymization on response quality: (i) ChatGPT 4o, and (ii) Llama 3.3:70b. While Llama can be locally deployed, we use it primarily to mimic proprietary AI systems, given its state-of-the-art performance, ensuring a controlled yet representative evaluation of anonymization effects.

Guardrail models: These models anonymize the text input. This first includes a NER model for entity masking and different LLMs to provide context or pseudonymize the entities. We specifically select open-source models for the guardrail tasks to enable deployment in controlled environments. The models used for these tasks are: Llamac3.3:70b, Llama 3.1:8b-instruct, Phi4:14b, and Mistral:7b.

2.1 Synthetic Prompt Generation

The first step in our workflow involved creating a dataset of prompts designed to assess response quality for personal tasks. Existing datasets in LLM anonymization research primarily focus on inferring personal information from text data or prompts (Yukhymenko et al., 2024). However, to the best of our knowledge, no dataset exists where user prompts explicitly request assistance for personal tasks that necessitate the inclusion of personal details such as names, locations, and affiliated organizations. We focus on three distinct personal tasks—personal introductions, cover letters, and business emails—as they represent common real-world scenarios in which users seek AI-generated text assistance while involving sensitive personal information.

Personal Introduction: Personal introductions are frequently used in professional and social settings, including networking events, biographies, and job-seeking platforms (Xu et al., 2023). These introductions typically contain personally identifiable information (PII) such as names, current and past employers, and locations.

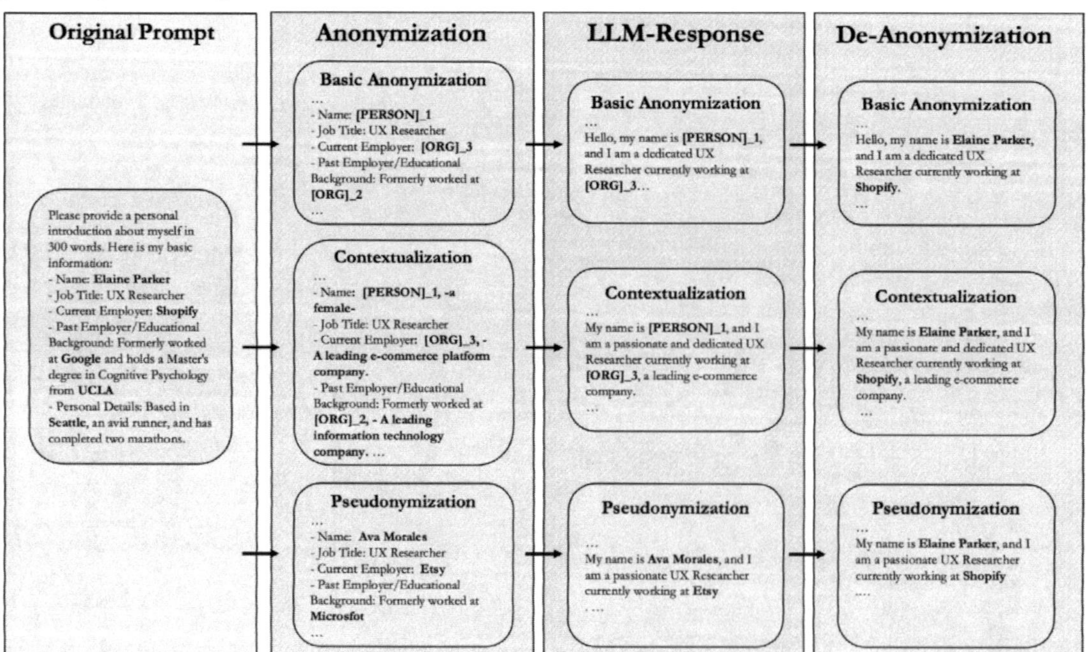

Figure 2. Overview of Anonymizations and Pseudonymizations

Cover Letter: Cover letters are a critical component of job applications and have been increasingly generated or refined using AI-powered writing assistants (Zinjad et al., 2024). Since cover letters include personal details such as work history, employer names, and sometimes personal aspirations, they provide a rich context for studying anonymization strategies in structured yet personalized texts.

Business Email: Email communication is a widely studied domain in NLP, particularly in business and professional settings (Jovic and Mnasri, 2024). Emails often contain sensitive information about organizations, job roles, and ongoing projects, making them a relevant task for evaluating anonymization methods while preserving coherence and intent.

By selecting these tasks, we aim to explore how anonymization affects the quality of LLM-generated outputs in contexts where personal information is integral to the content.

To create this dataset, we employed a meta-prompting approach, where an LLM was prompted to generate a single synthetic prompt for a given task. This process was repeated 50 times per task, resulting in a total of 150 prompts per LLM model. Importantly, all experimental steps were conducted twice, using two different LLMs—Llama3.3:70B and ChatGPT-4o—to generate independent prompt datasets.

Each meta-prompt included:

- Explicit task instructions (e.g., generating a personal introduction, cover letter, or email).
- A requirement to include realistic names, locations, and organizations that actually exist.
- A directive to ensure prompts were formulated from the perspective of a user seeking quick assistance, rather than overly refined or context-heavy instructions. This was done because initial trials revealed that the generated prompts were often too polished and provided a lot of context, resembling pre-written templates rather than spontaneous user queries.

2.2 Anonymize Prompts

In this study, we employ a BERT-based transformer model for Named Entity Recognition (NER) to anonymize prompts. Specifically, we utilize the *XLM-RoBERTa-large-finetuned-conll03-english* model (Conneau et al., 2020). Our choice of a BERT-based NER model is motivated by two primary factors: First, BERT-based models have achieved state-of-the-art results in various NER benchmarks (Conneau et al., 2020). Second, BERT-based models are increasingly being integrated into guardrail solutions to ensure safety and compliance in AI applications (Zheng et al. 2024).

Once the entities are identified, we anonymize the prompt text by systematically replacing each detected entity with a structured placeholder that preserves its semantic role. Specifically, named entities are substituted with generic category-based markers to maintain coherence and allow for later de-anonymization. Each entity type is assigned a unique identifier that follows a consistent pattern across all prompts. For instance, a detected organization (e.g., *Google*) is replaced with ORG_1, a location (e.g., *New York*) is replaced with LOCATION_1, and a person's name (e.g., *John Doe*) is substituted with PERSON_1. If multiple entities of the same category appear in a prompt, they are enumerated sequentially.

This structured anonymization approach ensures that the prompts retain their original syntactic and semantic integrity while eliminating personally identifiable information (PII). The placeholders allow for the preservation of relationships between entities.

2.3 Contextualization of Entities

Anonymization of entities often results in loss of contextual information, which can affect the quality and coherence of generated responses. For example, both *Google* and *Stanford University* would be anonymized as ORG_X, obscuring the distinction between a large software company and a university. To mitigate this issue, we implement a contextualization step where guardrail LLMs provide enriched descriptions of the masked entities. This approach ensures that the semantic role of entities remains intact, allowing the main LLM models to generate more coherent and informative responses despite anonymization.

Each anonymized entity is passed to the guardrail LLM, which is prompted to generate a concise description of the entity without revealing its name. For instance:

- *Google* → "a large software company"

- *Stanford University* → "a private research university"

For personal names, the contextualization is limited to gender classification, where the guardrail model predicts whether the name is typically male or female. This step helps in preserving pronoun consistency in text generation while avoiding re-identification of individuals.

2.4 Pseudonymization of Entities

In an alternative anonymization setup, instead of contextualizing the masked entities, we apply pseudonymization, where each entity is replaced with a comparable but non-identical alternative. This approach retains the structural integrity of the text while obfuscating specific details.

To achieve this, we prompt our guardrail LLM models to generate substitutes for entities identified by the NER model. The replacements are chosen to be semantically similar but distinct from the original entity. For example:

- *John Doe → Frank Miller*
- *Google → Microsoft*
- *New York → Chicago*

The goal of this approach is to preserve the context of the text while preventing direct entity recognition. Unlike contextualization, where descriptions replace entity names, pseudonymization maintains the original sentence structure, allowing the text to remain fluent and natural without explicit entity masking.

2.5 LLM Response Generation

After setting up the different prompts with various anonymization techniques, we input these prompts into the main LLM models to generate responses. In the system prompt, we inform the model that the input contains entity markers (with contextual information where applicable) or pseudonyms. Additionally, we instruct the model not to modify the format of these entity markers to ensure that they can be accurately mapped back in later stages. Overall, responses are generated for four different anonymization setups: (i) The original prompts (no anonymization), (ii) the anonymized prompts with simple masking, (iii) the anonymized prompts with contextualized information, and (iv) the pseudonymized prompts.

2.6 De-Anonymization

For prompts that underwent entity masking, each anonymized entity (e.g., ORG_1, LOCATION_1, PERSON_1) is replaced in the LLM responses with its original name based on the entity mapping from the anonymization step. Similarly, in the pseudonymized setup, each substituted entity (e.g., *Microsoft* in place of *Google*) is reverted to its original counterpart.

This step ensures that we can evaluate the quality of the generated text in its original form while analyzing whether anonymization strategies introduced any distortions or inconsistencies in the output.

2.7 Evaluating the Response Quality

To assess the quality of the generated responses, we use an automated evaluation approach based on the LLM-as-a-Judge method (Zheng et al., 2023), a widely used technique for evaluating LLM-generated text.

For the primary evaluation, we adopt the single answer grading approach, where the LLM is presented with a single prompt-response pair and asked to rate the response on a scale from 1 to 10. To ensure consistency, we use the official single answer grading prompt from Zheng et al. (2023).

While LLM-as-a-Judge typically provides an overall quality score, anonymization techniques may affect different aspects of response quality in varying ways. Therefore, in addition to a single score, we follow Zhong et al. (2022) and evaluate responses across four key dimensions:

- Coherence – Logical structure and connectedness of ideas.
- Consistency – Internal consistency and factual alignment with the prompt.
- Fluency – Grammatical correctness and naturalness of the language.
- Relevance – Appropriateness and relevance of the response to the given prompt.

We compute an average of these four scores to provide a secondary measure of overall quality. Based on recent findings, we use GPT-4o as the evaluation model, as it has been shown to exhibit high alignment with human preferences in LLM-as-a-Judge comparisons (Raju et al., 2024).

2.8 Privacy Evaluation

In addition to assessing response quality, we evaluate whether the anonymized text effectively preserves privacy. To measure this, we use two complementary approaches:

1. **Entity Matching** – We conduct a simple entity match by comparing the originally identified entities with those present in the anonymized prompts and responses. This allows us to check if any masked entities leak into the anonymized versions.
2. **LLM-Based Inference Attacks** – Inspired by Staab et al. (2023), we test whether an LLM (ChatGPT-4o) can infer masked or pseudonymized entities. The model is prompted to guess the original entities based on the anonymized text, simulating a potential privacy risk where an AI system could re-identify anonymized information.

Since the entities in our dataset were originally generated by LLMs, they tend to be commonly known entities (e.g., *Harvard University* or *Google*). This likely overestimates the model's ability to predict masked entities, as real-world anonymization would often involve more unique or less widely known names. Nevertheless, this measure provides a useful benchmark for comparing the relative differences between anonymization setups, particularly in assessing whether adding contextual descriptions or pseudonyms increases the likelihood of entity re-identification.

For both privacy measures, we define privacy as the inverse of the number of identified entities, calculated as:

$$Privacy = 1 - \frac{Identified\ Entities}{Total\ Entities}$$

When comparing the effectiveness of different anonymization strategies, we measure privacy before de-anonymization since de-anonymization occurs outside the "unsafe environment" in our setup.

3 Results

3.1 Evaluation of Anonymization Strategies

Table 1 presents the results for utility and privacy across different anonymization strategies. As expected, responses to original (non-anonymized) prompts achieve the highest scores across utility metrics, with an LLM-as-a-Judge score of 9.95 (ChatGPT-4o) and 9.76 (Llama 3.3:70B). Privacy scores are naturally low, as all original entities remain intact.

Across all specifications, we observe that anonymized and pseudonymized responses (without de-masking) exhibit lower quality scores. For example, basic anonymization results in a drop in utility, with ChatGPT-4o scoring 3.09 and Llama 3.3:70B scoring 3.19 in overall LLM-as-a-Judge evaluations. This is unsurprising, as these transformations alter the structure of the original prompt, potentially reducing the coherence and contextual accuracy with the initial prompt.

However, once the initial entities are reinserted into the anonymized or pseudonymized responses (i.e., after de-anonymization), response quality significantly improves. The LLM-as-a-Judge score of de-anonymized responses reaches 9.37 (ChatGPT-4o) and 8.41 (Llama 3.3:70B), indicating that while anonymization impacts output quality, de-anonymization can effectively restore much of the lost information.

When comparing different anonymization techniques, we find that simple anonymization followed by de-anonymization performs surprisingly well. Notably, for Llama 3.3:70B-generated responses, this basic anonymization-de-anonymization approach outperforms all other anonymization strategies.

For GPT-4o-generated responses, however, the results vary depending on the guardrail model used. We find that for all guardrail models except Mistral 7B, contextualized anonymization slightly outperforms the simple masking technique. For instance, the contextualized de-anonymized responses using Phi-4 14B achieve an LLM-as-a-Judge score of 9.70 (ChatGPT-4o), slightly higher than 9.37 for basic de-anonymization.

Regarding privacy scores, we observe that Llama-generated contextualization perform comparable to simple anonymization-de-anonymization when assessed using entity matching. Specifically, Llama 3.3:70B contextualized anonymization retains a privacy score of 0.99 (entity match), similar to basic anonymization. However, for Phi-4 and Mistral-generated contexts, a slightly higher number of tagged entities appear in responses, suggesting an increased risk of entity leakage when adding contextual information. For instance, the privacy score (entity match) of Phi4:14b drops to 0.95. Similarly, we find high risk of revealing entities for Phi and Mistral generated pseudonymization.

Using the LLM inference method to assess privacy risks, we find an increased privacy risk for all contextualization methods. For example, ChatGPT-4o contextualization (Phi-4 14B) has an

Table 1: Utility and Privacy Scores by Anonymization Strategy

LLM Response Model	ChatGPT				Llama			
Dimension	Utility		Privacy		Utility		Privacy	
Metric	Avg 4D	Score	Entity Match	LLM Inf.	Avg 4D	Score	Entity Match	LLM Inf.
Baseline: Original Response	9.97	9.95	0.00	0.10	9.89	9.76	0.00	0.11
Basic Anonymization								
Anonymized Response	6.72	3.09	0.97	0.83	6.35	3.19	0.99	0.86
De-Anonymized Response	9.75	9.37	0.97	0.83	9.41	8.41	0.99	0.86
Contextualization (Anonymized)								
Contextualization: Phi4 14b	7.18	3.18	0.88	0.46	6.50	3.49	0.95	0.42
Contextualization: Llama3.3 70b	7.10	3.20	0.97	0.62	6.48	3.47	0.99	0.61
Contextualization: Llama3.1 8b	7.07	3.17	0.97	0.59	6.49	3.37	0.99	0.58
Contextualization: Mistral 7b	7.18	3.19	0.94	0.54	6.13	3.24	0.97	0.53
Contextualization (De-Anonymized)								
Contextualization: Phi4 14b	9.86	9.70	0.88	0.46	9.17	8.03	0.95	0.42
Contextualization: Llama3.3 70b	9.83	9.53	0.97	0.62	9.11	7.51	0.99	0.61
Contextualization: Llama3.1 8b	9.82	9.60	0.97	0.59	9.16	7.72	0.99	0.58
Contextualization: Mistral 7b	9.72	9.46	0.94	0.54	8.79	7.14	0.97	0.53
Pseudonymization (Pseudonyms)								
Pseudonymization: Phi4 14b	3.86	1.58	0.78	0.85	3.64	1.32	0.82	0.87
Pseudonymization: Llama3.3 70b	3.81	1.48	0.97	0.98	3.64	1.23	0.98	0.99
Pseudonymization: Llama3.1 8b	3.85	1.60	0.95	0.97	3.61	1.23	0.98	0.98
Pseudonymization: Mistral 7b	3.93	1.79	0.77	0.87	3.60	1.23	0.78	0.82
Pseudonymization (De-Anonymized))								
Pseudonymization: Phi4 14b	7.77	6.04	0.78	0.85	7.27	5.06	0.82	0.87
Pseudonymization: Llama3.3 70b	9.29	8.57	0.97	0.98	9.01	7.43	0.98	0.99
Pseudonymization: Llama3.1 8b	9.37	8.69	0.95	0.97	8.75	7.03	0.98	0.98
Pseudonymization: Mistral 7b	6.65	4.61	0.77	0.87	5.38	3.21	0.78	0.82

Utility reflects response ratings using the LLM-as-a-Judge method. Avg. 4D corresponds to the average score of 4 dimensions of response quality: Coherence, consistency, fluency, and relevance. Score reflects a single overall score for the output.

LLM inference score of 0.46, while basic anonymization is at 0.83, suggesting that adding descriptions makes it easier for an LLM to reconstruct the original entities. In contrast, pseudonymization decreases this risk, with Llama3.3:70b pseudonymization reaching privacy scores of 0.98 (ChatGPT-4o) and 0.99 (Llama 3.3:70B), indicating that substituting entities with comparable alternatives can be an effective method to obscure true entities.

3.2 Evaluation by Task Type

We also analyzed differences in response quality and privacy scores across task types. Figure 3 presents response quality (measured as the average score across four dimensions) and privacy (measured using LLM inference) for selected anonymization strategies.

Overall, we found that results remained consistent across task types. However, for both GPT-4o and Llama-generated responses, the drop in response quality of anonymized prompts was most pronounced in cover letter. This is unsurprising, as cover letters require personalized and highly structured writing, making anonymization more disruptive to specific entity information. Consistent with this, we observe that contextualization had a strong positive effect on cover letters, particularly for GPT-4o, where it outperformed simple masking. For Llama-generated responses, contextualization also had a

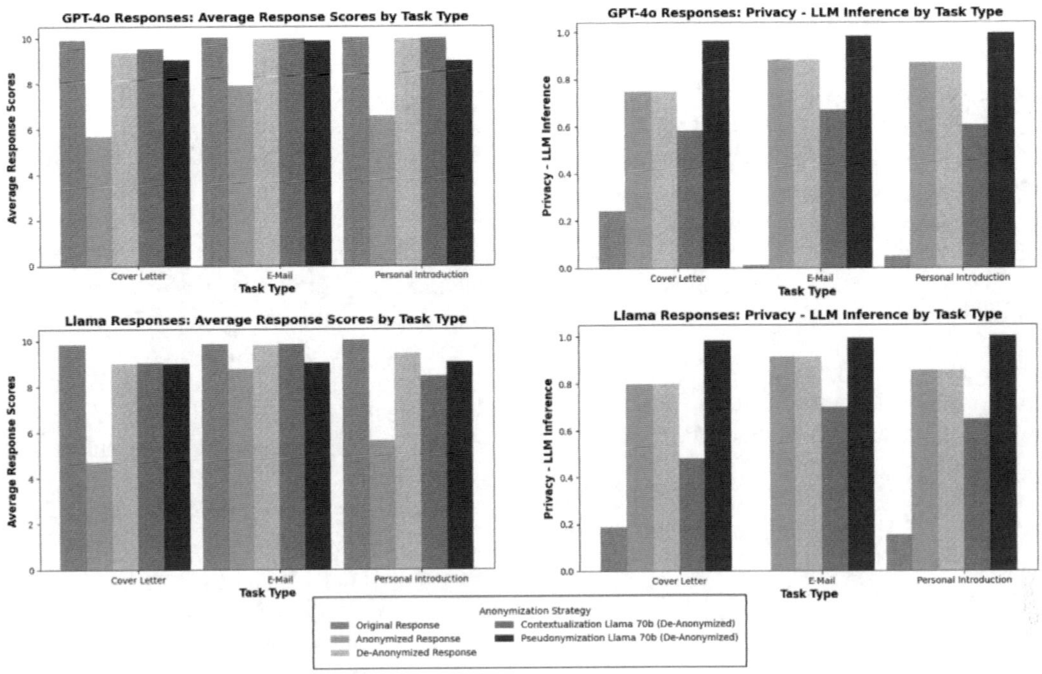

Figure 3. Evaluations by Task Type

moderate positive effect on cover letters, though its impact was smaller than for GPT-4o.

However, for Llama-generated responses, we found a notable drop in response quality for personal introductions when using contextualization. This suggests that while contextual descriptions help preserve coherence in structured tasks where tailoring responses for entities matters like cover letters, they may introduce unintended biases or distortions in more flexible, open-ended tasks like personal introductions.

Regarding privacy, we found that for both GPT-4o and Llama models, cover letters had the lowest privacy scores. This indicates that the contextual and job-specific details present in cover letter prompts may make it easier for LLMs to infer the original entities, reducing the effectiveness of simple anonymization strategies. Hence, for cover letters, we require strategies that better obscure entity identities, such as pseudonymization, which proved to be effective in preventing LLM inferences across all task types.

4 Discussion

Our results demonstrate that anonymization can effectively protect sensitive information while maintaining response quality in personalized LLM tasks. Across different anonymization strategies, we observe a minimal reduction in response quality (roughly 1 point on a 10-point scale), while achieving 97%-99% entity masking, indicating a strong privacy gain.

Interestingly, simple anonymization and de-anonymization methods (e.g., direct entity masking and backmapping) yield the best results for Llama-generated responses, suggesting that additional context can introduce unnecessary variability. Although prompts clarify that contextual information is provided solely as background information, we found that models often over-integrate these details into responses, such as mentioning that the user lives in an *East Coast city* in a cover letter. In contrast, GPT-4o benefits from contextualized anonymization, where entity replacements include descriptive labels. This indicates that some models may better leverage contextual cues to compensate for missing specific entity references.

Our findings highlight the importance of tailoring anonymization strategies to specific LLM architectures and task types, as different models interpret masked entities and contextual information differently. Additionally, we show that effective anonymization does not necessarily require complex transformations, as simpler techniques achieve comparable privacy protection with minimal response degradation.

This study underscores the feasibility of deploying automated anonymization workflows for real-world, privacy-sensitive LLM applications. Future work could explore adaptive anonymization techniques, where models dynamically adjust anonymization levels based on task sensitivity and model behavior.

5 Limitations

While our study provides valuable insights into the effects of anonymization on LLM-generated responses, several limitations should be considered when interpreting our findings.

First, our analysis is limited to ChatGPT-4o and Llama models, meaning the results may not generalize to other large language models, such as Claude, Gemini, or Mistral, which may process anonymized prompts differently. Different LLM architectures may exhibit varying sensitivity to entity masking, contextualization, or pseudonymization, potentially leading to different response quality and privacy trade-offs. Future work could expand the analysis to a broader range of models to assess generalizability across LLM ecosystems.

Second, while we employ the LLM-as-a-Judge method to automate response quality evaluation, our study does not incorporate human raters. Although recent work suggests that ratings with GPT-4o align well with human preferences, LLM-based scoring may not fully capture nuances such as subtle coherence issues, tone, or factual correctness. Similarly, our evaluation does not explicitly assess truthfulness or detect hallucinations in de-anonymized responses. For example, a de-anonymized cover letter could introduce fabricated details not present in the original prompt. Future research could incorporate human evaluations and factual consistency checks to ensure that anonymization does not introduce unintended distortions or hallucinated content that may not be detected by AI-based scoring.

Third, our dataset consists of synthetically generated prompts rather than real user queries. While this allows for an automated workflow, real-world user prompts may introduce greater variation, ambiguity, or complexity that could affect both anonymization performance and response generation. In particular, one challenge is anonymizing lesser-known entities, such as small businesses or less prominent organizations, which LLM-based techniques may struggle to recognize. Since our synthetic prompts are LLM-generated, they may overrepresent well-known entities, whereas real-world inputs may include more unique or less widely recognized names that could be more challenging to identify and anonymize effectively. Future research could explore real-world anonymization cases to assess how different anonymization strategies perform in practical applications.

Moreover, while our privacy evaluation effectively quantifies entity masking and assesses re-identification risks using LLM inference, it does not fully capture the severity of a single entity leakage. The current approach assumes that privacy loss is proportional to the number of entities disclosed, but in real-world applications, even a single leaked entity (such as a person's name) could constitute a significant privacy risk. This is particularly critical in tasks like cover letters and business emails, where context may allow an adversary to infer personal details even if only one entity is revealed.

Finally, our study employs a single anonymization approach, using a BERT-based NER model for entity recognition. While this approach is effective for structured anonymization, other anonymization techniques exist, including LLM-based NER. In addition, recent privacy-preserving prompt sanitization techniques, such as Casper (Chong et al., 2024), extend beyond NER by incorporating topic-based anonymization and rule-based filters. Future research could explore how different anonymization methods interact with various LLMs, assessing trade-offs between privacy effectiveness and response degradation.

Acknowledgments

This research was supported by the Culture, Sports, and Tourism R&D Program through a Korea Creative Content Agency grant funded by the Ministry of Culture, Sports, and Tourism in 2024 (Project Name: Development of multimodal UX evaluation platform technology for XR spatial responsive content optimization; Project Number: RS-2024-00361757).

References

AWS. (2023). Foundational data protection for enterprise LLM acceleration with Protopia AI Available at: https://aws.amazon.com/

Azure. (2024). Data, privacy, and security for Azure OpenAI Service Available at: https://learn.microsoft.com/en-us/legal/cognitive-services/openai/data-privacy?tabs=azure-portal

Chen, Y., Li, T., Liu, H., & Yu, Y. (2023). Hide and seek (has): A lightweight framework for prompt privacy protection. *arXiv preprint arXiv:2309.03057*.

Chong, C. J., Hou, C., Yao, Z., & Talebi, S. M. S. (2024). Casper: Prompt Sanitization for Protecting User Privacy in Web-Based Large Language Models. *arXiv preprint arXiv:2408.07004*.

Conneau, A., Baevski, A., Collobert, R., Mohamed, A., & Auli, M. (2020). Unsupervised cross-lingual representation learning for speech recognition. *arXiv preprint arXiv:2006.13979*.

European Data Protection Supervisor. (2025). Large Language Models (LLM). Available at: https://www.edps.europa.eu/data-protection/technology-monitoring/techsonar/large-language-models-llm_en

Igamberdiev, T., & Habernal, I. (2023). DP-BART for privatized text rewriting under local differential privacy. *arXiv preprint arXiv:2302.07636*.

Jovic, M., & Mnasri, S. (2024). Evaluating AI-Generated Emails: A Comparative Efficiency Analysis. *World Journal of English Language*, *14*(2).

Mao, Y., Liao, X., Liu, W., & Yang, A. (2024). A Practical and Privacy-Preserving Framework for Real-World Large Language Model Services. *arXiv preprint arXiv:2411.01471* .

Pasch, S. (2025). LLM Content Moderation and User Satisfaction: Evidence from Response Refusals in Chatbot Arena. *arXiv preprint arXiv:2501.03266*.

Raju, R., Jain, S., Li, B., Li, J., & Thakker, U. (2024). Constructing domain-specific evaluation sets for llm-as-a-judge. *arXiv preprint arXiv:2408.08808*.

Riabi, A., Mahamdi, M., Mouilleron, V., & Seddah, D. (2024). Cloaked classifiers: Pseudonymization strategies on sensitive classification tasks. *arXiv preprint arXiv:2406.17875*.

Staab, R., Vero, M., Balunović, M., & Vechev, M. (2023). Beyond memorization: Violating privacy via inference with large language models. *arXiv preprint arXiv:2310.07298*.

Sun, X., Liu, G., He, Z., Li, H., & Li, X. (2024). DePrompt: Desensitization and Evaluation of Personal Identifiable Information in Large Language Model Prompts. *arXiv preprint arXiv:2408.08930*.

Yermilov, O., Raheja, V., & Chernodub, A. (2023). Privacy-and utility-preserving nlp with anonymized data: A case study of pseudonymization. *arXiv preprint arXiv:2306.05561*.

Yukhymenko, H., Staab, R., Vero, M., & Vechev, M. (2024). A Synthetic Dataset for Personal Attribute Inference. *arXiv preprint arXiv:2406.07217*.

Xu, C., Li, J., Li, P., & Yang, M. (2023). Topic-guided self-introduction generation for social media users. *arXiv preprint arXiv:2305.15138*.

Zheng, A., Rana, M., & Stolcke, A. (2024). Lightweight Safety Guardrails Using Fine-tuned BERT Embeddings. *arXiv preprint arXiv:2411.14398*.

Zheng, L., Chiang, W. L., Sheng, Y., Zhuang, S., Wu, Z., Zhuang, Y., ... & Stoica, I. (2023). Judging llm-as-a-judge with mt-bench and chatbot arena. *Advances in Neural Information Processing Systems*, *36*, 46595-46623.

Zhong, M., Liu, Y., Yin, D., Mao, Y., Jiao, Y., Liu, P., ... & Han, J. (2022). Towards a unified multi-dimensional evaluator for text generation. *arXiv preprint arXiv:2210.07197*.

Zinjad, S. B., Bhattacharjee, A., Bhilegaonkar, A., & Liu, H. (2024, July). Resumeflow: An llm-facilitated pipeline for personalized resume generation and refinement. In *Proceedings of the 47th International ACM SIGIR Conference on Research and Development in Information Retrieval* (pp. 2781-2785).

Named Entity Inference Attacks on Clinical LLMs: Exploring Privacy Risks and the Impact of Mitigation Strategies

Adam Sutton[1] and **Xi Bai**[1,2] and
Kawsar Noor[1,2] and **Thomas Searle**[1] and **Richard Dobson**[1]
[1]Department of Biostatistics and Health Informatics,
Institute of Psychiatry, Psychology and Neuroscience, King's College London, London, UK
[2]National Institute for Health and Care Research Biomedical Research Centre,
University College London Hospitals, National Health Service Foundation Trust, London, UK

Abstract

Transformer-based Large Language Models (LLMs) have achieved remarkable success across various domains, including clinical language processing, where they enable state-of-the-art performance in numerous tasks. Like all deep learning models, LLMs are susceptible to inference attacks that exploit sensitive attributes seen during training. AnonCAT, a RoBERTa-based masked language model, has been fine-tuned to de-identify sensitive clinical textual data. The community has a responsibility to explore the privacy risks of these models. This work proposes an attack method to infer sensitive named entities used in the training of AnonCAT models. We perform three experiments; the privacy implications of generating multiple names, the impact of white-box and black-box on attack inference performance, and the privacy-enhancing effects of Differential Privacy (DP) when applied to AnonCAT. By providing real textual predictions and privacy leakage metrics, this research contributes to understanding and mitigating the potential risks associated with exposing LLMs in sensitive domains like healthcare.

1 Introduction

Various fields have seen the benefits of applying transformer-based Large Language Models (LLM) to NLP tasks (Wang et al., 2018). The medical domain is one such field that has applied LLMs to various tasks and achieved state-of-the-art performance (Peng et al., 2019). Due to the increased number of training parameters; training such models can be expensive in terms of computation, data, and time. To alleviate these issues, pre-training is done via a general language modelling task, and this "base" model is distributed to be fine-tuned (Devlin, 2018). The result of the pre-training and fine-tuning process is a language model that achieves a high level of performance for a specific task within a specific domain.

AnonCAT is a RoBERTa-based LLM that has been fine-tuned for the task of de-identifying clinical textual data (Kraljevic et al., 2023; Liu, 2019). The purpose of AnonCAT is to protect patient privacy within healthcare records and to provide a framework that is adaptable between hospitals, departments, and other healthcare agencies. AnonCAT is available through the MedCAT GitHub[1] (Kraljevic et al., 2021).

Textual data containing sensitive personal information can be encoded in the model during pretraining (Huang et al., 2022) and fine tuning (Qi et al., 2023), and this may be exploitable by inference attacks. Clinical textual data will often have highly sensitive attributes that a model will see during training, such as names, dates of birth, medications, family, and lifestyle. Motivated attackers may be able to infer such sensitive attributes via white-box (direct access to the model) (Wang et al., 2024) and black-box (access to model outputs only) attacks (Huang and Zhang, 2019). Inference attempts are more commonly applied to generative models in comparison to alternative textual models (such as masked language models) (Gu et al., 2023).

Efforts have been made to reduce the amount of training that can be leaked from inference attacks; such as regularization, differential privacy, confidence masking, and knowledge distillation (Hu et al., 2022). In particular, differential privacy (DP) is a common defence against data leakage from LLMs (Anil et al., 2021), where individual data points are aimed at being obfuscated while maintaining the statistical information of the underlying dataset.

In this work, our aim is to look at AnonCATs susceptibility to a "name inference attack", a variant of an attribute inference attack. We also provide two methods to measure the privacy of the model.

[1]https://github.com/CogStack/MedCAT

Proceedings of the Sixth Workshop on Privacy in Natural Language Processing, pages 42–52
April 4, 2025 ©2025 Association for Computational Linguistics

A name inference attack is an attempt by a motivated attacker to infer the named entities of a given de-identified text. We look to answer the following questions:

1. Can a decoder architecture be used to attack AnonCAT via a name inference attack, extracting names from de-identified text?

2. Are there additional privacy leaks from generating multiple names?

3. How does a name inference attack perform as a white-box attack compared to a black-box attack?

4. What are the privacy benefits of a model that has been trained with Differential Privacy when subject to a name inference attack?

2 Related Works

Language models have been well established in their susceptibility to inference attacks (Mireshghallah et al., 2022). Among large language models, causal language models have been shown to leak more information compared to masked language models (Jagannatha et al., 2021).

Membership inference attacks are a somewhat common method of attack explored. The work focuses mainly on inferring if the samples were part of the victim models training set (Duan et al., 2024). This attack will not directly infer sensitive attributes and will instead attempt to ascertain only the presence of the sample being in the training set. "Group" level attacks infer sensitive information with a higher privacy leakage compared to a single sample.

Attribute inference attacks are an alternative method in which an attacker can infer sensitive features from samples (Jayaraman and Evans, 2022). These samples are assumed to be from the training set, or at least statistically similar to training samples.

Another method of attack is embedding inversion, where, given the embedding parameters, sensitive tokens or phrases can be recovered (Morris et al., 2023).

These methods generally do not target the most sensitive of training information - such as names and dates of birth. Some works look at inferring sensitive information at a "group" level as opposed to a single sample, which achieves a higher leakage of relative privacy (Jagannatha et al., 2021).

Attackers also have multiple avenues to expose vulnerabilities and gain access to training data. White-box and black-box attacks cover large amounts of potential attacks, with varying levels of access to victim models and source weights (Chen et al., 2021; Song and Raghunathan, 2020). Datasets used in the attack are similarly varied according to their task and availability (Yeom et al., 2018).

To combat this, work has been done to enable the application of DP in deep learning on a large scale, where privacy is maintained and the impact on predictive performance is minimised (Abadi et al., 2016). This has been extended to the realm of NLP, where DP has been deployed in an attempt to preserve the privacy encoded in hidden states while maintaining the utility of the model(Coavoux et al., 2018). Efforts have also been made to ensure the privacy of fine-tuning datasets through techniques applied during the fine-tuning process (Yu et al., 2021).

2.1 AnonCAT

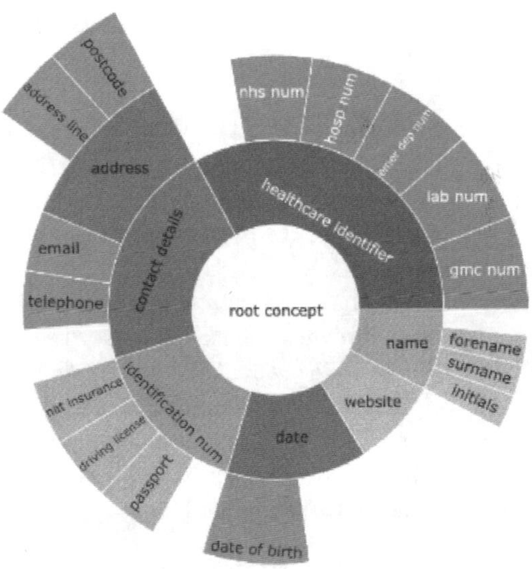

Figure 1: Sunburst hierarchical ontology structure of terms for redaction from the AnonCAT de-identification model. There is a shared root concept, with leaf nodes being more specific than its inherited parent.

"AnonCAT" is a transformer language model approach to text redaction (Kraljevic et al., 2023). It employs localised fine-tuning of a pre-trained model to improve performance of de-identifying clinical text, to further improve the performance at local sites. AnonCATs transformer model is a masked language model based on RoBERTa (Liu, 2019). The method is proposed to enhance the privacy protection of all entities within healthcare organisations and contribute to the safety of healthcare data when used in research and development.

3 Methods

3.1 Attack Definition

Algorithm 1 Attribute Inference Attack

Inputs: AnonCAT model $\mathbf{\Phi}$ with:
output hidden representation h,
Textual sample x which contains:
non-sensitive attributes x^{ns} and
sensitive attributes x^{s}
Obtain $h(x^{ns})$ via querying $\mathbf{\Phi}(x^{ns})$
Train: Train an attack model ϕ that aims to predict x^{s}
Output: $\hat{x^s} = \phi(h(x^{ns}))$

Given a sample x which is comprised of it's sensitive and non-sensitive attributes (in this case tokens) such that: $x = [x^{ns}, x^{s}]$ where x^{ns} refers to its non-sensitive attributes and x^{s} refers to its sensitive counterparts. We define the attack algorithm in Alg. 1.

The hidden states $h(x^{ns})$ provided by $\mathbf{\Phi}$ are used as input for the attribute inference attack, where the trained parameters of $\mathbf{\Phi}$ are frozen so as not to poison the attack model with ground truth from the attack dataset.

ϕ represents the learned name attack model to infer sensitive attributes that have been used as part of the training of the AnonCAT model $\mathbf{\Phi}$. The model weights are updated for each training sample of non-sensitive and sensitive textual pairs. $\hat{x^s}$ is the predicted textual sensitive attributes that a potential attacker would aim to be x^{s}.

3.2 Attack Model Architecture

Fig. 2 describes the model architecture for performing an attribute entity attack on an AnonCAT / masked language model. Before the attack model is used the de-identified text will be passed through the victim AnonCAT model. The raw AnonCAT architecture without being part of an attack is described in App. A.

The attack model encodes and embeds the prefix and suffix entries to be fed along with the AnonCAT models hidden states. The attack model parameters are randomly initialised, as a pre-trained models training would not be beneficial to the hidden states passed from the victim model.

The attack model uses a causal language model (or a "decoder model") which is used to predict the next token given previous tokens. In a standard setup for causal language models, next token predictions will occur for each token given the preceding tokens. In the attack model variant, the only tokens generated are those that contain the sensitive names in the suffix.

3.3 Generation

3.3.1 Generation Sampling

Various generation strategies, such as greedy sampling, multinomial sampling, or beam search, still consider all possible tokens where the tail distribution heavily outweighs likely tokens. The large number of potential samples from the tail distribution will also include tokens that are impossible to include in the prediction. To force these more likely tokens to be sampled, we will remove the less likely tokens from consideration by top-K sampling, as first performed in (Gu et al., 2023):

$$\mathcal{C} = argsort(\mathcal{P})[:k] \quad (1)$$

$$q_i = \frac{e^{P_{c_i}/t}}{\sum_j e^{P_{c_j}/t}} \forall c_i \in \mathcal{C} \quad (2)$$

$$\mathcal{P}' = [q_1, q_2, ...q_k] \quad (3)$$

The top-k most likely indices are retrieved by sorting by logits, giving us $\mathcal{C}$. The probabilities for each potential token are then returned via the softmax function. We denote our top-k tokens to be sampled as $\mathcal{P}'$. For our experiments, we set k at 50 and the temperature (t) at 3.

We scaled the logits for each potential token by a temperature value (to promote diversity when choosing from the top-k predicted tokens). The diversity of an increased temperature value is better suited to generating the first few tokens. We reduce the temperature for each token after the first linearly until the 10th token, where it is 1 for the remainder of the generation process.

We limit the length of all generated text to a maximum of 15 tokens. The maximum number of tokens required to encode a name in the dataset is 11. The ability to correctly generate consistent words or phrases is also greatly reduced after 15 tokens.

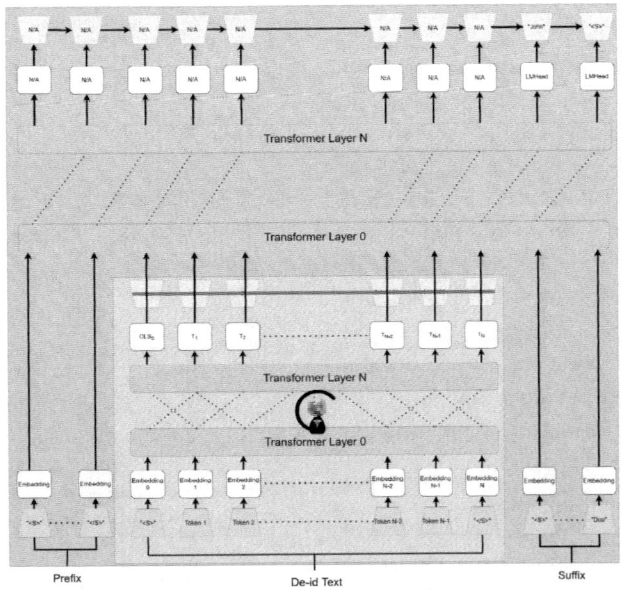

Figure 2: A single sample of the proposed decoder model for a name entity attack predicting the de-identified name. The blue represents a standard AnonCAT model that performs entity recognition, and the parameters in this model are frozen. The predictions for entities are ignored, and the hidden states are passed to the attack model. The attack model also has prefixes and suffixes that are concatenated to sample of de-identified text before predicting the entities name.

3.3.2 Top n sampling

At each forward step that generates text, there are tens of thousands of potential tokens at a single forward step and multiple consecutive tokens to be generated. This results in a large number of potential names being generated as part of the attack. Depending on the motivations of an attacker, partial predictions or predictions that are highly likely but not the first prediction may be "good enough".

To simulate this, we will continue to predict with the n most likely tokens at each forward step. After the final tokens have been generated, the n most likely sequences will be used as the final names inferred. The values of n used in this work are 1,2,5 and 10. These values have been explicitly chosen to see the impact of n on attack performance.

4 Experiments

4.1 Datasets

4.1.1 AnonCAT Dataset

The model is initialised with the "RoBERTa-base" pre-trained model, which was trained on five datasets (BookCorpus, English Wikipedia, CC-NEWS, OpenWebText, Stories) (Liu et al., 2019). The dataset that was used in the process to fine-tune the AnonCAT de-identification models has been independently validated and approved for ongoing usage as part of a de-identification pipeline for ongoing research studies at University College London Hospital. This dataset was generated through two rounds of annotation sessions, focusing on 10 critical Personally Identifiable Information (PII) concepts in accordance with the Health Insurance Portability and Accountability Act (HIPPA) guidance on de-identification and privacy rules. This dataset consists of 560 documents in which the 10 PII concepts were manually annotated. The AnonCAT model achieved >0.95 F1 across all PII categories.

4.1.2 Attack Dataset

The attack model is randomly initialised, so no dataset is used in the pre-training step of the attack model. The dataset for the "fine-tuning" step of the attribute inference attack is from the 2014 i2b2 / UTHealth shared task of natural language (Stubbs and Uzuner, 2015; Stubbs et al., 2015). One track of the shared task focuses on a set of 1304 longitudinal medical records describing 296 patients, where the task is de-identification for longitudinal clinical records. This corpus has since been used commonly in de-identification tasks as a gold standard dataset.

4.2 Experimental Setup

The following hyper-parameters are set for each model created for a fair comparison between them. The models are trained for 64 epochs, with a batch size of 8. The learning rate is set to 5e-5 and the weight decay is set to 0.01. Due to the length of some documents and multiple names that exist in most documents, a maximum window size of 200 has been chosen. This window size is empirically chosen based on the expected best performance so multiple entities don't have identical text entered into the model and to avoid some documents being too long to fit all text. In these experiments, the only de-identified attributes predicted across all models are patient names.

Tab.1 shows a textual example of a training sample. When generating predictions outside of the training set, the label is not provided. The model also only performs backpropagation on the label tokens during training. Some files have multiple occurrences of patient names, along with different variants of the patient's name (i.e., "John Doe", "John", "Mr. Doe" all being present within the same document). In the interest of fairness, these variants have been altered to the full name as the ground truth label.

4.2.1 White-Box Attack

The white-box attack model has access to 771 files where patient names are available and labelled. We perform an 80/20 train/test split to have 616 training files and 155 test files. We split at the file level to avoid poisoning the model with ground truth labels from the test dataset in the training step. With our split of 771 files we have 1079 training samples, and 236 testing samples.

4.2.2 Black-Box Attack

If the model weights are not exposed and access to the victim model is limited via an API a white-box attack is impossible. In this case a model extraction attack is performed on the black-box API, this will generate a model where the attribute inference attack can instead be performed on this generated model. Fig. 3 demonstrates the process used in a model extraction attack to generate labels that will be used to generate labels for a training dataset.

To generate a model for the black-box attack, we need a textual dataset that can be used to query the API to obtain labelled data. This dataset must still have names present in the dataset. "n2c2" has hosted multiple clinical challenges in the past,

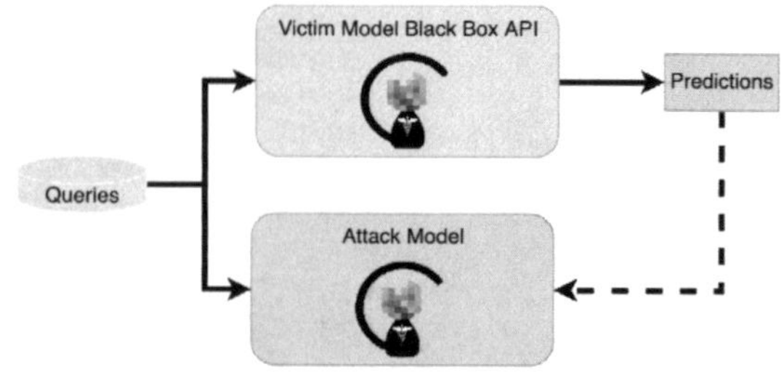

Figure 3: The workflow of a model extraction attack to be used when white-box access to the model is not available and only prediction labels are returned to the attacker. This will be used to create a model which will then be used as part of an attribute inference attack. Queries are fed to the black-box API, where predictions are paired with their corresponding queries to make input and label pairs.

and two challenges still have names in the dataset (Uzuner et al., 2011, 2010b,a). After querying the API with these samples, the generated labels will be used as ground-truth labels to pair with their respective texts. These pairs will be used to train another AnonCAT model.

4.2.3 Differential Privacy Models

The AnonCAT model is a RoBERTa transformer model, trained via the masked language model method. To fine-tune the model with differential privacy (DP), we employed dp-transformers (Yu et al., 2021)[2], which provides a high-level interface for conducting DP-related operations such as adding a noise multiplier and clipping gradients at the lower level of the training loop.

Three variants of the DP model were fine-tuned, where the target epsilon (privacy budget) is set to 0.1, 2 and 8. All other configurable parameters are constant throughout the three training rounds to ensure a fair comparison. We observed that as the epsilon values decreased (with an increased level of privacy), the utility of the model degraded on the basis of the evaluation metrics.

Tab. 2 shows the performance of multiple models used with varying levels of privacy. As the privacy budget decreases, more noise is introduced to the model weights during training and is considered to have increased privacy at the cost of model utility. In real-world usage of DP models, values of epsilon above 1 are considered to be insufficiently private, while values below 1 are considered safer.

[2]https://github.com/microsoft/dp-transformers

Prefix	"<s> Predict the name of the person in the following text: </s>"
De-identified text	"<s> ...seeing your patient Mr in followup for episodes of dyspnea... </s>"
Suffix	"<s> Name of the person is: </s><s>
Label	**John Doe</s>**

Table 1: A textual example of what is passed to the model during a training step. The sample will be in the order of; prefix, de-identified text, suffix, and label. The model only learns from predicting tokens that occur in the label, previous tokens in the input are ignored. When using the model outside of training, text is generated after the final <s> token in the suffix.

Model	Precision	Recall	F1
No privacy	0.965	0.989	0.976
epsilon 8	0.760	0.781	0.769
epsilon 2	0.760	0.784	0.770
epsilon 0.1	0.636	0.699	0.653

Table 2: Performance metrics of models with varying privacy budgets. Generally, a lower epsilon results in increased privacy, at the cost of performance. An epsilon lower than 1 is generally considered "suitably private".

4.3 Model Evaluation

Evaluation loss isn't a suitable metric for evaluating model performance; in a forward step tokens are generated given a perfect ground truth of preceding tokens. Later tokens will be poisoned by earlier predictions, being replaced by the ground truth. To fairly evaluate the models ability to infer names, names should be generated given a test sample with personal information removed. Our generation method as described in Sec. 3.3.1 is used. Two metrics are measured to evaluate the performance of a model. A binary classification metric, and a sliding Hamming distance. The binary classification metric is derived from seeing if the true label is a sublist of the predicted tokens. The Hamming distance will be formed via a sliding window; with the ground truth being compared to all consecutive sublists of the predicted tokens. Examples of this are provided in Tab. 3.

These metrics were chosen manually through experiments that generate text using the model. Often, the model and generation method would not prioritise generating an end-of-string token. This would often result in repeating tokens after a name has been fully predicted. On other occasions, the correct full entity would be predicted part way through a generated prediction. The sliding Hamming distance is included for partial predictions of names.

4.4 Results

4.4.1 Top n Samples

Generating specific token sequences is inherently challenging, as there are many potential labels at each step, and later labels depend on preceding predictions, which can propagate and amplify uncertainty. As potential attackers will not know the names of potential victims during attacks, they could generate multiple names to increase their chances of success.

Fig. 4a and Fig. 4d show the performance of various values of the n most likely names inferred by a white-box attack model. Smaller values of n are always subsets of larger values, so an increase in the number of most likely predictions can only result in an increase or equal predictive performance.

Both the Hamming distance and the binary classification performance show a similar pattern of performance, between all values of n. Performance peaks at the 22nd epoch, and decreases and plateaus. This may be a sign of over-fitting from the model. A deviation in later epochs shows increases in binary classification performance that is not matched in the average sliding Hamming distance.

4.4.2 White-Box vs Black-Box

We contrast the performance of a white-box model attack versus a black-box model attack. The black-box model has been generated via a model extraction attack as explained in Sec. 4.2.2. The source model is the same as the model used in the white-box attack. Fig. 4b and Fig. 4e compare the performance of a black-box and white-box name inference attack. In this experiment n is set to 5 for both models.

Both Hamming distance and binary classification performance show that the white-box attack model outperforms the black-box attack model at inferring names from de-identified text, as should be expected. Although binary classification does

Prediction	Tokenised	Binary	Hamming Distance
"John Doe"	[610, 28484]	1	0
"John Doe Doe Doe"	[610, 28484, 28484, 28484]	1	0
"Jane Doe"	[7343, 28484]	0	0.5

Table 3: Examples of predictions for the ground truth label "John Doe". Metrics are generated during evaluation of name inference models. The tokens ids from a generated name are compared to the ground truth label tokens ids. There are two methods of evaluation - a binary evaluation and a hamming distance. The binary classification checks if the ground truth list of tokens is a sublist of the generated set. The hamming distance metric creates a rolling window over the predicted text, and returns the largest hamming distance value normalised by the length of the label.

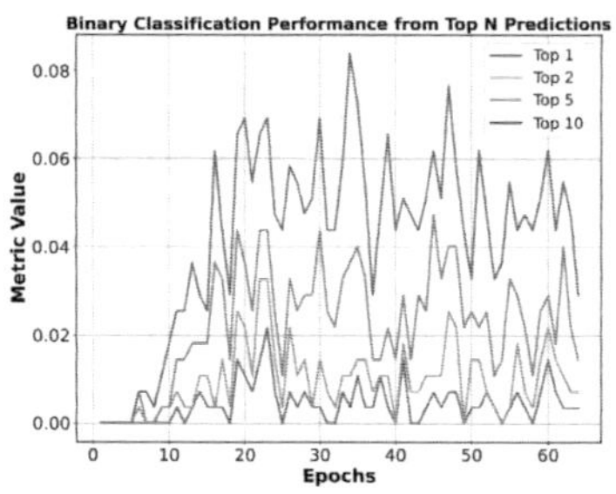

(a) Top-n performance in binary classification for correctly inferring names from de-identified text.

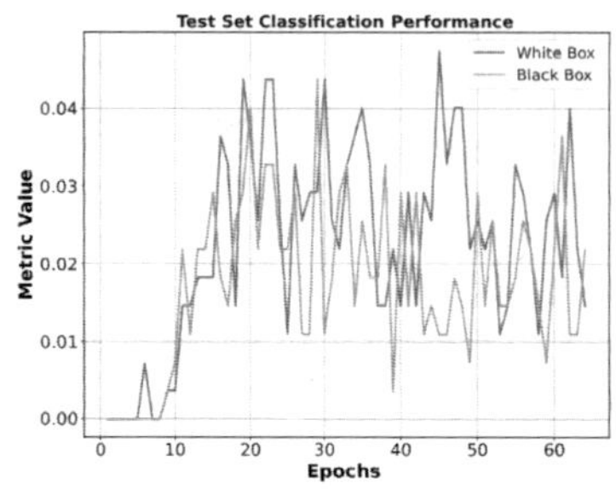

(b) Comparison of binary classification performance between black-box and white-box name inference attacks (n=5).

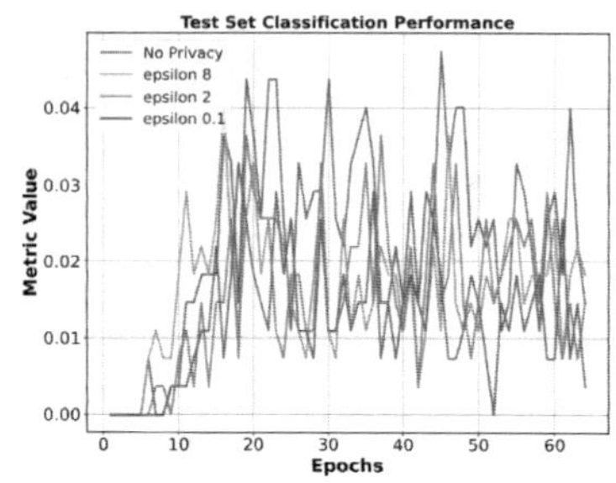

(c) Comparison of binary classification performance of models with varying levels of privacy (defined by "epsilon") and a baseline model (n=5).

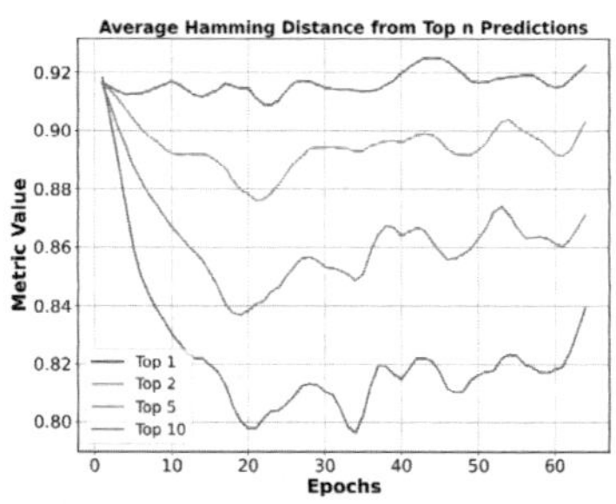

(d) Top-n average sliding Hamming distance for correctly inferring names from de-identified text.

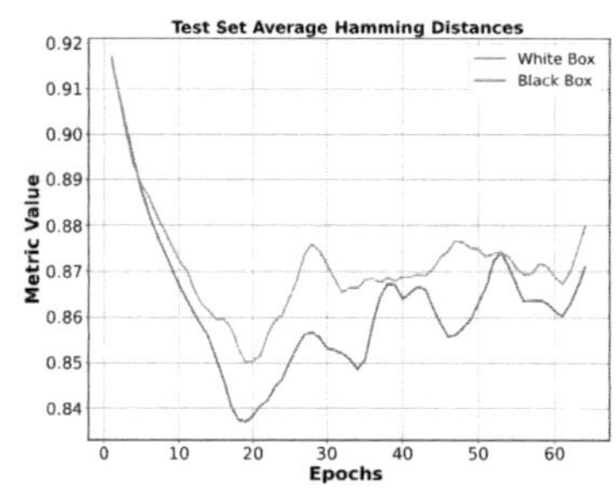

(e) Average sliding Hamming distance for name inference from de-identified text using white-box and black-box models (n=5).

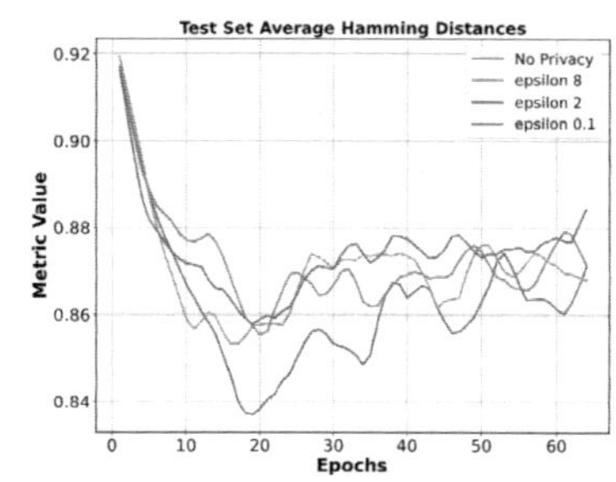

(f) Comparison of average sliding Hamming distance across models with varying privacy levels (defined by Epsilon) and a baseline model (n=5).

Figure 4: Performance metrics comparing predictions of names between various models. Fig.4a and Fig.4d show the attack performance when returning the models n most likely names as generated by the attack model from a single model with no additional privacy considerations.

not have a large performance gap, the Hamming distance shows a larger difference.

4.4.3 Differential Privacy

We compare three models that employ differential privacy, where the privacy parameter, epsilon, is set to 0.1, 2, 8. A lower epsilon results in a more "private" model. We also compare this with attacking a model with no differential privacy as a baseline comparison. In this experiment n is set to 5 for all models.

Fig. 4c and Fig. 4f show the performance of multiple name inference attacks on models with varying levels of privacy. The baseline model outperforms all the models in which DP is deployed. Furthermore, as epsilon decreases (and privacy should increase), the predictive performance of the models is also degraded. This also shows a trade-off balance between varying levels of epsilon and the desired performance.

5 Conclusion

We have demonstrated the "named inference attack", an attribute inference attack that focuses on generating the names that were used as part of the training process. We demonstrated our attack on de-identification models trained using "AnonCAT", showing that we can predict approximately 2% of names from an attack dataset when using only the most likely generated label. Finally, we compared the performance of the attack with models with differing levels of privacy, such as a black-box attack or differential privacy.

Various works have presented different methods of inference attacks on machine learning models (Chen et al., 2021; He et al., 2022; Yeom et al., 2018). All of these works show a small, but potentially significant, data leakage. The same has been demonstrated in this work, with perhaps the most sensitive attribute - names.

When only the most likely prediction is generated, name inference attacks perform similarly (~2%) to other works that attempt to infer sensitive attributes in similar masked language models (Jagannatha et al., 2021).

Although generating multiple predictions for a single input is not standard practice in traditional machine learning models, this approach can be particularly useful in attribute inference attacks. By generating more names for a single input, the model's performance improves, potentially increasing the risk of sensitive attribute disclosure. This may also show that generating text via a causal language model is a difficult task compared to other tasks where output labels are limited.

This type of attack is measured in terms of absolute leakage. Conventionally, leakage is measured in relative terms compared to random guessing (Guo et al., 2023; Song and Mittal, 2021; Feng et al., 2022). The attribute space for the type of attack demonstrated here has too many possibilities. Random guessing can be assumed to have a performance of 0%, and thus absolute performance is a suitable metric.

Consensus on an acceptable level of information leakage may be difficult to reach. Although any level of leakage is not ideal, different fields may have different tolerances for privacy leakage. Ultimately, acceptable leakage is contextually defined by the interaction of technical limits, risk assessments, regulatory requirements, and specific downstream use.

Whilst there is no direct 'acceptable' level of leakage or privacy, the UK's Information Commissioner's Office has previously suggested in correspondence that 95% accuracy of the de-id model itself would be acceptable given that these models are being deployed into environments with many additional security and privacy constraints. Hospitals such as University College London Hospitals are using these guidelines as part of their information governance.

There is a minor improvement in privacy during the black-box attack compared to a white-box attack using the binary classification metric. The rolling hamming distance shows greater privacy provided by limiting access to model weights.

Differential privacy shows a trade-off between model utility and privacy. As inference attack performance degrades in line with privacy budget increase, the predictive performance decreases when attempting to de-identify text. The small differences in attack model performance between different budgets may indicate that the inherent difficulty of inference attacks on masked language models may only require a smaller allocation of a privacy budget compared to other models.

Consideration should be given to the goals and objectives of potential attackers, especially in fields such as healthcare, where there is low tolerance for information leakage. Little has been formalised about hypothetical attackers conducting inference attacks, and less about real-world attackers performing real attacks. Are they seeking to infer as much private information as possible or targeting specific individuals? Are their motivations financial, political, or something else?

This work can validate models and APIs, enabling their secure external exposure while using real-world data. By understanding the risk of sharing data and models, information governance teams can define tolerable thresholds of privacy risk, facilitating access to resources for fields such as healthcare and research.

In our experiments, we assume that the attack training data follows a distribution similar to the victim model's data. Although this assumption cannot be guaranteed, it provides some security, as an information leakage ceiling of $2-8\%$ reduces the confidence of potential attackers. Moreover, if a large-scale attack were to take place, it would be difficult for such an attack to isolate the true positives from the false positive results. However, further attacks that target both true and false positives may achieve some success.

Future work could explore vulnerabilities beyond names, such as addresses, ages, and other sensitive attributes that may also be inferable. Identifying these risks is critical to protecting privacy and equipping policy makers to make informed decisions.

This work has focused on inferring names that have been used in the process of training AnonCAT; where the pre-training step is a masked language model. Other models can be explored in future work, such as generative language models, which have become more prevalent as conversational AIs become more common.

For a fully secure environment, we recommend that red-team inference attacks not be the sole focus of security considerations. This approach should be used in conjunction with other measures to ensure both model and data privacy. AnonCAT is deployed within secure data environments and enhanced with additional security measures, such as restrictive access controls and active monitoring of access and usage.

5.1 Limitations

The data used to train victim models comes from hospitals based in the United Kingdom, where the inference attack models data are from n2c2, which is predominantly a US based dataset. Clinical texts may come from different distributions. Future work could investigate differences in the geographic distributions of clinical texts.

Name inference attacks only focus on names, as opposed to all potential personality identifiable data. Other types of attributes may be better suited to different model architectures (such as a regression head for numbers like age).

Finally, the attack model has been trained only for transformer model architectures. This work cannot indicate whether these types of attack models can generalise to other architectures.

References

Martin Abadi, Andy Chu, Ian Goodfellow, H Brendan McMahan, Ilya Mironov, Kunal Talwar, and Li Zhang. 2016. Deep learning with differential privacy. In *Proceedings of the 2016 ACM SIGSAC conference on computer and communications security*, pages 308–318.

Rohan Anil, Badih Ghazi, Vineet Gupta, Ravi Kumar, and Pasin Manurangsi. 2021. Large-scale differentially private bert. *arXiv preprint arXiv:2108.01624*.

Chen Chen, Xuanli He, Lingjuan Lyu, and Fangzhao Wu. 2021. Killing one bird with two stones: Model extraction and attribute inference attacks against bert-based apis. *arXiv preprint arXiv:2105.10909*.

Maximin Coavoux, Shashi Narayan, and Shay B Cohen. 2018. Privacy-preserving neural representations of text. *arXiv preprint arXiv:1808.09408*.

Jacob Devlin. 2018. Bert: Pre-training of deep bidirectional transformers for language understanding. *arXiv preprint arXiv:1810.04805*.

Michael Duan, Anshuman Suri, Niloofar Mireshghallah, Sewon Min, Weijia Shi, Luke Zettlemoyer, Yulia Tsvetkov, Yejin Choi, David Evans, and Hannaneh Hajishirzi. 2024. Do membership inference attacks work on large language models? *arXiv preprint arXiv:2402.07841*.

Tiantian Feng, Raghuveer Peri, and Shrikanth Narayanan. 2022. User-level differential privacy against attribute inference attack of speech emotion recognition in federated learning. *arXiv preprint arXiv:2204.02500*.

Kang Gu, Ehsanul Kabir, Neha Ramsurrun, Soroush Vosoughi, and Shagufta Mehnaz. 2023. Towards sentence level inference attack against pre-trained language models. *Proceedings on Privacy Enhancing Technologies*.

Chuan Guo, Alexandre Sablayrolles, and Maziar Sanjabi. 2023. Analyzing privacy leakage in machine learning via multiple hypothesis testing: A lesson from fano. In *International Conference on Machine Learning*, pages 11998–12011. PMLR.

Xuanli He, Chen Chen, Lingjuan Lyu, and Qiongkai Xu. 2022. Extracted bert model leaks more information than you think! *arXiv preprint arXiv:2210.11735*.

Hongsheng Hu, Zoran Salcic, Lichao Sun, Gillian Dobbie, Philip S Yu, and Xuyun Zhang. 2022. Membership inference attacks on machine learning: A survey. *ACM Computing Surveys (CSUR)*, 54(11s):1–37.

Jie Huang, Hanyin Shao, and Kevin Chen-Chuan Chang. 2022. Are large pre-trained language models leaking your personal information? *arXiv preprint arXiv:2205.12628*.

Zhichao Huang and Tong Zhang. 2019. Black-box adversarial attack with transferable model-based embedding. *arXiv preprint arXiv:1911.07140*.

Abhyuday Jagannatha, Bhanu Pratap Singh Rawat, and Hong Yu. 2021. Membership inference attack susceptibility of clinical language models. *arXiv preprint arXiv:2104.08305*.

Bargav Jayaraman and David Evans. 2022. Are attribute inference attacks just imputation? In *Proceedings of the 2022 ACM SIGSAC Conference on Computer and Communications Security*, pages 1569–1582.

Zeljko Kraljevic, Thomas Searle, Anthony Shek, Lukasz Roguski, Kawsar Noor, Daniel Bean, Aurelie Mascio, Leilei Zhu, Amos A Folarin, Angus Roberts, Rebecca Bendayan, Mark P Richardson, Robert Stewart, Anoop D Shah, Wai Keong Wong, Zina Ibrahim, James T Teo, and Richard J B Dobson. 2021. Multi-domain clinical natural language processing with MedCAT: The medical concept annotation toolkit. *Artif. Intell. Med.*, 117:102083.

Zeljko Kraljevic, Anthony Shek, Joshua Au Yeung, Ewart Jonathan Sheldon, Haris Shuaib, Mohammad Al-Agil, Xi Bai, Kawsar Noor, Anoop D Shah, Richard Dobson, et al. 2023. Validating transformers for redaction of text from electronic health records in real-world healthcare. In *2023 IEEE 11th International Conference on Healthcare Informatics (ICHI)*, pages 544–549. IEEE.

Yinhan Liu. 2019. Roberta: A robustly optimized bert pretraining approach. *arXiv preprint arXiv:1907.11692*.

Yinhan Liu, Myle Ott, Naman Goyal, Jingfei Du, Mandar Joshi, Danqi Chen, Omer Levy, Mike Lewis, Luke Zettlemoyer, and Veselin Stoyanov. 2019. Roberta: A robustly optimized BERT pretraining approach. *CoRR*, abs/1907.11692.

Fatemehsadat Mireshghallah, Kartik Goyal, Archit Uniyal, Taylor Berg-Kirkpatrick, and Reza Shokri. 2022. Quantifying privacy risks of masked language models using membership inference attacks. *arXiv preprint arXiv:2203.03929*.

John X Morris, Volodymyr Kuleshov, Vitaly Shmatikov, and Alexander M Rush. 2023. Text embeddings reveal (almost) as much as text. *arXiv preprint arXiv:2310.06816*.

Yifan Peng, Shankai Yan, and Zhiyong Lu. 2019. Transfer learning in biomedical natural language processing: An evaluation of bert and elmo on ten benchmarking datasets. In *Proceedings of the 2019 Workshop on Biomedical Natural Language Processing (BioNLP 2019)*.

Xiangyu Qi, Yi Zeng, Tinghao Xie, Pin-Yu Chen, Ruoxi Jia, Prateek Mittal, and Peter Henderson. 2023. Fine-tuning aligned language models compromises safety, even when users do not intend to! *arXiv preprint arXiv:2310.03693*.

Congzheng Song and Ananth Raghunathan. 2020. Information leakage in embedding models. In *Proceedings of the 2020 ACM SIGSAC conference on computer and communications security*, pages 377–390.

Liwei Song and Prateek Mittal. 2021. Systematic evaluation of privacy risks of machine learning models. In *30th USENIX Security Symposium (USENIX Security 21)*, pages 2615–2632.

Amber Stubbs, Christopher Kotfila, and Özlem Uzuner. 2015. Automated systems for the de-identification of longitudinal clinical narratives: Overview of 2014 i2b2/uthealth shared task track 1. *Journal of biomedical informatics*, 58:S11–S19.

Amber Stubbs and Özlem Uzuner. 2015. Annotating longitudinal clinical narratives for de-identification: The 2014 i2b2/uthealth corpus. *Journal of biomedical informatics*, 58:S20–S29.

Özlem Uzuner, Imre Solti, and Eithon Cadag. 2010a. Extracting medication information from clinical text. *Journal of the American Medical Informatics Association*, 17(5):514–518.

Özlem Uzuner, Imre Solti, Fei Xia, and Eithon Cadag. 2010b. Community annotation experiment for ground truth generation for the i2b2 medication challenge. *Journal of the American Medical Informatics Association*, 17(5):519–523.

Özlem Uzuner, Brett R South, Shuying Shen, and Scott L DuVall. 2011. 2010 i2b2/va challenge on concepts, assertions, and relations in clinical text. *Journal of the American Medical Informatics Association*, 18(5):552–556.

Alex Wang, Amanpreet Singh, Julian Michael, Felix Hill, Omer Levy, and Samuel R Bowman. 2018. Glue: A multi-task benchmark and analysis platform for natural language understanding. *arXiv preprint arXiv:1804.07461*.

Jeffrey G Wang, Jason Wang, Marvin Li, and Seth Neel. 2024. Pandora's white-box: Increased training data leakage in open llms. *arXiv preprint arXiv:2402.17012*.

Samuel Yeom, Irene Giacomelli, Matt Fredrikson, and Somesh Jha. 2018. Privacy risk in machine learning: Analyzing the connection to overfitting. In *2018 IEEE 31st computer security foundations symposium (CSF)*, pages 268–282. IEEE.

Da Yu, Saurabh Naik, Arturs Backurs, Sivakanth Gopi, Huseyin A Inan, Gautam Kamath, Janardhan Kulkarni, Yin Tat Lee, Andre Manoel, Lukas Wutschitz, et al. 2021. Differentially private fine-tuning of language models. *arXiv preprint arXiv:2110.06500*.

A Standard AnonCAT Model

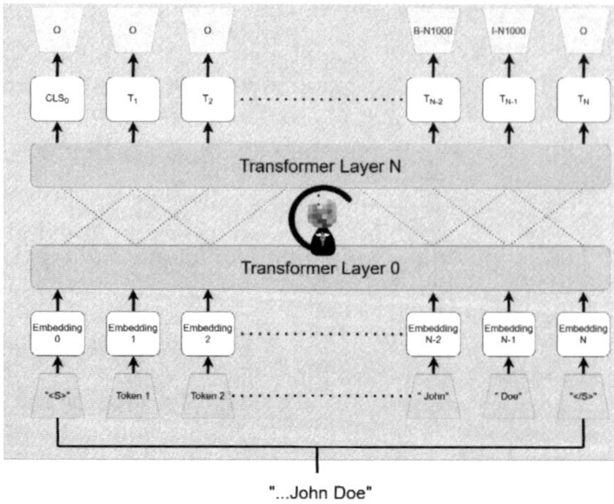

Figure 5: A standard AnonCAT model that would be used for identifying sensitive personal entities within text.

Inspecting the Representation Manifold of Differentially-Private Text

Stefan Arnold
Friedrich-Alexander-Universität Erlangen-Nürnberg
Lange Gasse 20, 90403 Nürnberg, Germany
stefan.st.arnold@fau.de

Abstract

Differential Privacy (DP) for text has recently taken the form of text paraphrasing using language models and temperature sampling to better balance privacy and utility. However, the geometric distortion of DP regarding the structure and complexity in the representation space remains unexplored. By estimating the intrinsic dimension of paraphrased text across varying privacy budgets, we find that word-level methods severely raise the representation manifold, while sentence-level methods produce paraphrases whose manifolds are topologically more consistent with human-written paraphrases. Among sentence-level methods, masked paraphrasing, compared to causal paraphrasing, demonstrates superior preservation of structural complexity, suggesting that autoregressive generation propagates distortions from unnatural word choices that cascade and inflate the representation space.

1 Introduction

Language Models (LMs) (Chowdhery et al., 2023) are trained on extensive corpora of text containing sensitive information. Several studies demonstrated that sensitive information can be extracted from LMs (Song and Shmatikov, 2019; Pan et al., 2020; Nasr et al., 2023; Carlini et al., 2023), raising significant privacy concerns and prompting the integration of privacy mechanisms.

To protect against unintended disclosure of information, *Differential Privacy* (DP) (Dwork et al., 2006) has been tailored to raw text (Fernandes et al., 2019; Feyisetan et al., 2020). Through a randomized mechanism, DP formalizes privacy through a notion of indistinguishability, ensuring that texts remain statistically unaffected by the addition or removal of individual samples in the text corpus.

While early randomized mechanisms exploit the distances between words in the embedding space (Mikolov et al., 2013) to replace words with a noisy approximation of their nearest neighbor, grammatical constraints associated with word-level privatization (Mattern et al., 2022) has led to a shift towards paraphrasing text at sentence-level by leveraging LMs (Igamberdiev and Habernal, 2023; Utpala et al., 2023; Meisenbacher et al., 2024).

Contribution. We inspect the representation geometry of text paraphrased under the privacy constraints of DP, accounting for different levels of privacy. Ansuini et al. (2019) discovered that high-dimensional signals reside on low-dimensional manifolds, a property that holds across neural representations (Tulchinskii et al., 2024). Building on *Intrinsic Dimensionality* (ID), we estimate the ID of texts and interpret ID shifts as a proxy for distortions on their structure and complexity. Specifically, we compare differentially-private transformations operating on word-level and sentence-level. We find that word-level DP deviates the most from human-authored paraphrases, significantly altering the underlying representation space. Concerning sentence-level DP, we argue that bidirectional paraphrasing based on masked substitution mitigates cascading errors that arise in sequential generation.

2 Background

We briefly provide the necessary foundations for differential privacy and intrinsic dimensionality.

2.1 Differential Privacy

Differential Privacy (DP) is a notion of privacy introduced by Dwork et al. (2006) under the term ε-indistinguishability. DP operates on the principle of adding noise calibrated to the sensitivity of adjacent datasets that differ by at most one record. The level of indistinguishability can be controlled by the privacy budget $\varepsilon \in (0, \infty]$, with declining privacy guarantees as $\varepsilon \to \infty$.

To mitigate the disclosure of authorship (Song and Shmatikov, 2019), DP is applied to perturb raw

Proceedings of the Sixth Workshop on Privacy in Natural Language Processing, pages 53–59
April 4, 2025

text either at word level or sentence level through noise injected into embedding models (Mikolov et al., 2013) and language models (Peters et al., 2018; Radford et al., 2018), respectively.

Word-level DP. Feyisetan et al. (2020) introduced a randomized mechanism in which a text is perturbed at the word level by mapping each word to another word located within a radius derived from an embedding space and governed by the privacy budget ε. This randomized mechanism was termed `MADLIB`. By scaling the notion of indistinguishability by a distance, `MADLIB` satisfies the axioms of metric DP (Chatzikokolakis et al., 2013). Despite many refinements regarding the preservation of utility (Carvalho et al., 2021; Xu et al., 2021b; Yue et al., 2021) and privacy (Xu et al., 2020, 2021a), `MADLIB` continues to suffers from syntactic errors (Mattern et al., 2022) and semantic drift (Arnold et al., 2023).

Sentence-level DP. Given the shortcomings of `MADLIB` and its recent refinements (Yue et al., 2021; Chen et al., 2023), researchers conceptualized the privatization of text as paraphrasing by utilizing sequence-to-sequence models (Bo et al., 2021; Krishna et al., 2021; Weggenmann et al., 2022; Igamberdiev and Habernal, 2023). Unlike word-level mechanisms, which perturb text on a word-by-word basis, sentence-level mechanisms paraphrase entire sentences. A defining characteristic shared is the injection of noise into the encoder representations, and learning of the decoder to generate fluent paraphrases while obfuscating stylistic identifiers that could otherwise compromise privacy.

Mattern et al. (2022) conjectured that temperature sampling in LMs can be interpreted as an instance of the exponential mechanism (McSherry and Talwar, 2007), where the scoring function corresponds to most probable word given a context. The probability of selecting a word follows the softmax distribution over the *logits*, which represent the likelihood of each word occurring in a given context. Since DP requires the sensitivity to be bounded, these logits are clipped in range.

Since paraphrasing is contingent upon the resemblance between the training text and the text subjected to privatization, Utpala et al. (2023) leverage the generalization capabilities of large-scale pretrained LMs to generate paraphrases via zero-shot prompting. Meisenbacher et al. (2024) depart from autoregressive generation and instead adopted the idea of temperature sampling to masked LMs. Unlike causal LMs, which sample text sequentially, this approach masks words and predicts its substitution bidirectionally from context.

2.2 Intrinsic Dimensionality

Grounded on the manifold hypothesis (Fefferman et al., 2016), the concept of intrinsic dimensionality characterizes the number of degrees of freedom for data in a representation space. Unlike extrinsic dimensionality, which corresponds to the overall dimensionality of the representation space, the intrinsic dimension (ID) corresponds to the minimum number of coordinates which are necessary to approximately capture the variability, revealing the structure and complexity of the manifold. This renders the ID as a geometric property (Valeriani et al., 2023) that describes how data points are distributed within the representation space.

Several methods have been developed to estimate intrinsic dimensionality, each differing in its underlying assumptions and formulations. Levina and Bickel (2004) uses maximum likelihood estimation to fit the likelihood on the distances from one point to each point within a *fixed* neighborhood structure. If the neighborhood is set too small in a dense region, the dimensionality might be underestimated. If the neighborhood is set too large in a sparse region, it might be overestimated. Farahmand et al. (2007) adapts the size of the neighborhood based on the geometry of the manifold.

Facco et al. (2017) exploits the expected ratio of distances between closest neighbors, observing that the distribution of distances of a point to its first neighbor is significantly smaller than to its second neighbor in lower dimensions, while in higher dimensions, the distance ratio is relatively close. By relying on the minimal information needed from the neighborhood, this approach alleviates the effects of variations in densities and curvatures within the manifold, providing stable ID estimates.

Recent studies have investigated how intrinsic dimensionality evolves and manifests through the layers (Ansuini et al., 2019), with connections to learning dynamics (Aghajanyan et al., 2021; Pope et al., 2021) and generalization (Birdal et al., 2021). Ansuini et al. (2019) demonstrated that data embedded in a high-dimensional space is progressively compressed into low-dimensional manifolds.

Table 1: Overview of prominent techniques for differentially-private text rewriting. Scope specifies whether the method applies DP at the word-level or sentence-level. Mechanism indicates the type of privacy mechanisms. Budget refers to the recommended range of the privacy budget. Approach describes the underlying substitution mechanism, including word embeddings, causal LMs, conditional LMs, or masked LMs. Fine-tuned specifies whether the LM was explicitly fine-tuned for paraphrasing or only leveraged pre-trained representations.

	Scope	Mechanism	Budget	Approach	Fine-tuned
Feyisetan et al. (2020)	Word-level	Exponential	~ 10	Word Embedding	no
Mattern et al. (2022)	Sentence-level	Exponential	~ 100	Causal LM	yes
Igamberdiev & Habernal (2023)	Sentence-level	Gaussian	~ 1000	Conditional LM	no
Utpala et al. (2023)	Sentence-level	Exponential	~ 100	Causal LM	no
Meisenbacher et al. (2024)	Sentence-level	Exponential	~ 100	Masked LM	no

3 Methodology

We aim to investigate how privacy-preserving transformations alter the geometry of paraphrases relative to those generated without privacy guarantees.

For our experiments, we utilize MRPC (Dolan and Brockett, 2005), a dataset containing sentence pairs labeled for semantic equivalence. We selected sentence pairs that provide a *reference* and *paraphrase* to ensure a controlled basis for assessing geometric distortions in representation subspaces.

3.1 Selection of Privacy Mechanisms

Table 1 outlines key characteristics of prominent approaches for differentially-private rewriting. To ensure comparability across privacy budgets, we focus on randomized mechanisms that implement the exponential mechanism. For word-level paraphrasing, we select Madlib (Feyisetan et al., 2020), which perturbs individual word in embedding space. For sentence-level paraphrasing, we select DP-PARAPHRASE (Mattern et al., 2022), DP-PROMPT (Utpala et al., 2023), and DP-MLM (Meisenbacher et al., 2024), covering causal and masked paraphrasing with temperate sampling. DP-PARAPHRASE and DP-PROMPT are powered by fine-tuned GPT-2 (Radford et al., 2019) and pre-trained LLaMA-3 (Touvron et al., 2023), respectively. DP-MLM employs RoBERTa (Liu et al., 2019). Table 2 presents an example sentence from MRPC along with its human-authored and differentially-private paraphrases.

3.2 Estimation of Intrinsic Dimension

Following Tulchinskii et al. (2024), we obtain embeddings for each word in a text using BERT (Devlin et al., 2019), treating each text as a point cloud of words spanning a manifold in the representation space. The ID of this point cloud is then estimated using TwoNN (Facco et al., 2017). To ensure that ID estimations reflect meaningful linguistic properties rather than artifacts of tokenization, we drop demarcation tokens as <CLS> and <SEP>. We also filtered short text sequences with less than 15 words and truncated long text sequences at 128 words. This stabilizes ID estimates by ensuring that estimations are based on sufficiently rich representations, while avoiding outlier effects from excessively short or long sentences.

Our investigation spans a range of privacy budgets $\varepsilon \in \{10, 15, 20, 25, 50, 100\}$, allowing us to weigh the geometric distortions with respect to the desired level of privacy. Since temperature sampling is probabilistic, we repeat the paraphrasing process three times per sample at each privacy level, ensuring robust ID estimations across multiple trials and reducing variance in the distortions.

4 Findings

Figure 1 presents the deviation in the number of ID as a function of the privacy budget. To establish a lower bound for ID shifts, we measure the ID difference between reference sentences and their human-authored paraphrases from MRPC. This yields an ID shift of approximately 0.12, indicating that naturally occurring paraphrasing introduces only minimal geometric distortions in the representation space. Any privacy-preserving transformation that deviates strongly from this baseline alters the structure and complexity of text representations beyond natural variation, potentially affecting readability.

Word-Level Perturbation. Since MADLIB is applied at word-level, its randomized mechanism perturbs words independently, disregarding sentence structure and grammatical coherence. This results in fragmented and disorganized text, a phe-

Table 2: Example from MRPC showing a sentence and its human-authored paraphrase. Note that differentially-private paraphrases at word-level are obtained using a privacy budget of $\varepsilon = 25$, whereas differentially-private paraphrases at sentence-level are obtained using a privacy budget of $\varepsilon = 100$.

Sentence	Amrozi accused his brother, whom he called " the witness ", of deliberately distorting his evidence.
Paraphrase	Referring to him as only " the witness ", Amrozi accused his brother of deliberately distorting his evidence.
Feyisetan et al. (2020)	Amrozi accused his brother , Tyler he warn the witness confined deliberately discolored muse evidence.
Mattern et al. (2022)	The person is Amrozi . aggression is evident even illustrates its extreme inflections over their close relative.
Utpala et al. (2023)	The witness had said his wife had left him when his wife was pregnant, his second daughter was not Alis.
Meisenbacher et al. (2024)	He alleged his nephew, whom he named _ the witness " of specifically distracting his testimony.

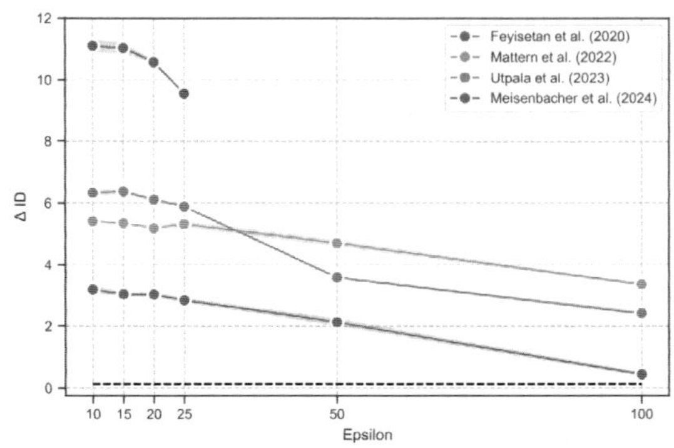

Figure 1: Shift in the estimated number of intrinsic dimensions, with a horizontal line representing a lower bound derived from human-authored paraphrases.

nomenon that can be observed through the highest ID shifts among all approaches. This observation reinforces a fundamental limitation of word-level perturbations, which induce severe distortions in representation subspaces, making them unsuitable for privacy-preserving paraphrasing.

Sentence-Level Perturbation. Unlike MADLIB, which perturbs words in isolation, sentence-level perturbation incorporates context when generating paraphrases. Across all privacy budgets, sentence-level perturbation introduces significantly less distortion, as indicated by their consistently lower ID shifts. This demonstrates that leveraging LMs produces more natural paraphrases.

Among causal paraphrasing, a mixed pattern emerges depending on the privacy regime. The ID shift of DP-PARAPHRASE remains stable across privacy budgets, whereas DP-PROMPT declines more sharply. At strict privacy regimes, DP-PARAPHRASE, which is explicitly fine-tuned for paraphrasing, outperforms DP-PROMPT, which learns paraphrasing implicitly from pre-training. At more relaxed privacy regimes, however, DP-PROMPT surpasses DP-PARAPHRASE by operating more within human-like representation geometry. Since privacy is enforced via temperature sampling, this trend suggests differing sensitivity to temperature values. DP-PARAPHRASE handles high temperatures more effectively, whereas DP-PROMPT tends to generate excessively complex paraphrases. Unlike autoregressive paraphrasing, DP-MLM adopts masked paraphrasing, reconstructing words bidirectionally rather than generating words sequentially. DP-MLM clearly excels across all privacy budgets, yielding more stable representation geometry.

Error Propagation We argue that a key factor driving the divergence between causal and masked paraphrasing stems from error propagation. Causal paraphrasing perturbs text in a fixed order, where each word conditions the selection of the next word, whereas masked paraphrasing operate bidirectionally, conditioning each word substitution on both preceding and following context. When differential privacy is enforced through temperature sampling, it introduces randomness, destabilizing generation by increasing the likelihood of unnatural word choices. Once a word has been poorly substituted, the language model must compensate to maintain fluency, leading to cascading errors which manifest in the form of drastic changes in the representation subspace. Since masked paraphrasing is not constrained by sequential consistency, distortion from a poorly chosen word does not propagate along the sentence, preventing error accumulation and producing more stable paraphrases.

5 Conclusion

We analyze the transformative effects of applying DP to text, focusing on how privacy constraints induce geometric distortions in the representation space. By leveraging the ID as a measure of structural complexity, we assess the extent to which prominent DP mechanisms alter latent subspaces and reshape linguistic representations. Our findings reveal that word-level DP introduces severe ID shifts, leading to drastically inflated representation manifolds. For sentence-level DP, we observe distinct differences between their representation geometry, depending on how words are substituted and whether errors from suboptimal word choices accumulate and propagate throughout a sentence.

Limitations. A limitation of our inspection is that ID estimation, while a powerful tool for inspecting representation geometry of text, does not directly capture linguistic quality. Although ID shifts provide evidence of geometric distortions, connecting these distortions to measures of fluency (Salazar et al., 2020) and adequacy (Zhang et al., 2019; Yuan et al., 2021) would complement our understanding of alterations induced by DP rewriting.

References

Armen Aghajanyan, Sonal Gupta, and Luke Zettlemoyer. 2021. Intrinsic dimensionality explains the effectiveness of language model fine-tuning. In *Proceedings of the 59th Annual Meeting of the Association for Computational Linguistics and the 11th International Joint Conference on Natural Language Processing (Volume 1: Long Papers)*, pages 7319–7328.

Alessio Ansuini, Alessandro Laio, Jakob H Macke, and Davide Zoccolan. 2019. Intrinsic dimension of data representations in deep neural networks. *Advances in Neural Information Processing Systems*, 32.

Stefan Arnold, Dilara Yesilbas, and Sven Weinzierl. 2023. Driving context into text-to-text privatization. In *Proceedings of the 3rd Workshop on Trustworthy Natural Language Processing (TrustNLP 2023)*, pages 15–25, Toronto, Canada. Association for Computational Linguistics.

Tolga Birdal, Aaron Lou, Leonidas J Guibas, and Umut Simsekli. 2021. Intrinsic dimension, persistent homology and generalization in neural networks. *Advances in Neural Information Processing Systems*, 34:6776–6789.

Haohan Bo, Steven H. H. Ding, Benjamin C. M. Fung, and Farkhund Iqbal. 2021. ER-AE: Differentially private text generation for authorship anonymization. In *Proceedings of the 2021 Conference of the North American Chapter of the Association for Computational Linguistics: Human Language Technologies*, pages 3997–4007, Online. Association for Computational Linguistics.

Nicholas Carlini, Daphne Ippolito, Matthew Jagielski, Katherine Lee, Florian Tramèr, and Chiyuan Zhang. 2023. Quantifying memorization across neural language models. In *The Eleventh International Conference on Learning Representations, ICLR 2023, Kigali, Rwanda, May 1-5, 2023*. OpenReview.net.

Ricardo Silva Carvalho, Theodore Vasiloudis, and Oluwaseyi Feyisetan. 2021. Tem: High utility metric differential privacy on text. *arXiv preprint arXiv:2107.07928*.

Konstantinos Chatzikokolakis, Miguel E Andrés, Nicolás Emilio Bordenabe, and Catuscia Palamidessi. 2013. Broadening the scope of differential privacy using metrics. In *International Symposium on Privacy Enhancing Technologies Symposium*, pages 82–102. Springer.

Sai Chen, Fengran Mo, Yanhao Wang, Cen Chen, Jian-Yun Nie, Chengyu Wang, and Jamie Cui. 2023. A customized text sanitization mechanism with differential privacy. In *Findings of the Association for Computational Linguistics: ACL 2023*, pages 5747–5758, Toronto, Canada. Association for Computational Linguistics.

Aakanksha Chowdhery, Sharan Narang, Jacob Devlin, Maarten Bosma, Gaurav Mishra, Adam Roberts, Paul Barham, Hyung Won Chung, Charles Sutton, Sebastian Gehrmann, et al. 2023. Palm: Scaling language modeling with pathways. *Journal of Machine Learning Research*, 24(240):1–113.

Jacob Devlin, Ming-Wei Chang, Kenton Lee, and Kristina Toutanova. 2019. BERT: Pre-training of deep bidirectional transformers for language understanding. In *Proceedings of the 2019 Conference of the North American Chapter of the Association for Computational Linguistics: Human Language Technologies, Volume 1 (Long and Short Papers)*, pages 4171–4186, Minneapolis, Minnesota. Association for Computational Linguistics.

Bill Dolan and Chris Brockett. 2005. Automatically constructing a corpus of sentential paraphrases. In *Third international workshop on paraphrasing (IWP2005)*.

Cynthia Dwork, Frank McSherry, Kobbi Nissim, and Adam Smith. 2006. Calibrating noise to sensitivity in private data analysis. In *Theory of cryptography conference*, pages 265–284. Springer.

Elena Facco, Maria d'Errico, Alex Rodriguez, and Alessandro Laio. 2017. Estimating the intrinsic dimension of datasets by a minimal neighborhood information. *Scientific reports*, 7(1):12140.

Amir Massoud Farahmand, Csaba Szepesvári, and Jean-Yves Audibert. 2007. Manifold-adaptive dimension estimation. In *Proceedings of the 24th international conference on Machine learning*, pages 265–272.

Charles Fefferman, Sanjoy Mitter, and Hariharan Narayanan. 2016. Testing the manifold hypothesis. *Journal of the American Mathematical Society*, 29(4):983–1049.

Natasha Fernandes, Mark Dras, and Annabelle McIver. 2019. Generalised differential privacy for text document processing. In *International Conference on Principles of Security and Trust*, pages 123–148. Springer, Cham.

Oluwaseyi Feyisetan, Borja Balle, Thomas Drake, and Tom Diethe. 2020. Privacy-and utility-preserving textual analysis via calibrated multivariate perturbations. In *Proceedings of the 13th International Conference on Web Search and Data Mining*, pages 178–186.

Timour Igamberdiev and Ivan Habernal. 2023. DP-BART for privatized text rewriting under local differential privacy. In *Findings of the Association for Computational Linguistics: ACL 2023*, pages 13914–13934, Toronto, Canada. Association for Computational Linguistics.

Satyapriya Krishna, Rahul Gupta, and Christophe Dupuy. 2021. ADePT: Auto-encoder based differentially private text transformation. In *Proceedings of the 16th Conference of the European Chapter of the Association for Computational Linguistics: Main Volume*, pages 2435–2439, Online. Association for Computational Linguistics.

Elizaveta Levina and Peter Bickel. 2004. Maximum likelihood estimation of intrinsic dimension. *Advances in neural information processing systems*, 17.

Yinhan Liu, Myle Ott, Naman Goyal, Jingfei Du, Mandar Joshi, Danqi Chen, Omer Levy, Mike Lewis, Luke Zettlemoyer, and Veselin Stoyanov. 2019. Roberta: A robustly optimized bert pretraining approach. *arXiv preprint arXiv:1907.11692*.

Justus Mattern, Benjamin Weggenmann, and Florian Kerschbaum. 2022. The limits of word level differential privacy. In *Findings of the Association for Computational Linguistics: NAACL 2022*, pages 867–881, Seattle, United States. Association for Computational Linguistics.

Frank McSherry and Kunal Talwar. 2007. Mechanism design via differential privacy. In *48th Annual IEEE Symposium on Foundations of Computer Science (FOCS'07)*, pages 94–103. IEEE.

Stephen Meisenbacher, Maulik Chevli, Juraj Vladika, and Florian Matthes. 2024. DP-MLM: Differentially private text rewriting using masked language models. In *Findings of the Association for Computational Linguistics: ACL 2024*, pages 9314–9328, Bangkok, Thailand. Association for Computational Linguistics.

Tomas Mikolov, Kai Chen, Greg Corrado, and Jeffrey Dean. 2013. Efficient estimation of word representations in vector space. *arXiv preprint arXiv:1301.3781*.

Milad Nasr, Nicholas Carlini, Jonathan Hayase, Matthew Jagielski, A Feder Cooper, Daphne Ippolito, Christopher A Choquette-Choo, Eric Wallace, Florian Tramèr, and Katherine Lee. 2023. Scalable extraction of training data from (production) language models. *arXiv preprint arXiv:2311.17035*.

Xudong Pan, Mi Zhang, Shouling Ji, and Min Yang. 2020. Privacy risks of general-purpose language models. In *2020 IEEE Symposium on Security and Privacy (SP)*, pages 1314–1331. IEEE.

Matthew Peters, Mark Neumann, Mohit Iyyer, Matt Gardner, Christopher Clark, Kenton Lee, and Luke Zettlemoyer. 2018. Deep contextualized word representations.

Phillip Pope, Chen Zhu, Ahmed Abdelkader, Micah Goldblum, and Tom Goldstein. 2021. The intrinsic dimension of images and its impact on learning. *9th International Conference on Learning Representations, ICLR*.

Alec Radford, Karthik Narasimhan, Tim Salimans, and Ilya Sutskever. 2018. Improving language understanding by generative pre-training.

Alec Radford, Jeffrey Wu, Rewon Child, David Luan, Dario Amodei, Ilya Sutskever, et al. 2019. Language models are unsupervised multitask learners. *OpenAI blog*, 1(8):9.

Julian Salazar, Davis Liang, Toan Q. Nguyen, and Katrin Kirchhoff. 2020. Masked language model scoring. In *Proceedings of the 58th Annual Meeting of the Association for Computational Linguistics*, pages 2699–2712, Online. Association for Computational Linguistics.

Congzheng Song and Vitaly Shmatikov. 2019. Auditing data provenance in text-generation models. In *Proceedings of the 25th ACM SIGKDD International Conference on Knowledge Discovery & Data Mining*, pages 196–206.

Hugo Touvron, Thibaut Lavril, Gautier Izacard, Xavier Martinet, Marie-Anne Lachaux, Timothée Lacroix, Baptiste Rozière, Naman Goyal, Eric Hambro, Faisal Azhar, et al. 2023. Llama: Open and efficient foundation language models. *arXiv preprint arXiv:2302.13971*.

Eduard Tulchinskii, Kristian Kuznetsov, Laida Kushnareva, Daniil Cherniavskii, Sergey Nikolenko, Evgeny Burnaev, Serguei Barannikov, and Irina Piontkovskaya. 2024. Intrinsic dimension estimation for robust detection of ai-generated texts. *Advances in Neural Information Processing Systems*, 36.

Saiteja Utpala, Sara Hooker, and Pin-Yu Chen. 2023. Locally differentially private document generation using zero shot prompting. In *Findings of the Association for Computational Linguistics: EMNLP 2023*, pages 8442–8457, Singapore. Association for Computational Linguistics.

Lucrezia Valeriani, Diego Doimo, Francesca Cuturello, Alessandro Laio, Alessio Ansuini, and Alberto Cazzaniga. 2023. The geometry of hidden representations of large transformer models. *Advances in Neural Information Processing Systems*, 36:51234–51252.

Benjamin Weggenmann, Valentin Rublack, Michael Andrejczuk, Justus Mattern, and Florian Kerschbaum. 2022. Dp-vae: Human-readable text anonymization for online reviews with differentially private variational autoencoders. In *Proceedings of the ACM Web Conference 2022*, WWW '22, page 721–731, New York, NY, USA. Association for Computing Machinery.

Nan Xu, Oluwaseyi Feyisetan, Abhinav Aggarwal, Zekun Xu, and Nathanael Teissier. 2021a. Density-aware differentially private textual perturbations using truncated gumbel noise. In *The International FLAIRS Conference Proceedings*, volume 34.

Zekun Xu, Abhinav Aggarwal, Oluwaseyi Feyisetan, and Nathanael Teissier. 2020. A differentially private text perturbation method using a regularized mahalanobis metric. *arXiv preprint arXiv:2010.11947*.

Zekun Xu, Abhinav Aggarwal, Oluwaseyi Feyisetan, and Nathanael Teissier. 2021b. On a utilitarian approach to privacy preserving text generation. *arXiv preprint arXiv:2104.11838*.

Weizhe Yuan, Graham Neubig, and Pengfei Liu. 2021. Bartscore: Evaluating generated text as text generation. *Advances in Neural Information Processing Systems*, 34:27263–27277.

Xiang Yue, Minxin Du, Tianhao Wang, Yaliang Li, Huan Sun, and Sherman S. M. Chow. 2021. Differential privacy for text analytics via natural text sanitization. In *Findings of the Association for Computational Linguistics: ACL-IJCNLP 2021*, pages 3853–3866, Online. Association for Computational Linguistics.

Tianyi Zhang, Varsha Kishore, Felix Wu, Kilian Q Weinberger, and Yoav Artzi. 2019. Bertscore: Evaluating text generation with bert. *International Conference on Learning Representations*.

Beyond Reconstruction: Generating Privacy-Preserving Clinical Letters

Libo Ren[1], **Samuel Belkadi**[2], **Lifeng Han**[1,3*]
Warren Del-Pinto[1], and **Goran Nenadic**[1]
[1] The University of Manchester, UK
[2] Cambridge University, UK
[3] LIACS & LUMC, Leiden University, NL
* *corresponding author*
l.han@lumc.nl, warren.del-pinto|g.nenadic@manchester.ac.uk
renlibo994, belkadisamuel@gmail.com

Abstract

Due to the sensitive nature of clinical letters, their use in model training, medical research, and education is limited. This work aims to generate diverse, de-identified, and high-quality synthetic clinical letters to enhance privacy protection. This study explores various pre-trained language models (PLMs) for text masking and generation, employing various masking strategies with a focus on Bio_ClinicalBERT. Both qualitative and quantitative methods are used for evaluation, supplemented by a downstream Named Entity Recognition (NER) task. Our results indicate that encoder-only models outperform encoder-decoder models. General-domain and clinical-domain PLMs exhibit comparable performance when clinical information is preserved. Preserving clinical *entities* and document *structure* yields better performance than fine-tuning alone. Masking stopwords enhances text quality, whereas masking nouns or verbs has a negative impact. BERTScore proves to be the most reliable quantitative evaluation metric in our task. Contextual information has minimal impact, indicating that synthetic letters can effectively replace original ones in downstream tasks. Unlike previous studies that focus primarily on reconstructing original letters or training a privacy-detection and substitution model, this project provides a framework for *generating diverse* clinical letters while embedding privacy detection, enabling sensitive dataset expansion and facilitating the use of real-world clinical data. Our codes and trained models will be publicly available at https://github.com/HECTA-UoM/Synthetic4Health

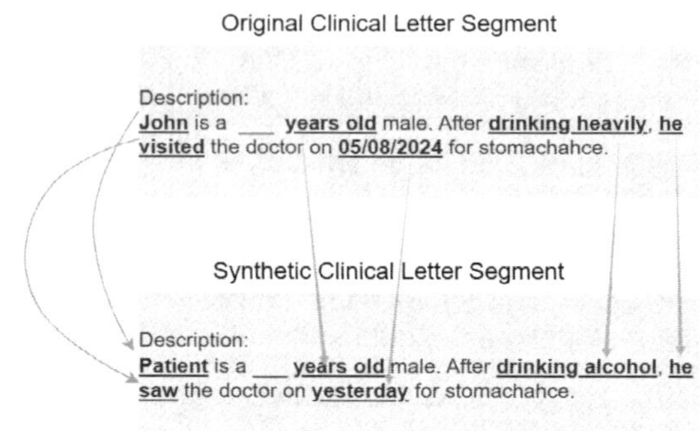

Figure 1: An Example of the Objective: generating more clinical letters from the original anonymised clinical letter segment with clinical soundness

1 Introduction

Electronic clinical letters play a crucial role in healthcare communication. However, their sensitive nature makes them challenging to share and limits their adoption in clinical education and research (Tarur and Prasanna, 2021; Tucker et al., 2016; Spasic and Nenadic, 2020). Although public datasets such as MIMIC and i2b2 provide de-identified clinical data, they are often restricted to specific regions and institutions, limiting their representativeness of diverse clinical conditions (Humbert-Droz et al., 2022).

To address these challenges, synthetic clinical letter generation has attracted growing interest. While existing methods primarily rely on structured data, Natural Language Generation (NLG) models provide a promising alternative by integrating linguistic and clinical knowledge (HÜSKE-KRAUS, 2003; Amin-Nejad et al., 2020a; Tang et al., 2023). Unlike previous studies, we go beyond training de-identification models to detect and substitute private information. This work focuses on leveraging NLG methods to generate synthetic clinical letters while indirectly minimising privacy risks. Although the dataset we used has been anonymised, we additionally apply a privacy detection and masking process as an additional verification step to further enhance the security of synthetic letters. Our findings contribute to bridging the gap in privacy-aware clinical letter generation, facilitating a more effective approach to processing real-world clinical

Proceedings of the Sixth Workshop on Privacy in Natural Language Processing, pages 60–74
April 4, 2025 ©2025 Association for Computational Linguistics

letters and addressing data scarcity in the medical domain.

A brief example of our objective is shown in Figure 1. To achieve this, we investigate different *model architectures*, *segmentation strategies*, and *masking* techniques and evaluate their effectiveness both qualitatively and quantitatively. Additionally, we assess their usability in *downstream* NLP tasks such as Named Entity Recognition (NER). We ensure compliance with ethical guidelines by using only de-identified clinical data and adhering to all data use agreements.

2 Related Work

Biomedical patient data privacy protection has been an important task for clinical research, especially when it comes to big data era. Developing privacy-preserving decision support tools has been a challenge for statisticians and clinical researchers (Tucker et al., 2016; Claerhout and DeMoor, 2005; Terry, 2012; Liu et al., 2015).

Recent studies in clinical Natural Language Processing (NLP) explored various tasks, including NER, de-identification, and NLG. Several tools, such as SciSpacy (Dernoncourt et al., 2017; Kovačević et al., 2024), are designed to enhance domain-specific entity recognition, while Philter (Norgeot et al., 2020) combines both traditional and modern NLP models to identify and remove Protected Health Information (PHI). Transformer-based architectures are widely used in clinical NLG, particularly in text rewriting, discharge summary generation, and data augmentation, (Vaswani et al., 2017). For instance, LT3 (Belkadi et al., 2023) improves label-to-text generation, while DeID-GPT (Liu et al., 2023) employs GPT-4 to identify and generate substitute words for private information. Micheletti et al. (2024) demonstrate that Masked Language Models (MLMs) outperform Causal Language Models (CLMs) in text masking tasks. Existing studies either focus on training models, utilize existing LLMs *identify* to identify *private* information, or concentrate solely on *NLG* without much attention in privacy. However, few studies integrate clinical text generation with privacy-preservation and diversity considerations, which is the focus of this study.

3 Methodology

To generate clinical letters that retain the original clinical narrative without being exact duplicates, we employed various PLMs. Sensitive data is masked by and substituted with contextually predicted tokens using PLMs. Additionally, we evaluate different masking strategies to de-identify potentially sensitive information as an additional validation step. We also considered how non-sensitive elements, such as stopwords, indirectly influence the effectiveness of de-identification. A brief workflow is presented in Figure 2.

3.1 Dataset

The dataset used in this research comprises 204 clinical letters and 51,574 manually annotated clinical entities from the SNOMED CT Entity Linking Challenge (A et al., 2000; Johnson et al., 2024, 2023). Protected health information (PHI) was manually reviewed and replaced with underscores to ensure privacy. The length of the clinical letters ranges from 360 to 3,329 words, with an average length of approximately 1,450 words. Each letter contains patient information, medical history, and follow-up instructions. They are also stored in CSV format with unique identifiers and textual content. Given the input constraints of language models, clinical letters are tokenised and segmented into smaller chunks for processing before being merged. The entity annotations, sourced from SNOMED CT, cover 5,336 distinct clinical concepts and are stored in CSV format. These annotations map entity positions in the text to their corresponding SNOMED CT concepts. An excerpt from the dataset is shown in Figure 3.

3.2 Clinical Information Preserving

3.2.1 Experimental Setup

The collected dataset consists of raw clinical letters and annotations, which were first merged into a unified DataFrame. Manually annotated entities were then extracted based on their index. Since PLMs such as BERT, RoBERTa, and T5 have a token limit (typically 512 (Zeng et al., 2022)), we employed a *variable-length chunking* strategy (Subsection 3.2.2) rather than fixed-length truncation. All experiments were conducted using Google Colab Pro+ environment equipped with a T4 GPU (16GB VRAM), 52GB of system RAM, and 225GB of disk space, running Python 3.10, PyTorch 2.3.1, and Hugging Face Transformers 4.42.4.

For *feature* extraction, we used word_tokenize to preserve word integrity, which is crucial for retaining clinical entities. For masking and generation, we followed each model's native tokeniza-

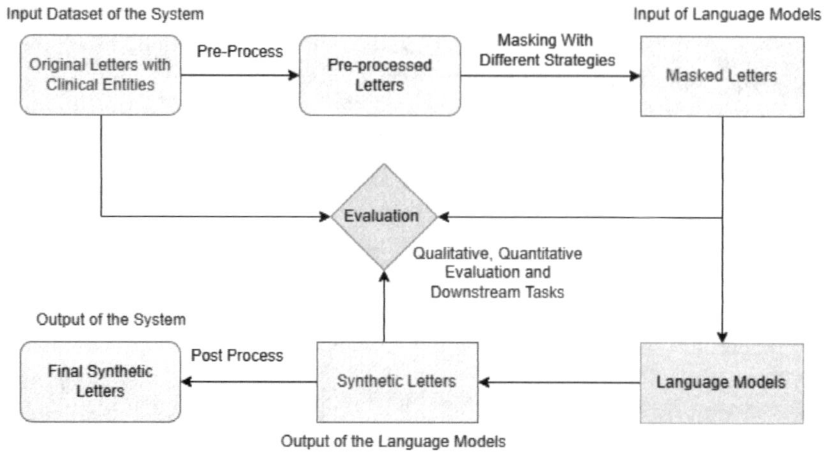

Figure 2: Overall Workflow

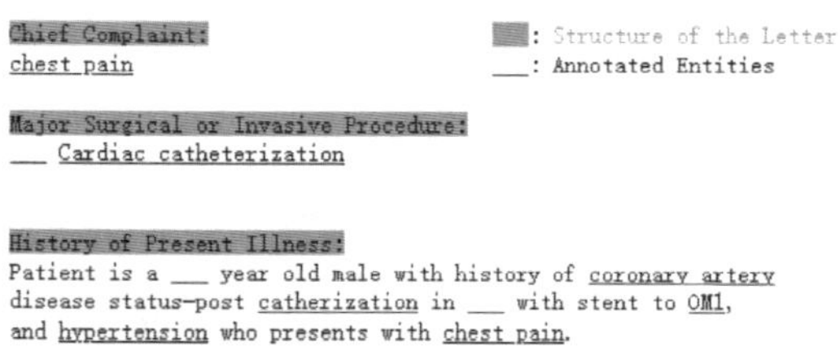
Chief Complaint:
chest pain

Major Surgical or Invasive Procedure:
___ Cardiac catheterization

History of Present Illness:
Patient is a ___ year old male with history of coronary artery disease status-post catherization in ___ with stent to OM1, and hypertension who presents with chest pain.

: Structure of the Letter
___: Annotated Entities

Figure 3: Text Excerpt from the Original Letter (A et al., 2000; Johnson et al., 2024, 2023) ('note_id': '17656866-DS-6')

tion method. BERT-based models utilize WordPiece tokenization, which is effective for handling out-of-vocabulary words and masked predictions. T5-based models employ Sentence-Piece tokenization, which better handles abbreviations and non-standard characters (e.g., "COVID-19")—common in clinical letters—as it does not rely on spaces for splitting. The pre-processing pipeline is shown in Figure 4.

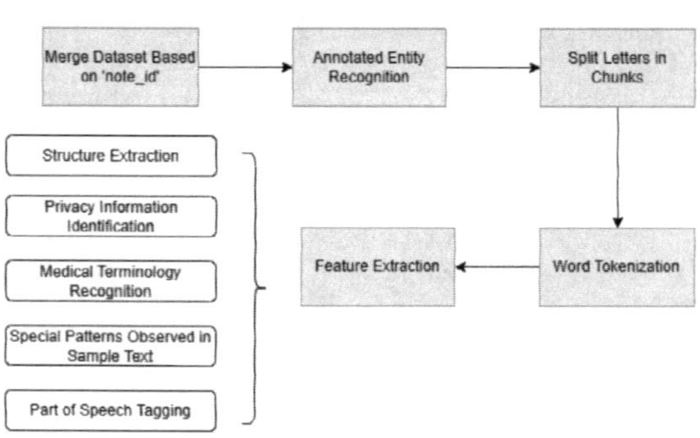

Figure 4: Pre-Processing Pipeline

3.2.2 Splitting Letters into Variable-Length Chunks

As mentioned above, pre-trained language models (PLMs) such as BERT, RoBERTa, and T5 have a token limit (typically 512 (Zeng et al., 2022)), requiring an effective strategy to process longer clinical letters. To preserve the full semantics of medical text, we adopted a Variable-Length Chunking approach based on *semantic boundaries*, instead of using tradition truncation methods like fixed-length or discarding tokens (Hou et al., 2022).

Initially, each letter was processed at the sentence level. However, this approach proved inefficient and lacked sufficient contextual information for inference. To address this, we segmented letters into *paragraph-sized chunks* while maintaining sentence integrity. Rather than strictly restricting each paragraph by '`max_tokens`' limit for each paragraph, we prioritised preserving complete sentences. To constrain fragmenting sentences, we introduced a '`max_lines`' threshold. If adding a sentence exceeds either the '`max_lines`' or `max_tokens` limit, it is moved to the next chunk. However, adhering to the `max_tokens` constraint should be our primary consideration due to model requirements. Therefore, if a single sentence does not exceed '`max_lines`' but surpasses the '`max_tokens`' limit, it is further segmented based on '`max_tokens`'. To detect sentence boundaries, we used the NLTK library. Figure 5 illustrates this process.

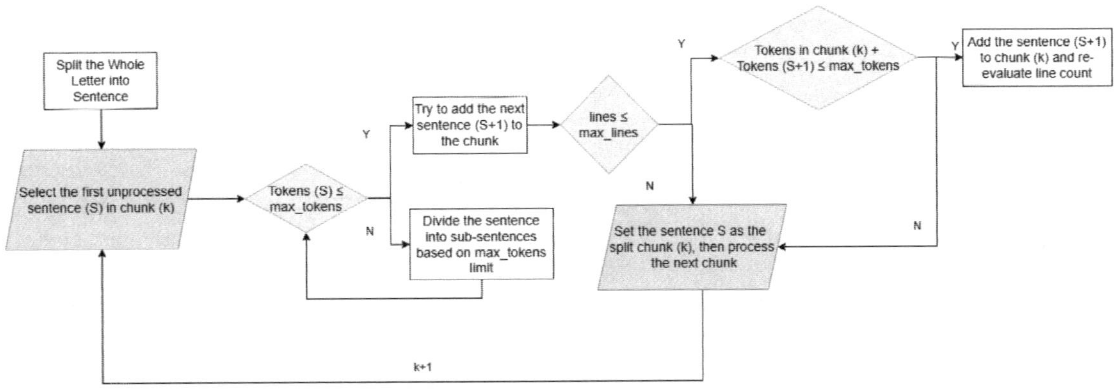

Figure 5: Text Chunking Workflow

3.2.3 Feature Extraction

To generate de-identified clinical letters while maintaining clinical narratives, we extracted key features before masking and generation. These features include:

- **Document Structure:** structural elements often correspond to capitalized headers and colons (:). They should be preserved as they define the document's format.
- **Privacy Information Identification:** An NER model (Stanza (Qi et al., 2020)) detected entities such as Name, Date, and Location, while regex masked structured data like phone numbers and emails.
- **Medical Terminology:** An NER model pretrained on i2b2 (Zhang et al., 2021) supplemented manual annotations by recognizing medical terms (e.g., Test, Treatment, Problem).
- **Special Patterns:** Medication dosages (e.g., enoxaparin 40 mg/0.4 mL) and abbreviations (e.g., b.i.d.) were retained unless classified as private.
- **POS Tagging:** To assess the impact of POS tagging on the model's understanding of clinical text, we employed a MIMIC-III-based model (Zhang et al., 2021), which outperformed NLTK and SpaCy in clinical syntactic comprehension.

3.3 Clinical Letters Generation

Our objective is to generate synthetic clinical letters that *differ* from the originals rather than producing near-identical copies, as repeated statement may indirectly reveal the patients' privacy. While fine-tuning improves precision and semantic comprehension, it risks overfitting, leading to outputs too closely aligned with the original dataset and reducing generalisability. Therefore, simply fine-tuning a model is suboptimal if PLMs can already generate readable text. Instead, the focus should be on protecting *clinical* terms and narratives while preventing *privacy* breaches. Since decoder-only models struggle with long-text processing (Amin-Nejad et al., 2020b) and require substantial computational resources, we explored both encoder-only and encoder-decoder PLMs with random masking. After evaluating their ability to generate synthetic letters, we selected Bio_ClinicalBERT for its strong domain adaptation and tested various masking strategies, as detailed in Appendix A. Additionally, given the discussion in Subsection 3.2.2, we assessed the impact of variable-length chunking on generation quality with Bio_ClinicalBERT.

3.3.1 Encoder-Only Models

Standard masked language modelling (MLM) was used in this study. First, tokens were selected for masking and then corrupted, resulting in masked text containing both masked and unmasked tokens. The model then predicted the masked tokens, replacing them with the most probable candidates. We predict all masked tokens in *parallel* within a single forward pass for each clinical letter. If processed sequentially, it might generate more coherent text, but the computational complexity would increase significantly (from $O(N)$ to $O(N!)$). Given the clinical focus of this task, we explored models fine-tuned on clinical or biomedical datasets. However, since no clinically fine-tuned RoBERTa (Zhuang et al., 2021)

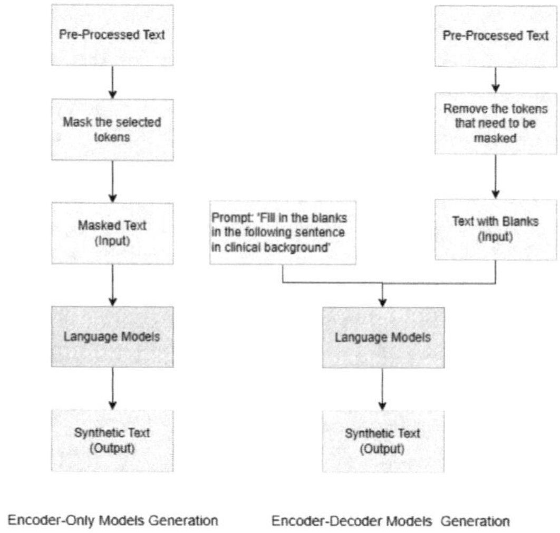

Figure 6: Comparison of Encoder-Only and Encoder-Decoder Model Architectures

variant was available, RoBERTa-base was used for comparison. The encoder-only models we evaluated include Bio_ClinicalBERT (Alsentzer et al., 2019), medicalai/ClinicalBERT (Wang et al., 2023), RoBERTa-base (Zhuang et al., 2021), and Clinical-Longformer (Li et al., 2023).

3.3.2 Encoder-Decoder Models

Although encoder-decoder models are not typically used for MLM, they excel in coherent text generation, particularly T5. Therefore, we included T5 family models in our comparisons. Unlike BERT, which replaces masked tokens with '<mask>', the T5 family models indexing masked words as 'extra_id_x'. The text, with these words removed, serves as input for generation, referred to as "text with blanks". For consistency, '<mask>' was later used when displaying masked text. Additionally, a **structured prompt** was required, formatted as "Fill in the blanks in the following sentence in clinical background" + text with blanks. Like encoder-only models, masked tokens are *predicted in parallel* across clinical letters. In this part, we experimented with T5-base (Raffel et al., 2020), Clinical-T5-Base (Eric and Johnson, 2023; Goldberger et al., 2000), Clinical-T5-Sci (Eric and Johnson, 2023; Goldberger et al., 2000), and Clinical-T5-Scratch (Eric and Johnson, 2023; Goldberger et al., 2000) for comparison. The architectures of encoder-only and encoder-decoder models are shown in Figure 6.

3.4 Evaluation

Both quantitative and qualitative methods are used to evaluate performance. Additionally, a downstream NER task assesses whether synthetic clinical letters can replace raw data. The evaluation pipeline is illustrated in Figure 8 of the Appendix.

3.4.1 Quantitative Evaluation

To assess the quality of synthetic letters, we conduct quantitative evaluation across multiple dimensions, including inference performance, readability, and similarity to raw data.

- **Standard NLG Metrics:** ROUGE, BERT Score, and METEOR assess textual similarity while ensuring generated text differs from the original. Synthetic text is compared with the original, and a baseline is established by comparing masked text to the original. The evaluation score should exceed the baseline but stay below 1.
- **Readability Metrics:** SMOG, Flesch Reading Ease, and Flesch-Kincaid Grade Level assess readability, with SMOG prioritised for clinical relevance.
- **Advanced Text Quality Metrics:** Perplexity, subjectivity, and information entropy are used to evaluate informativeness and subjectivity.
- **Invalid Prediction Rate:** Measures the ratio of invalid token predictions (e.g., subwords, punctuation) to assess the model's ability to generate meaningful text.
- **Inference Time:** Records generation time per letter, with shorter times indicating improved computational efficiency for large-scale deployment.

3.4.2 Qualitative Evaluation

While some synthetic texts performed well on most metrics, they did not always appear satisfactory upon visual inspection, whereas others with average scores appeared more natural. Although human evaluation is the most reliable method for assessing clinical letters, it is limited by time constraints and workload demands. Thus, combining qualitative and quantitative evaluations helps the identification of the most effective quantitative metrics for model evaluation. Once identified, one metric can serve as the benchmark standard, while others function

	Model Evaluation			
	RoBERTa-base	medicalai / ClinicalBERT	Clinical-Longformer	Bio _ Clinical-BERT
ROUGE-1				
Generation Performance	86.54	88.46	89.52	84.91
Baseline	84.91	84.91	84.91	84.91
ROUGE-2				
Generation Performance	74.51	78.43	79.61	73.08
Baseline	73.08	73.08	73.08	73.08
ROUGE-L				
Generation Performance	86.54	88.46	89.52	84.91
Baseline	84.91	84.91	84.91	84.91
BERTScore F1				
Generation Performance	0.81	0.83	0.84	0.85
Baseline	0.79	0.65	0.79	0.65
METEOR				
Generation Performance	0.87	0.88	0.90	0.86
Baseline	0.85	0.85	0.85	0.85
Flesch Reading Ease				
Generation Performance	10.24	18.70	9.22	16.67
Baseline (Original)	8.21	8.21	8.21	8.21
Baseline (Mask)	16.67	16.67	16.67	16.67

Table 1: Encoder-Only Models Comparison at the Sentence Level (The 'Baseline' without annotations was calculated by comparing masked text to the original text)

as complementary indicators. To address this, we selected a representative sample of clinical letters based on evaluation results, analysed the impact of different generation methods on these outcomes, and validated the findings with six additional samples to verify their consistency with quantitative metrics.

3.4.3 Downstream NER task

Beyond qualitative and quantitative evaluation, synthetic clinical letters were tested in a downstream NER task to assess their quality and potential as replacements for real clinical data. As shown in Figure 7, entities were first extracted from clinical letters using ScispaCy [1] and then used to train a base SpaCy [2] model. The trained model was applied to the test set, and the extracted entities were compared with those initially identified by ScispaCy to evaluate the consistency of entity recognition between synthetic and original clinical letters.

4 Results and Discussion

4.1 Model Comparison and Evaluation Metric Selection

4.1.1 Qualitative Results

Among encoder-only models, all four successfully generated meaningful words for masked input, correctly inferring 'r' from 'R ankle', demonstrating strong contextual understanding. Bio_ClinicalBERT further introduced relevant words absent from the input (e.g., "admitted") while maintaining clinical coherence, producing clinically sound sentences even without direct token matches, and effectively retaining clinical information while introducing diversity.

For encoder-decoder models, T5-base outperformed other variants but produced irrational outputs, including incomplete or nonsensical phrases (e.g., "open is a ___ yo male"). The other three T5 family models frequently generated de-identification (DEID) tags instead of meaningful replacements due to corpus biases. Overall, encoder-only models outperformed encoder-decoder models, aligning with previous research (Micheletti et al., 2024) showing that Masked Language Modelling (MLM) outperforms Causal Language Modelling (CLM) in medical text generation.

4.1.2 Quantitative Results

For **sentence-level** results, among encoder-only models, clinical-related models consistently outperform general domain RoBERTa-base, aligning with qualitative observations. **Bio_ClinicalBERT**, despite having no word overlap in this sample, achieves **the highest BERTScore** while maintaining a **clinically coherent output**. The encoder-decoder models generally perform poorly in most metrics compared to encoder-only models, except for METEOR. Their BERTScores are significantly

[1]https://allenai.github.io/scispacy/
[2]https://spacy.io/

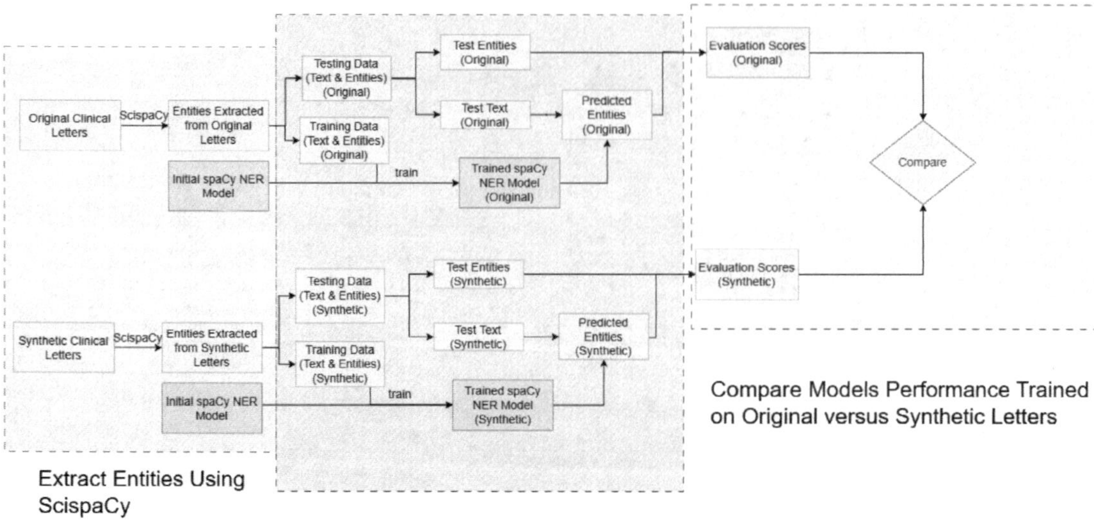

Figure 7: Workflow of Downstream NER Task

lower than the baseline, suggesting a large deviations from the original meaning. These findings further support the validity of BERTScore as the primary evaluation metric, with other metrics serving as supplementary references.

On the **full dataset**, **all encoder-only models performed similarly**, contradicting our hypothesis that clinical-related models would outperform base models. This suggests that training in clinical data does not significantly improve synthetic letter quality, likely because most clinical tokens were preserved, leaving only general tokens masked in our settings. BERTScore remains a reliable primary metric, as qualitative and quantitative evaluations align at both the sentence and dataset levels.

4.2 Variable-Length Chunk Segmentation

As mentioned in Subsection 3.2.2, we set 'max_lines' as a variable parameter and assigned a fixed value of 256 to 'max_tokens'. We tested increasing 'max_lines' values until the average tokens per chunk peaked, indicating that more clinical information could be preserved. Due to time constraints, the initial experiment on seven letters showed that 41 was the optimal 'max_lines value', where inference time decreased up to this point but rose beyond it (Table 3). This trend was consistent in 10- and 30-letter samples. However, inference time reflects only a general trend rather than precise measurements, as it is influenced by multiple factors, including chunk size and network conditions.

4.3 Masking Strategies

4.3.1 Random Masking

We evaluated the impact of masking ratios (i.e., masked tokens / total tokens) on the quality of synthetic clinical letters using Bio_ClinicalBERT. As expected, higher masking ratios led to lower similarity metrics, but all evaluation values remained above the baseline while staying below 1.0, indicating that the model preserves clinical context and generates understandable text. Notably, at a 1.0 masking ratio, BERTScore increased from 0.29 to 0.63, demonstrating Bio_ClinicalBERT's ability to *retain meaningful clinical information* despite *extensive masking*.

4.3.2 Masking Only Nouns

Masking nouns, which often correspond to Personally Identifiable Information (PII), helps verify de-identification while retaining clinical context. We found that *masking fewer nouns led to better performance across all metrics*, consistent with random masking. When the noun masking ratio reached 1.0, BERTScore increased from 0.70 to 0.89, indicating meaningful noun predictions. All evaluations are higher than the baseline but lower than 1.0. However, as the noun masking ratio increased further, BERTScore decreased significantly. To generate synthetic clinical letters that retain clinical information while being distinguishable, we

	Model Evaluation			
	T5-base	Clinical-T5-base	Clinical-T5-Scratch	Clinical-T5-Sci
		ROUGE-1		
Gencration Performance	86.79	85.19	87.38	80.36
Baseline	73.77	73.77	73.77	73.77
		ROUGE-2		
Generation Performance	75.00	71.70	75.25	69.09
Baseline	63.33	63.33	63.33	63.33
		ROUGE-L		
Generation Performance	84.91	83.33	87.38	80.36
Baseline	73.77	73.77	73.77	73.77
		BERTScore F1		
Generation Performance	0.44	0.40	0.45	0.40
Baseline	0.50	0.50	0.50	0.50
		METEOR		
Generation Performance	0.85	0.83	0.83	0.82
Baseline	0.85	0.85	0.85	0.85
		Flesch Reading Ease		
Generation Performance	8.21	8.21	19.71	8.21
Baseline (Original)	8.21	8.21	8.21	8.21
Baseline (Mask)	8.21	8.21	8.21	8.21

Table 2: Encoder-Decoder Models Comparison at the Sentence Level (The Baseline without annotations was calculated by comparing masked text to the original text)

max_lines	**10**	**20**	**30**	**35**	**40**	**41**	**42**	**45**	**50**
Inference Time (min)	13:47	8:10	6:44	5:24	5:10	5:01	5:12	5:54	6:05
Average Tokens Per Chunk	51.59	90.23	131.26	136.55	144.34	146.43	146.43	146.43	146.43

Table 3: Comparison for different Chunk Size

recommend masking around 80% of nouns to maintain balanced evaluation scores. Full noun masking significantly reduces synthetic letter quality.

4.3.3 Masking Only Verbs

Masking verbs also help identify appropriate token types for masking while retaining clinical meaning. Although verbs are crucial for describing clinical events, they can often be inferred from context. Therefore, masking verbs may have a slight effect on the synthetic clinical letters quality, but can also introduce some variation. From our experimental investigations, masking verbs followed a similar trend to other masking strategies, with *both invalid prediction rates and NLG metrics decreasing as the masking ratio increased.* This is likely due to two factors: the model prioritises generating coherent sentences and may be less sensitive to verbs due to their relative scarcity in the raw data. **BERTScore remained high at 0.95** when **all** verbs were masked, compared to 0.89 when all nouns were masked.

4.3.4 Masking Only Stopwords

Masking **stopwords** aims to **reduce noise**, allowing the model to focus on clinically relevant information while enhancing **generalisation** in synthetic clinical letters to *distinguish* them from actual letters. Additionally, **varying syntax** by masking stopwords mitigates the risk of PHI reconstruction from adversarial attacks. It is often combined with other masking strategies to strengthen privacy protection. From our experiments, the results follow a similar trend to random masking, where a higher masking ratio leads to lower ROUGE Score and BERTScore. Notably, the Invalid Prediction Rate is lowest at a medium masking ratio, as higher ratios cause information loss, while lower ratios make small prediction errors more impactful. The overall **low Invalid Prediction Rate** and **high BERTScore** suggest that stopwords have minimal influence on the model's contextual understanding.

4.3.5 Comparison of Identical Actual Masking Ratios

To further observe how different masking strategies influence the generation of clinical letters, we compared the results using the same actual masking ratios but with different strategies, where the number of masked tokens remained constant. Masking only stopwords resulted in the highest BERTScore and lowest invalid prediction rate, confirming that **stopwords** have **minimal impact** on meaning. Conversely, masking **nouns and verbs** performed **worse** than random masking, suggesting that excessive masking of these token types can **compromise** the clinical information preservation.

4.3.6 Hybrid Masking

Hybrid masking strategies are compared at the same actual masking ratio. Masking **only stopwords** yielded the **best** performance, while *adding noun masking reduced* performance, confirming that masking nouns negatively affects results. However, it still outperformed random masking, suggesting that stopwords have a greater influence than nouns. Additionally, when verbs were further masked alongside nouns and stopwords, performance deteriorated further, indicating that verbs also *negatively* impact model performance.

4.3.7 Comparison with and without Entity Preservation

To assess the impact of entity preservation, we compared results with a baseline model that did not retain entities. When 40% of nouns were masked while preserving entities, the models outperformed those without entity preservation. Additionally, with a 0.3 masking ratio, entity-preserving models had lower ROUGE-1 and ROUGE-2 scores but higher ROUGE-L and BERTScores, indicating less direct overlap with the original text but better narrative retention. These findings confirm that *preserving entities and document structure enhances model performance*, matching our goal of generating clinically coherent yet diverse synthetic letters.

4.3.8 Downstream NER Task

We evaluated whether synthetic letters can replace original (anonymised) clinical letters in NER tasks for research and model training. SpaCy models trained on synthetic letters performed similarly to those trained on original letters, achieving comparable evaluation scores with an F1 score close to ScispaCy's 0.843. This suggests that *unmasked context does not significantly impact model understanding*. Therefore, synthetic letters can be effectively used in NER tasks to replace real-world clinical letters, ensuring data privacy.

Metric	spaCy Trained on Original Letters	spaCy Trained on Synthetic Letters	Performance Delta (Δ)
F1	0.855	0.853	-0.002
P	0.865	0.863	-0.002
R	0.846	0.843	-0.003

Table 4: Comparisons on Downstream NER Task (Precision, Recall, F1)

5 Conclusion

This study explores de-identified synthetic clinical letters that preserve *document structure and clinical narratives* while enhancing diversity. Encoder-only models outperformed encoder-decoder models, with base models performing *comparable* to **clinical-specific** models when clinical terms were preserved. Variable-length chunking strategy effectively maintained sentence meaning, and POS-based masking influenced output quality. Masking *stopwords* improved text quality, whereas masking *nouns and verbs* had negative impacts. BERTScore was identified as the primary evaluation metric, aligning well with both quantitative and qualitative evaluations. A **downstream NER task** demonstrated the feasibility of replacing real-world letters with synthetic ones for this task. Unlike existing research that focuses on improving similarity through model fine-tuning or training a privacy detection and substitution model, this study *emphasises preserving clinically relevant information* while maintaining **diversity**. It provides a framework for better utilisation of real-world datasets while mitigating privacy risks.

Limitations

Although the strategies outlined above facilitate the generation of diverse, de-identified synthetic clinical letters, several limitations remain. One primary concern is the *quality of the data set*, which is affected by spelling errors, ambiguous polysemous words, and limited data volume, potentially impacting generalisability. Additionally, the model struggles with long-tail phenomena, frequently failing to comprehend novel words that are common in the clinical domain. Moreover, processing shorthand and abbreviations presents an additional challenge, often resulting in misinterpretations of key medical terms.

Moreover, the *limited scope of the dataset*, which includes only 204 letters, constraints generalising the findings to broader clinical scenarios. Furthermore, the *evaluation framework*, primarily based on BERTScore, focuses on textual similarity and fails to comprehensively evaluate other critical aspects such as privacy protection efficacy, text diversity, and clinical soundness.

Future work should focus on evaluating de-identification performance using non-anonymous datasets, developing a comprehensive evaluation benchmark and enhancing clinical and general knowledge integration, e.g. (Shaji et al., 2025). The evaluation benchmark should include:

- Privacy protection evaluation using alternative PHI detection models, Membership Inference Attacks, and Model Inversion Attacks (Fang et al., 2024; Ying et al., 2020).
- Diversity evaluation through TF-IDF cosine similarity or Dependency Tree Edit Distance (Thompson et al., 2015; Tsarfaty et al., 2012).
- Clinical soundness evaluation using MEDNLI (Medical Natural Language Inference) or GPT-based assessments (Romanov and Shivade, 2018).

Additionally, techniques such as synonymous substitution, entity linking to SNOMED CT, and specialised spelling correction could be leveraged to enhance the quality and diversity of synthetic clinical letters, e.g. (Romero et al., 2025). Another potential direction is leveraging models to predict and replace privacy-sensitive content that was originally substituted with underscores.

Impact Statement

We use only de-identified clinical data from MIMIC and strictly adhere to all data use agreements. The dataset has already been anonymised, and in this project, we further applied dual anonymisation and re-generation techniques to enhance privacy protection. These strategies are described in Appendix A.

All code used in this project, which will be released, is adapted from well-known language models open-sourced in Hugging Face. However, if applied to real-world clinical letters, it must be reviewed prior to release to mitigate potential data privacy risks. Synthetic clinical letters can be reproduced using the MIMIC-IV dataset and the code provided. However, if users apply this method to process privately collected clinical letters, they should ensure compliance with data protection regulations and clarify copyright ownership.

Our findings help bridge the gap in NLG-based clinical letter generation, facilitating better utilisation of real-world clinical letters by re-generating text while masking sensitive information. This approach helps address data scarcity in medical research and education. However, challenges inherent to LLMs, such as hallucinations and data bias, still persist.

Acknowledgements

LH, WDP, and GN are grateful for the support from the grant "Assembling the Data Jigsaw: Powering Robust Research on the Causes, Determinants and Outcomes of MSK Disease", and the grant "Integrating hospital outpatient letters into the healthcare data space" (EP/V047949/1; funder: UKRI/EPSRC). LH is grateful for the 4D Picture EU project (`https://4dpicture.eu/`) on cancer patient journey support.

References

Goldberger A, Amaral L, Glass L, Hausdorff J, Ivanov PC, Mark R, Mietus JE, Moody GB, Peng CK, and Stanley HE. 2000. Physiobank, physiotoolkit, and physionet: Components of a new research resource for complex physiologic signals. `https://physionet.org/content/`.

Emily Alsentzer, John Murphy, William Boag, Wei-Hung Weng, Di Jindi, Tristan Naumann, and Matthew McDermott. 2019. Publicly available clinical bert embeddings. In *Proceedings of the 2nd Clinical Natural Language Processing Workshop*, pages 72–78.

Ali Amin-Nejad, Julia Ive, and Sumithra Velupillai. 2020a. Exploring transformer text generation for medical dataset augmentation. In *Proceedings of the Twelfth Language Resources and Evaluation Conference*, pages 4699–4708.

Ali Amin-Nejad, Julia Ive, and Sumithra Velupillai. 2020b. Exploring transformer text generation for medical dataset augmentation. In *Proceedings of the Twelfth Language Resources and Evaluation Conference*, pages 4699–4708, Marseille, France. European Language Resources Association.

Samuel Belkadi, Nicolo Micheletti, Lifeng Han, Warren Del-Pinto, and Goran Nenadic. 2023. Generating medical instructions with conditional transformer. In *NeurIPS 2023 Workshop on Synthetic Data Generation with Generative AI.*

Brecht Claerhout and Georges JE DeMoor. 2005. Privacy protection for clinical and genomic data: The use of privacy-enhancing techniques in medicine. *International Journal of Medical Informatics*, 74(2-4):257–265.

Franck Dernoncourt, Ji Young Lee, Ozlem Uzuner, and Peter Szolovits. 2017. De-identification of patient notes with recurrent neural networks. *Journal of the American Medical Informatics Association*, 24(3):596–606.

Lehman Eric and Alistair Johnson. 2023. Clinical-T5: Large Language Models Built Using MIMIC Clinical Text. PhysioNet.

Hao Fang, Yixiang Qiu, Hongyao Yu, Wenbo Yu, Jiawei Kong, Baoli Chong, Bin Chen, Xuan Wang, Shu-Tao Xia, and Ke Xu. 2024. Privacy leakage on dnns: A survey of model inversion attacks and defenses. *arXiv preprint arXiv:2402.04013*.

Ary L. Goldberger, Luis A. N. Amaral, Leon Glass, Jeffrey M. Hausdorff, Plamen Ch. Ivanov, Roger G. Mark, Joseph E. Mietus, George B. Moody, Chung-Kang Peng, and H. Eugene Stanley. 2000. Physiobank, physiotoolkit, and physionet. *Circulation*, 101(23):e215–e220.

Le Hou, Richard Yuanzhe Pang, Tianyi Zhou, Yuexin Wu, Xinying Song, Xiaodan Song, and Denny Zhou. 2022. Token dropping for efficient bert pretraining. In *Proceedings of the 60th Annual Meeting of the Association for Computational Linguistics (Volume 1: Long Papers)*, pages 3774–3784.

Marie Humbert-Droz, Pritam Mukherjee, and Olivier Gevaert. 2022. Strategies to address the lack of labeled data for supervised machine learning training with electronic health records: Case study for the extraction of symptoms from clinical notes. *JMIR Medical Informatics*, 10(3):e32903.

D HÜSKE-KRAUS. 2003. Text generation in clinical medicine: A review. *Methods of information in medicine*, 42(1):51–60.

Alistair Johnson, Lucas Bulgarelli, Tom Pollard, Brian Gow, Benjamin Moody, Steven Horng, Leo Anthony Celi, and Roger Mark. 2024. Mimic-iv.

Alistair EW Johnson, Lucas Bulgarelli, Lu Shen, Alvin Gayles, Ayad Shammout, Steven Horng, Tom J Pollard, Sicheng Hao, Benjamin Moody, Brian Gow, et al. 2023. Mimic-iv, a freely accessible electronic health record dataset. *Scientific data*, 10(1):1.

Aleksandar Kovačević, Bojana Bašaragin, Nikola Milošević, and Goran Nenadić. 2024. De-identification of clinical free text using natural language processing: A systematic review of current approaches. *Artificial Intelligence in Medicine*, page 102845.

Zenon Lamprou, Frank Pollick, and Yashar Moshfeghi. 2022. Role of punctuation in semantic mapping between brain and transformer models. In *International Conference on Machine Learning, Optimization, and Data Science*, pages 458–472. Springer.

Yikuan Li, Ramsey M Wehbe, Faraz S Ahmad, Hanyin Wang, and Yuan Luo. 2023. A comparative study of pretrained language models for long clinical text. *Journal of the American Medical Informatics Association*, 30(2):340–347.

Ximeng Liu, Rongxing Lu, Jianfeng Ma, Le Chen, and Baodong Qin. 2015. Privacy-preserving patient-centric clinical decision support system on naive bayesian classification. *IEEE journal of biomedical and health informatics*, 20(2):655–668.

Zhengliang Liu, Yue Huang, Xiaowei Yu, Lu Zhang, Zihao Wu, Chao Cao, Haixing Dai, Lin Zhao, Yiwei Li, Peng Shu, et al. 2023. Deid-gpt: Zero-shot medical text de-identification by gpt-4. *arXiv preprint arXiv:2303.11032*.

Nicolo Micheletti, Samuel Belkadi, Lifeng Han, and Goran Nenadic. 2024. Exploration of masked and causal language modelling for text generation. *CoRR*, abs/2405.12630.

Beau Norgeot, Kathleen Muenzen, Thomas A Peterson, Xuancheng Fan, Benjamin S Glicksberg, Gundolf Schenk, Eugenia Rutenberg, Boris Oskotsky, Marina Sirota, Jinoos Yazdany, et al. 2020. Protected health information filter (philter): accurately and securely de-identifying free-text clinical notes. *NPJ digital medicine*, 3(1):57.

Peng Qi, Yuhao Zhang, Yuhui Zhang, Jason Bolton, and Christopher D Manning. 2020. Stanza: A python natural language processing toolkit for many human languages. In *Proceedings of the 58th Annual Meeting of the Association for Computational Linguistics: System Demonstrations*, pages 101–108.

Colin Raffel, Noam Shazeer, Adam Roberts, Katherine Lee, Sharan Narang, Michael Matena, Yanqi Zhou, Wei Li, and Peter J. Liu. 2020. Exploring the limits of transfer learning with a unified text-to-text transformer. *Journal of Machine Learning Research*, 21(140):1–67.

Alexey Romanov and Chaitanya Shivade. 2018. Lessons from natural language inference in the clinical domain. In *Proceedings of the 2018 Conference on Empirical Methods in Natural Language Processing*, pages 1586–1596.

Pablo Romero, Lifeng Han, and Goran Nenadic. 2025. INSIGHTBUDDY-AI: Medication Extraction and Entity Linking using Pre-Trained Language Models and Ensemble Learning. In *NAACL-SRW, Forthcoming*, New Mexico, USA. ACL.

Dhivin Shaji, Angel Paul, Lifeng Han, Warren Del-Pinto, Goran Nenadic, and Suzan Verberne. 2025. De-identifying Clinical Texts using Biomed-Clinical BERTs and Comprehensive Risk Assessment. In *IEEE-ICHI 2025, Forthcoming*, Calabria, Italy. IEEE.

Irena Spasic and Goran Nenadic. 2020. Clinical text data in machine learning: Systematic review. *JMIR medical informatics*, 8(3):e17984.

Ruixiang Tang, Xiaotian Han, Xiaoqian Jiang, and Xia Hu. 2023. Does synthetic data generation of llms help clinical text mining? *ArXiv*, abs/2303.04360.

Sumitha Udayashankar Tarur and Sudhakar Prasanna. 2021. clinical case letter. *Indian Pediatr*, 58(188):189.

Nicolas P Terry. 2012. Protecting patient privacy in the age of big data. *UMKC L. Rev.*, 81:385.

Victor U Thompson, Christo Panchev, and Michael Oakes. 2015. Performance evaluation of similarity measures on similar and dissimilar text retrieval. In *2015 7th International Joint Conference on Knowledge Discovery, Knowledge Engineering and Knowledge Management (IC3K)*, volume 1, pages 577–584. IEEE.

Reut Tsarfaty, Joakim Nivre, and Evelina Andersson. 2012. Cross-framework evaluation for statistical parsing. In *Proceedings of the 13th Conference of the European Chapter of the Association for Computational Linguistics*, pages 44–54.

Katherine Tucker, Janice Branson, Maria Dilleen, Sally Hollis, Paul Loughlin, Mark J Nixon, and Zoë Williams. 2016. Protecting patient privacy when sharing patient-level data from clinical trials. *BMC medical research methodology*, 16:5–14.

Ashish Vaswani, Noam Shazeer, Niki Parmar, Jakob Uszkoreit, Llion Jones, Aidan N. Gomez, Łukasz Kaiser, and Illia Polosukhin. 2017. Attention is all you need. In *Proceedings of the 31st International Conference on Neural Information Processing Systems*, NIPS'17, page 6000–6010, Red Hook, NY, USA. Curran Associates Inc.

Guangyu Wang, Xiaohong Liu, Zhen Ying, Guoxing Yang, Zhiwei Chen, Zhiwen Liu, Min Zhang, Hongmei Yan, Yuxing Lu, Yuanxu Gao, et al. 2023. Optimized glycemic control of type 2 diabetes with reinforcement learning: a proof-of-concept trial. *Nature Medicine*, 29(10):2633–2642.

Zuobin Ying, Yun Zhang, and Ximeng Liu. 2020. Privacy-preserving in defending against membership inference attacks. In *Proceedings of the 2020 Workshop on Privacy-Preserving Machine Learning in Practice*, pages 61–63.

Wang Zeng, Sheng Jin, Wentao Liu, Chen Qian, Ping Luo, Wanli Ouyang, and Xiaogang Wang. 2022. Not all tokens are equal: Human-centric visual analysis via token clustering transformer. In *Proceedings of the IEEE/CVF Conference on Computer Vision and Pattern Recognition*, pages 11101–11111.

Yuhao Zhang, Yuhui Zhang, Peng Qi, Christopher D Manning, and Curtis P Langlotz. 2021. Biomedical and clinical English model packages for the Stanza Python NLP library. *Journal of the American Medical Informatics Association*.

Liu Zhuang, Lin Wayne, Shi Ya, and Zhao Jun. 2021. A robustly optimized BERT pre-training approach with post-training. In *Proceedings of the 20th Chinese National Conference on Computational Linguistics*, pages 1218–1227, Huhhot, China. Chinese Information Processing Society of China.

A Different Masking Strategies

To make the synthetic letters more readable, clinically sound, and privacy-protective, different masking strategies are experimented based on the following principles.

- **Retain Annotated Entities:** Preserve clinical knowledge and context.
- **Preserve Extracted Structures:** Keep templates for clinical letters intact.
- **Mask Detected Private Information:** Useful for de-identification, especially in real-world applications.
- **Preserve Medical Terminology:** Ensure essential clinical terms remain unmasked.
- **Preserve Non-Private Numbers:** Keep medical-related numbers (e.g., dosage, heart rate) while masking private ones (e.g., phone numbers, postal codes).
- **Preserve Punctuation:** Maintain punctuation marks such as periods ('.') and underscores ('___') to improve text clarity and coherence (Lamprou et al., 2022).
- **Retain Special Patterns in Samples:** Retain clinically relevant patterns (e.g. 'Ibuprofen > 200 mg', etc) identified from raw sample letters to preserve important clinical details.

Based on the principles above, different masking strategies were experimented with:

- **Mask Randomly:** Tokens are randomly masked in 10% increments (0%-100%) to assess how the number of masked tokens affects synthetic letter quality and provides a baseline for other masking strategies.
- **Mask Based on POS Tagging:** Tokens are masked based on their part-of-speech (POS) category (e.g., only nouns, only verbs) in 10% increments to analyse POS influence on context understanding.
- **Mask Stopwords:** Stopwords are masked to reduce noise and enhance text diversity while ensuring that crucial clinical information remains intact. This approach can also serve as an indirect strategy to prevent reconstruction by attackers leveraging the same syntactic patterns.

- **Hybrid Masking Using Different Ratio Settings:** Combines different masking strategies at varying ratios (e.g., 50% nouns + 50% stopwords) to evaluate their combined effects.

B Evaluation Pipeline

The detailed evaluation pipeline is shown in Figure 8.

C More Evaluation Details

We evaluated the performance of encoder-only and encoder-decoder models at both the sentence level (using the sample sentence in Table 1 and Table 2) and the full dataset level in Table 5. Although SMOG is commonly used for medical datasets, it is less suitable for sentence-level analysis; thus, Flesch Reading Ease was used instead.

As shown in Table 7 and Table 8, readability metrics showed minor variations, with SMOG and Flesch-Kincaid scores occasionally falling below both the masked and original baselines, likely due to punctuation or spacing errors at high masking ratios. Perplexity remained stable, suggesting that synthetic letters are effective for training clinical models, while information entropy was preserved regardless of masking ratios. Subjectivity scores remained consistent, mitigating concerns about model bias.

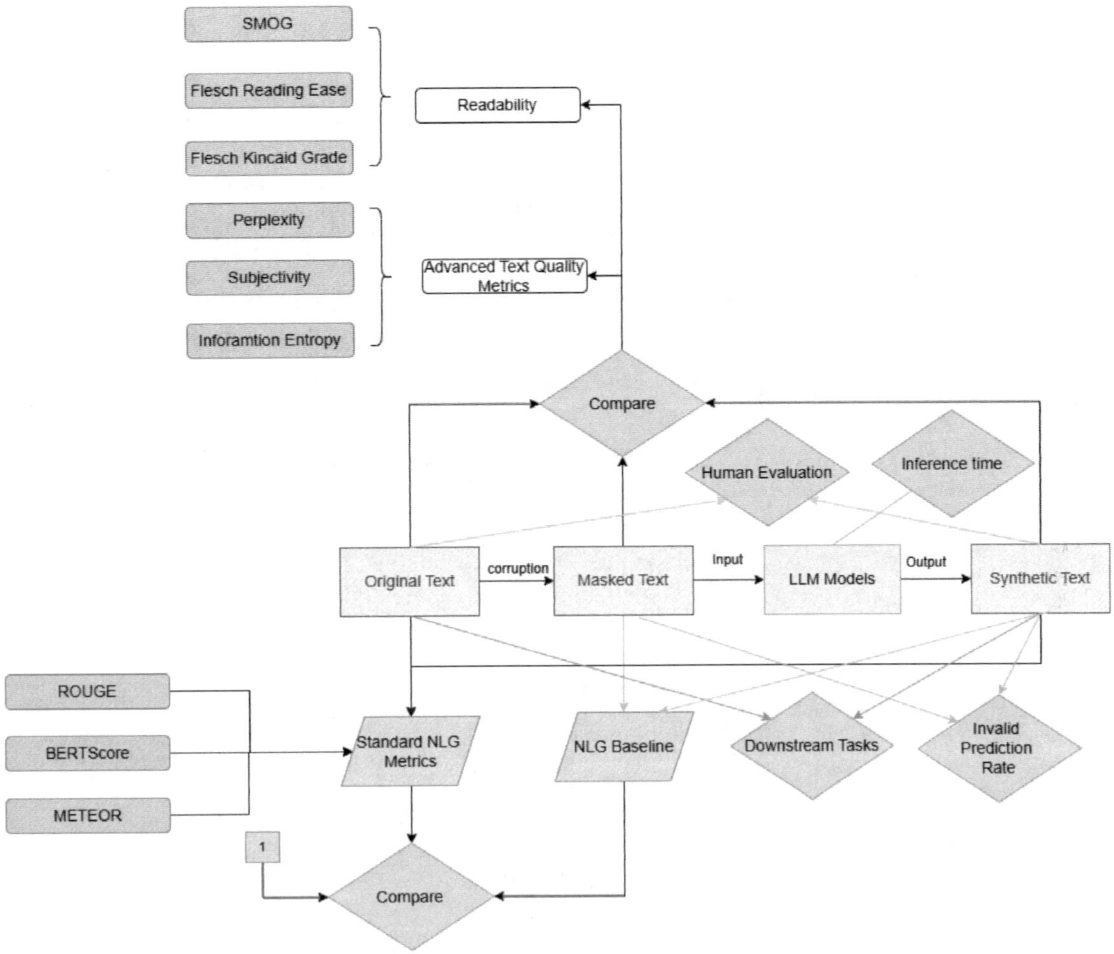

Figure 8: Evaluation Pipeline

	Model Evaluation			
	RoBERTa-base	medicalai / ClinicalBERT	Clinical-Longformer	Bio_ Clinical-BERT
ROUGE-1				
Generation Performance	92.98	93.63	94.66	93.18
Baseline	85.64	85.44	85.64	85.61
ROUGE-2				
Generation Performance	86.10	87.42	89.50	86.50
Baseline	74.96	74.64	74.96	74.92
ROUGE-L				
Generation Performance	92.54	93.22	94.38	92.71
Baseline	85.64	85.44	85.64	85.61
BERTScore F1				
Generation Performance	0.91	0.90	0.92	0.90
Baseline	0.82	0.63	0.82	0.63

Table 5: Encoder-Only Models Comparison on the Full Dataset with Masking Ratio 0.4 (The Baseline was calculated by comparing masked text to the original text)

Bio_ClinicalBERT	Masking Ratio					
	1.0	**0.8**	**0.6**	**0.4**	**0.2**	**0.0**
	ROUGE-1					
Generation Performance	76.28	83.75	88.91	93.18	96.76	99.51
Baseline	64.05	71.56	78.56	85.61	92.63	99.22
	ROUGE-2					
Generation Performance	62.60	70.77	78.81	86.50	93.42	99.02
Baseline	51.72	57.88	65.38	74.92	86.27	98.61
	ROUGE-L					
Generation Performance	74.33	81.69	87.71	92.71	96.65	99.50
Baseline	64.05	71.56	78.56	85.61	92.63	99.22
	BERTScore					
Generation Performance	0.63	0.75	0.83	0.90	0.95	0.99
Baseline	0.29	0.39	0.50	0.63	0.79	0.98
	METEOR					
Generation Performance	0.70	0.80	0.87	0.93	0.97	1.00
Baseline	0.66	0.72	0.78	0.85	0.92	0.99

Table 6: Standard NLG Metrics Across Different Masking Ratios Using Bio_ClinicalBERT (The Baseline was calculated by comparing masked text to the original text)

Bio_ClinicalBERT	Masking Ratio					
	1.0	**0.8**	**0.6**	**0.4**	**0.2**	**0.0**
	SMOG					
Generation Performance	8.91	9.18	9.50	9.79	10.00	10.13
Baseline (Original)	10.16	10.15	10.15	10.15	10.15	10.15
Baseline (Mask)	9.04	9.29	9.52	9.74	9.95	10.13
	Flesch Reading Ease					
Generation Performance	63.77	63.44	61.41	59.54	58.06	57.02
Baseline (Original)	56.85	56.87	56.87	56.87	56.87	56.87
Baseline (Mask)	70.11	67.39	64.75	62.15	59.62	57.13
	Flesch-Kincaid Grade					
Generation Performance	7.32	7.70	8.24	8.66	9.01	9.22
Baseline (Original)	9.26	9.26	9.26	9.26	9.26	9.26
Baseline (Mask)	7.41	7.79	8.16	8.52	8.87	9.22

Table 7: Readability Metrics Across Different Masking Ratios Using Bio_ClinicalBERT (The Baseline without annotations was calculated by comparing masked text to the original text)

Bio_ClinicalBERT	Masking Ratio					
	1.0	**0.8**	**0.6**	**0.4**	**0.2**	**0.0**
	Perplexity					
Generation Performance	2.24	2.32	2.31	2.30	2.29	2.29
Baseline (Original)	2.22	2.28	2.28	2.28	2.28	2.28
Baseline (Mask)	250.37	65.42	24.29	8.95	4.03	2.39
	Information Entropy					
Generation Performance	5.46	5.80	5.92	5.96	5.98	5.98
Baseline (Original)	5.98	5.98	5.98	5.98	5.98	5.98
Baseline (Mask)	4.51	4.93	5.29	5.60	5.85	5.97
	Subjectivity					
Generation Performance	0.32	0.32	0.32	0.32	0.33	0.33
Baseline (Original)	0.33	0.33	0.33	0.33	0.33	0.33
Baseline (Mask)	0.41	0.39	0.38	0.37	0.35	0.33

Table 8: Advanced Text Quality Metrics Across Different Masking Ratios Using Bio_ClinicalBERT (The Baseline without annotations was calculated by comparing masked text to the original text)

Beyond De-Identification: A Structured Approach for Defining and Detecting Indirect Identifiers in Medical Texts

Ibrahim Baroud[1,2], **Lisa Raithel**[1,2,3], **Sebastian Möller**[1,2], **Roland Roller**[2]
[1]Quality & Usability Lab, Technische Universität Berlin
[2]German Research Center for Artificial Intelligence (DFKI), Berlin
[3]BIFOLD - Berlin Institute for the Foundations of Learning and Data
ibrahim.baroud@tu-berlin.de

Abstract

Sharing sensitive texts for scientific purposes requires appropriate techniques to protect the privacy of patients and healthcare personnel. Anonymizing textual data is particularly challenging due to the presence of diverse unstructured direct and indirect identifiers. To mitigate the risk of re-identification, this work introduces a schema of nine categories of indirect identifiers designed to account for different potential adversaries, including acquaintances, family members and medical staff. Using this schema, we annotate 100 MIMIC-III discharge summaries and propose baseline models for identifying indirect identifiers. We release the annotation guidelines, annotation spans (6,199 annotations in total) and the corresponding MIMIC-III document IDs to support further research in this area.[1]

> [...] Patient is a *33-year-old* male, admitted at *12:20* after a *motor vehicle accident*.
> [...] He *works as a carpenter* and *lives with his 28-year-old girlfriend in assisted living*. No known *health insurance*, and he is *currently on disability assistance*. [...] He was noted to be *obese (BMI 32)* with a *height of 178 cm* and *weight of 110 kg*.
> [...] He was evaluated by the *Emergency Department team* and consulted with *Orthopedics* for suspected fractures. [...] Patient reports *playing basketball once a week* [...].

Figure 1: A snippet of a fictitious discharge summary with annotations according to our IPI schema in red.

1 Introduction

Access to data remains a major bottleneck in developing machine learning models for healthcare. Since data contains sensitive details about individuals, it cannot be shared readily outside hospitals. Interactions with legal departments and data security can be cumbersome, and regulations are somewhat unclear, particularly where text is concerned. However, the concept of de-identification is well-defined: according to HIPAA,[2] it requires the removal of a list of direct identifiers, known as protected health information (PHI),[3] including names and addresses.

Classical de-identification of text data has been explored for many years with various approaches (Sweeney, 1996; Gupta et al., 2004; He et al., 2015; Kocaman et al., 2023) and state-of-the-art de-identification systems achieve an F_1-score $\geq 95\%$ on academic benchmarks (Kocaman et al., 2023; Yogarajan et al., 2020). However, additional manual effort is needed to remove remaining PHIs, and more importantly, unstructured text often contains **additional information beyond PHIs** that can reveal an individual's identity (Feder et al., 2020), making the manual inspection process even more complex.

The concept of anonymization goes further: it is defined as an irreversible procedure that is applied to the data such that no information can be linked to any specific individual anymore (Meystre et al., 2010). While the terms de-identification and anonymization are often used interchangeably, they refer to distinct concepts (Chevrier et al., 2019). De-identification focuses solely on removing direct identifiers, whereas anonymization must also address indirect identifiers. Indirect identifiers are pieces of information that are potentially publicly known about an individual but do not lead to reidentification when considered alone. However, in combination with other background or external knowledge, they can be used to uniquely identify an individual (Pilán et al., 2022). Figure 1 shows a synthetic discharge summary with highlighted information (beyond direct identifiers) that may help reveal a person's identity.

[1]https://zenodo.org/records/15044596

[2]The U.S. Health Insurance Portability and Accountability Act of 1996.

[3]https://www.hhs.gov/hipaa/for-professionals/special-topics/de-identification/index.html

Proceedings of the Sixth Workshop on Privacy in Natural Language Processing, pages 75–85
April 4, 2025

Despite the importance of anonymization, relatively few studies have systematically addressed text anonymization beyond traditional PHI detection. Gardner and Xiong (2008) developed a system for extracting and suppressing sensitive information other than PHIs, but it was limited to diagnoses. Kolditz et al. (2019) created a dataset with PHIs and added more categories, namely medical units, relatives and typists. Feder et al. (2020) annotated a set of demographic traits in clinical notes and proposed a framework for detecting sentences that include such traits. Pilán et al. (2022) presented a benchmark dataset comprising annotations of court cases and evaluation metrics to assess the performance of anonymization methods. The annotations cover categories such as names and quantities, and annotators mark each of the entities as a direct or indirect identifier. Moreover, Yang et al. (2024) proposed a framework for text anonymization based on large language models (LLMs). This framework measures anonymization success simply by checking whether an adversarial LLM can guess the name of the person to whom the text belongs.

Building on prior work, our study defines and identifies information beyond traditional personal health identifiers within a controlled framework. We introduce a schema of indirect personal identifiers (IPIs) optimized for a medical context and apply it to annotate relevant spans in discharge summaries from the Medical Information Mart for Intensive Care (MIMIC-III) dataset (Johnson et al., 2016). We define the problem of structurally identifying IPIs as a span classification problem, rather than a sentence classification problem as in Feder et al. (2020), to avoid removing whole sentences (which might include other medical information) and to reduce information loss during anonymization. Finally, we evaluate the performance of various models in detecting the annotated identifiers.

2 Indirect Personal Identifiers (IPI)

The type of information that may lead to re-identification in a given text is domain-dependent and requires unique analysis (Sweeney, 2000). In the following, we introduce a schema covering aspects of indirect personal identifiers (IPI) and use it to annotate spans in discharge summaries from MIMIC-III. To construct our dataset, we randomly sampled 100 summaries with lengths ranging from 500 to 2,500 words.[4]

2.1 IPI Schema

Our proposed schema builds on related work by Kolditz et al. (2019) and Feder et al. (2020), as well as our own manual analysis of discharge summaries. From prior work, we incorporate concepts like *medical unit* (Kolditz et al., 2019), expanding it to include medical services, teams and medical personnel. We adapt *family structure* from Feder et al. (2020), broadening it to include family decisions. We also integrate *living arrangements* into a new category, DETAILS, which covers indirect identifiers such as addresses (e.g., 'lives in prison'), dates ('he turned 18 right before COVID started'), and references to other PHIs like license numbers.

Additionally, we adapt the category *occupation* into SEC, which covers socio-economic and criminal history. Our LFSTL category includes habits, sports and diet alongside the *drug* category from Feder et al. (2020). We redefine the category *casually noticeable* in our category APPEARANCE to specifically cover body piercings, tattoos and scars. Based on our manual analysis, we introduce TIME to capture time-related expressions such as timestamps for taking lab values, admission days and time references around events such as surgeries. A brief overview of our final categories is provided below,[5] with further details available in Appendix A.

APPEARANCE Descriptions of appearance, e.g. *freshly healed scar behind right ear*, and mentions of weight, height or body modifications.

CIRCUMSTANCES Any mention of an event (e.g. an accident) that caused an injury or happened in a medical facility. This category also includes specific statements or behavior, e.g. *crashed his car into a dumpster* or *refused medication because she does not believe in it.*

SEC Mentions of information concerning socio-economic or criminal history, such as employment (e.g. *is a retired police officer*), health insurance (e.g. *has no health insurance*) or social/legal status (*does not have valid papers*).

FAMILY Any mention of family-related information, such as being adopted, as well as the

[4] More details on the dataset in Appendix B.

[5] The following examples were created by the authors to avoid presenting data from MIMIC-III directly.

family's medical history or involvement (e.g. *daughter serves as her health care proxy*).

FCLT_PERSONNEL Mentions of healthcare facilities (*ICU*) or medical personnel (*nursing team*).

TIME All mentions of age or time-related information (e.g., *postoperative day number 5*).

LFSTL Regular activities and habits, such as sports or diet (e.g. *reports sticking to low-sodium diet*), but also tobacco, alcohol or substance use.

DETAILS All mentions of PHIs that were not detected, or a description of a PHI (e.g. *lives in a halfway house*, which reveals information about the person's address).

OTHER All other kinds of non-medical but infrequent information that might be sensitive, e.g. languages, ethnicity or sexual orientation.

2.2 Data Annotation

Two annotators independently labelled the same set of 100 de-identified discharge summaries using the nine categories described above. The annotations were then consolidated, meaning that all annotations from both annotators were discussed and resolved into one final version of the corpus presented here. Inter-annotator agreement (IAA) was calculated using the average pairwise relaxed F_1-score between the annotators' marked entities.[6] We chose F_1-score for calculating agreement as it proved to be a more usable and interpretable measure for annotations such as span classification, where the number of negative examples is very large (or unknown) and the probability of chance agreement on positive examples (the desired spans) is close to zero (Hripcsak and Rothschild, 2005). The overall agreement resulted in an F_1-score of 0.87. Table 4 in Appendix B lists the scores for each category. The annotators achieved the highest agreement in the categories TIME ($F_1 = 0.89$), LFSTL ($F_1 = 0.88$) and FAMILY ($F_1 = 0.87$), and the lowest on DETAILS ($F_1 = 0.41$).

The finalized dataset consists of 6,199 annotations, the majority of them belonging to the categories TIME (64.62%) and FCLT_PERSONNEL (22.92%). This is expected, as most discharge summaries contain detailed temporal descriptions, department consultations and precise timestamps, such as when lab values were recorded. In contrast, information such as spoken languages or accident details appeared less frequently, as they were case-dependent and varied based on the typist's preference. Table 1 shows the number of annotations per category and their percentage in the overall annotations.

Category	#Annotations	Proportion
FAMILY	273	4.4%
APPEARANCE	132	2.13%
CIRCUMSTANCES	99	1.6%
SEC	59	0.95%
FCLT_PERSONNEL	1421	22.92%
TIME	4006	64.62%
LFSTL	144	2.32%
DETAILS	32	0.52%
OTHER	33	0.53%

Table 1: Number of annotations per category in 100 discharge summaries from MIMIC-III.

2.3 Data Characteristics

Overall, we focused on identifying indirect identifiers on the span level that may either be publicly known or describe a person's status, behaviour or appearance. Our final curated annotations reveal various such risks. For example, spans labeled as CIRCUMSTANCES contain descriptive information about accidents that could facilitate re-identification by witnesses. These details may enable an adversary to retrieve additional information about the patient, e.g. by searching online to find reports about the incident. Moreover, this category might encompass other sensitive or memorable descriptions, such as instances of patient aggression toward staff or refusal of medication.

The 59 annotations from the SEC category reveal information about a person's criminal history, which is public information in the U.S. (Jacobs and Larrauri, 2012) and therefore easy to look up even for a layperson. This category covers mentions of the patient being incarcerated, which may, in some cases, reveal the patient's exact address. Finally, the annotations include various information about patients' social status, such as being homeless or not having health insurance, or lifestyle, such as information about drinking, smoking or sports. Although these mentions are relatively infrequent in the dataset, they may pose a high re-identification risk. Unique or rare characteristics –

[6] Details about the annotators and IAA can be found in Appendix B.

especially those that distinguish an individual from the broader population – can drastically narrow down the pool of potential matches, making re-identification more feasible.

3 Experiments

To provide a first baseline for the automatic detection of the proposed set of indirect identifiers in medical texts, we experimented with BERT (Devlin et al., 2019) as well as open-source LLMs. We split the data into training (60%), development (15%) and test (25%) sets, and used the dev set for hyperparameter optimization. Table 2 shows statistics about the final data split.

We fine-tuned a BERT model for span classification using the HuggingFace library (Wolf et al., 2020). For the LLM experiments, we used Llama-3.1-8b-Instruct, Mistral-7B-Instruct-v0.3 and Qwen2.5-14B-Instruct in both zero-shot and three-shot settings leveraging Declarative Self-improving Python (DSPy) (Khattab et al., 2024) to automatically refine and optimize the prompt and Pydantic[7] to obtain structured and type-validated output from the LLMs. An example prompt is shown in Appendix E. We implemented an LLM agent for each category and provided DSPy with the description of each category as defined in the annotation guidelines. Model performance was assessed using relaxed precision, recall and F_1-score. Further details on data preprocessing, model fine-tuning and evaluation can be found in Appendix C.

	train	dev	test	total
#documents	60	15	25	100
#sections	592	162	253	1007
#annotations	3712	927	1560	6199

Table 2: Statistics for the train, development and test sets. '#sections' represents the number of sections the documents were split into for each set.

3.1 Results

Detailed evaluation results for the BERT model can be found in Table 3. Notably, recall is higher than precision in almost all cases. Phrases containing socio-economic or criminal information (SEC), medical facilities and personnel (FCLT_PERSONNEL) and time expressions (TIME) achieve higher scores than the other categories; i.e. less frequent categories tend to have a lower F_1-score, which was also true for the IAA scores. The lightweight LLMs, which are explored here for the first time for this specific task, performed poorly on the test set with F_1-score $\leq 51\%$ (micro) and recall $\leq 47\%$ (more details in Table 5). The 3-shot setting did not always improve performance. Interestingly, performance dropped in some cases when providing the models with examples. A similar phenomenon was also observed in Kwon et al. (2024) when using Llama3 for information extraction: the model achieved better results in some cases in the zero-shot setting in comparison to few-shot. This and the overall low performance of the LLMs in comparison to BERT highlights our doubts about the suitability and effectiveness of using LLMs for extracting our proposed categories of indirect identifiers. Moreover, our evaluation showed that the LLMs sometimes failed to follow the pre-defined output format and preserve the originality of the spans in the original texts. Moreover, they frequently hallucinated and extracted irrelevant or non-existent information.

Category	P	R	F_1	Support
DETAILS	0.13	0.50	0.21	4
FAMILY	0.67	0.96	0.79	73
APPEARANCE	0.52	0.59	0.55	29
CIRCUMSTANCES	0.18	0.23	0.20	30
SEC	0.59	0.71	0.65	14
FCLT_PERSONNEL	0.80	0.92	0.85	362
TIME	0.84	0.97	0.90	1006
LFSTL	0.57	0.86	0.68	35
OTHER	0.20	0.14	0.17	7
micro average	0.78	0.93	0.85	1560
macro average	0.50	0.65	0.55	1560

Table 3: Evaluation results on the test set for the **BERT-based** system in **P**recision, **R**ecall, and $\mathbf{F_1}$ score. Support shows the number of examples in the test set.

4 Discussion

As expected, the BERT-based model clearly outperformed the lightweight LLMs in both zero-shot and 3-shot settings, corroborating the results of Naguib et al. (2024) about BERT superiority against LLMs for span classification. This suggests that LLMs may be more powerful as supportive tools used to validate anonymization systems through inferring hidden information as proposed by Staab et al. (2024) rather than being used for span classification.

The BERT model shows a satisfactory micro

[7]https://pypi.org/project/pydantic/

F_1-score, with its comparably high recall being particularly advantageous for anonymization, as missing sensitive information can have serious consequences. However, the low macro F_1-score combined with the strong imbalance of the annotated categories indicates that the model struggles to detect less frequent, yet more critical, categories.

One reason for this may be the limited amount of training data, hampering the model's ability to learn robust representations for rare categories. Additionally, the inherent linguistic complexity within categories further complicates the task. In contrast to PHIs, such as names or addresses, which usually follow similar patterns across documents, IPIs exhibit greater lexical and semantic diversity. This not only makes them more challenging, but also highlights the urgency of accurately identifying them for effective anonymization. Given that annotating additional documents is both time- and resource-intensive, especially when rare events must be captured in sufficient numbers, it may be more realistic to investigate methods that perform well in low-resource scenarios.

5 Conclusion

In this work, we introduced a dataset along with an annotation schema designed to capture a wide range of indirect identifiers in medical texts. The schema is inspired by medical records, but is adaptable to other domains and text genres with minimal modifications. We evaluated the performance of BERT and LLMs in detecting the proposed categories. The overall performance of the models highlights the inherent difficulty of this task, particularly in identifying less frequent and diverse indirect identifiers. However, our work provides a foundation for further exploration and adaptation, with an eye to improving privacy through structural information detection. In future work, we aim to develop a framework that (k-)anonymizes the proposed indirect identifiers and study the utility of the anonymized texts on downstream tasks.

Acknowledgements

We thank the anonymous reviewers for their constructive feedback on this paper. This research was supported by the German Federal Ministry of Education and Research (BMBF) through the project Medinym (16KISA006 and 16KISA007) and the grant BIFOLD25B.

Limitations

Our list of categories is diverse; however, indirect identifiers should not be limited to it, and further studies should explore more potential risks in unstructured data that do not fall under these categories. We plan to test the scalability of our schema to other datasets, languages and domains (such as legal or financial), but accessing similar relevant data is very limited due to privacy concerns, especially in languages other than English.

The LLM experiments are intended to provide a different baseline approach rather than to compare performance with the BERT model, as such a comparison would be unfair in a zero- or few-shot setting. The LLM approach could be improved, for example, by using bigger models or performing an instruction tuning using the training set instead of evaluating the models in a zero- or few-shot setting. We plan to use LLMs to augment the training set with synthetically generated examples to solve the problem of low numbers of examples for certain categories, which also did not suffice to train the BERT model.

BERT-based models have been shown to work well in NER tasks; however, they cannot be fully relied on for finding all instances of potentially sensitive information. Instead, these models can be used as a complement to help humans speed up the process of enhancing privacy. As for LLMs, we would not trust them to produce complete and reliable results since our experiments showed unfaithful output in terms of format (which hinders a structured evaluation) and "hallucinations."

We did not experiment with a hybrid approach (e.g., combining regular expressions and the approaches described) to improve the detection of categories with formulaic patterns for which we expect a better performance using regular expression, such as TIME.

Ethical Considerations

The data used in the above work is publicly available, de-identified data from the MIMIC-III database and therefore does not expose any patients or medical staff. It is only available after registration and training. We state that we only annotated potential indirect identifiers and did not attempt to re-identify any patients. All examples in this paper were created by the authors. They resemble texts from MIMIC-III, but are not copied from real discharge summaries. We only release the annotations and document IDs from MIMIC-III, but **not** the documents themselves.

Broader Impact Statement

This work contributes to protecting patient privacy by identifying and categorizing indirect personal identifiers in medical discharge summaries which are not considered in de-identification. Our annotated dataset offers a valuable resource for developing and evaluating privacy-enhancing machine learning models. Despite being optimized for medical discharge summaries, we encourage the further use and development of our schema in other domains, e.g., the legal and finance domain, to enhance data privacy and data sharing.

References

Raphaël Chevrier, Vasiliki Foufi, Christophe Gaudet-Blavignac, Arnaud Robert, and Christian Lovis. 2019. Use and understanding of anonymization and de-identification in the biomedical literature: scoping review. *Journal of medical Internet research*, 21(5):e13484.

Jacob Devlin, Ming-Wei Chang, Kenton Lee, and Kristina Toutanova. 2019. BERT: Pre-training of Deep Bidirectional Transformers for Language Understanding. In *North American Chapter of the Association for Computational Linguistics*.

Amir Feder, Danny Vainstein, Roni Rosenfeld, Tzvika Hartman, Avinatan Hassidim, and Yossi Matias. 2020. Active deep learning to detect demographic traits in free-form clinical notes. *Journal of Biomedical Informatics*, 107:103436.

James Gardner and Li Xiong. 2008. HIDE: an integrated system for health information DE-identification. In *2008 21st IEEE international symposium on computer-based medical systems*, pages 254–259. IEEE.

Dilip Gupta, Melissa Saul, and John Gilbertson. 2004. Evaluation of a deidentification (De-Id) software engine to share pathology reports and clinical documents for research. *American journal of clinical pathology*, 121(2):176–186.

Bin He, Yi Guan, Jianyi Cheng, Keting Cen, and Wenlan Hua. 2015. CRFs based de-identification of medical records. *Journal of biomedical informatics*, 58:S39–S46.

George Hripcsak and Adam S Rothschild. 2005. Agreement, the f-measure, and reliability in information retrieval. *Journal of the American medical informatics association*, 12(3):296–298.

James B Jacobs and Elena Larrauri. 2012. Are criminal convictions a public matter? The USA and Spain. *Punishment & Society*, 14(1):3–28.

Alistair EW Johnson, Tom J Pollard, Lu Shen, Li-wei H Lehman, Mengling Feng, Mohammad Ghassemi, Benjamin Moody, Peter Szolovits, Leo Anthony Celi, and Roger G Mark. 2016. MIMIC-III, a freely accessible critical care database. *Scientific data*, 3(1):1–9.

Omar Khattab, Arnav Singhvi, Paridhi Maheshwari, Zhiyuan Zhang, Keshav Santhanam, Sri Vardhamanan, Saiful Haq, Ashutosh Sharma, Thomas T. Joshi, Hanna Moazam, Heather Miller, Matei Zaharia, and Christopher Potts. 2024. DSPy: Compiling Declarative Language Model Calls into Self-Improving Pipelines.

Veysel Kocaman, D Talby, and H Ul Hak. 2023. RWD143 Beyond Accuracy: Automated De-Identification of Large Real-World Clinical Text Datasets. *Value in Health*, 26(12):S532.

Tobias Kolditz, Christina Lohr, Johannes Hellrich, Luise Modersohn, Boris Betz, Michael Kiehntopf, and Udo Hahn. 2019. Annotating German clinical documents for de-identification. In *MEDINFO 2019: Health and Wellbeing e-Networks for All*, pages 203–207. IOS Press.

Yeonsu Kwon, Jiho Kim, Gyubok Lee, Seongsu Bae, Daeun Kyung, Wonchul Cha, Tom Pollard, Alistair Johnson, and Edward Choi. 2024. EHRCon: Dataset for Checking Consistency between Unstructured Notes and Structured Tables in Electronic Health Records. *ArXiv*, abs/2406.16341.

Stephane M Meystre, F Jeffrey Friedlin, Brett R South, Shuying Shen, and Matthew H Samore. 2010. Automatic de-identification of textual documents in the electronic health record: a review of recent research. *BMC medical research methodology*, 10:1–16.

Ines Montani and Matthew Honnibal. Prodigy: A modern and scriptable annotation tool for creating training data for machine learning models.

Marco Naguib, Xavier Tannier, and Aurélie Névéol. 2024. Few shot clinical entity recognition in three languages: Masked language models outperform LLM prompting. *arXiv preprint arXiv:2402.12801*.

Ildikó Pilán, Pierre Lison, Lilja Øvrelid, Anthi Papadopoulou, David Sánchez, and Montserrat Batet. 2022. The Text Anonymization Benchmark (TAB): A Dedicated Corpus and Evaluation Framework for Text Anonymization. *Computational Linguistics*, 48(4):1053–1101.

Isabel Segura-Bedmar, Paloma Martínez, and María Herrero-Zazo. 2013. SemEval-2013 task 9 : Extraction of drug-drug interactions from biomedical texts (DDIExtraction 2013). In *Second Joint Conference on Lexical and Computational Semantics (*SEM), Volume 2: Proceedings of the Seventh International Workshop on Semantic Evaluation (SemEval 2013)*, pages 341–350, Atlanta, Georgia, USA. Association for Computational Linguistics.

Robin Staab, Mark Vero, Mislav Balunović, and Martin Vechev. 2024. Beyond Memorization: Violating Privacy via Inference with Large Language Models. In *The Twelfth International Conference on Learning Representations*.

Latanya Sweeney. 1996. Replacing personally-identifying information in medical records, the Scrub system. In *Proceedings of the AMIA annual fall symposium*, page 333. American Medical Informatics Association.

Latanya Sweeney. 2000. Simple Demographics Often Identify People Uniquely.

Thomas Wolf, Lysandre Debut, Victor Sanh, Julien Chaumond, Clement Delangue, Anthony Moi, Pierric Cistac, Tim Rault, Remi Louf, Morgan Funtowicz, Joe Davison, Sam Shleifer, Patrick von Platen, Clara Ma, Yacine Jernite, Julien Plu, Canwen Xu, Teven Le Scao, Sylvain Gugger, Mariama Drame, Quentin Lhoest, and Alexander Rush. 2020. Transformers: State-of-the-art natural language processing. In *Proceedings of the 2020 Conference on Empirical Methods in Natural Language Processing: System Demonstrations*, pages 38–45, Online. Association for Computational Linguistics.

Tianyu Yang, Xiaodan Zhu, and Iryna Gurevych. 2024. Robust Utility-Preserving Text Anonymization Based on Large Language Models. *arXiv preprint arXiv:2407.11770*.

Vithya Yogarajan, Bernhard Pfahringer, and Michael Mayo. 2020. A review of automatic end-to-end de-identification: Is high accuracy the only metric? *Applied Artificial Intelligence*, 34(3):251–269.

A Detailed Descriptions of the IPI Categories

APPEARANCE Mention of a person's (also infant's) weight, height or a description of a person's body or body modifications, e.g., a scar under the eye, very tall, very short, gained/lost weight over a specific period of time, tattoos, piercings, etc.

CIRCUMSTANCES Any mention or description of an event (accident, storm, wildfire, etc.) that caused, e.g., a person's injury or happened in the clinical center such as patient being aggressive, rejecting help or medicine, leaving AMA (including discussions about the decision with persons outside the family) or injuring hospital staff. Additionally, details about how the person was brought into the hospital or mentions of statements, requests or complaints expressed by the person.

SEC Any mention of specific information about the person's employment (e.g., *is a retired police officer*) or criminal history, health insurance (e.g., *has no health insurance* or *has a legal guard*) or social status such as homelessness or living in subsidized housing.

FAMILY All mentions of detailed family-related information about the person such as being adopted, having a twin sibling or having had an in vitro fertilization pregnancy. Furthermore, specific descriptions of the family's medical history (e.g., *parent died at age 40*) or involvement (e.g., *patient's daughter serves as her health care proxy*).

FCLT_PERSONNEL All mentions of hospital names, hospital units, labs, departments, facilities, consulting services/teams, floor and rooms, medical branches, outside doctors.

TIME Mentions of age or time-related information, e.g. *postoperative day number 2*, *day of delivery number 13*, *day of life 6*, exact mentions of times when lab values were taken, or exact times about when medications should be taken. Do not consider times related to the medical condition itself, e.g., *stopped breathing for 30 secs*.

LFSTL Hobbies and Lifestyle: such as sports or playing an instrument. Lifestyle: e.g. information about the patient's diet or private lifestyle.

DETAILS All mentions of PHIs that were not detected and de-identified automatically or an abstract/indirect description of a PHI, for instance regarding address (e.g., *lives in a halfway house* or *lives in prison*). Any information not related to PHIs such as weight or medical units are not part of this category and should be annotated as described in the other categories above. For consistency, the following are the PHIs to consider for this category: Name, email addresses, geographic details, dates directly related to the individual, telephone, fax numbers, social security numbers, medical record numbers, health plan beneficiary numbers, account numbers, certificate and license numbers, vehicle and device identifiers, biometric identifiers and facial photograph, URL, IP addresses.

OTHER Other kinds of non-medical information that may be too sensitive to keep in the data e.g. languages, ethnicity (e.g., *Caucasian*, *AAF* etc.) and sexual orientation.

B Data and Annotation Details

Data The discharge summaries we use for demonstrating our schema are randomly sampled from the Medical Information Mart for Intensive Care (MIMIC-III) dataset (Johnson et al., 2016). It comprises health-related data from over 40,000 patients who stayed in critical care units of the Beth Israel Deaconess Medical Center between 2001 and 2012. Among other types of data, such as patient demographics, the database also includes various types of textual data, such as diagnostic reports and discharge summaries. We chose discharge summaries for our study, since these are richer in information than other notes in MIMIC-III.

Annotation Tool For annotation, we used Prodigy (Montani and Honnibal), version 1.11.11. It was run on a secure, lab-internal server; access was only permitted to the authors.

Annotators The annotation team included one female and one male researcher, each with a different cultural background. Both annotators are fluent in English, though it is not their native language. One has expertise in computer science and data anonymization, and the other has experience in biomedical natural language processing. Neither has formal medical training, but both have experience in computational research and have contributed to various annotation projects in a research setting. Both annotators were compensated as part of their regular researcher roles.

Inter-Annotator Agreement The reported pairwise F_1-score is based on partial matches: a true positive exists when the compared spans overlap with at least one token and have the same label. We focus on partial matches because the exact span is not as important as in other entity recognition tasks; the main difficulty lies in finding the relevant information and removing it—anonymizing a longer span does not hurt the patient.

Category	F_1-Score
DETAILS	0.41
FAMILY	0.87
APPEARANCE	0.62
CIRCUMSTANCES	0.59
SEC	0.78
FCLT_PERSONNEL	0.85
TIME	0.89
LFSTL	0.88
OTHER	0.52
micro average	0.87
macro average	0.71

Table 4: Inter-annotator agreement overall and per category using partial match pairwise F_1-scores (Hripcsak and Rothschild, 2005).

C Model Training and Evaluation Details

Data Preprocessing In order to train an NER model, we converted the Prodigy annotations (each represented with a span start and end) to word-level annotations. Words annotated as part of a category received label prefixes `B` when they are at the beginning of a category, `I` when they lie within the category, and finally, words that were not part of any category received the label `O` (out). Since BERT cannot handle sequences longer than 512 sub-tokens, we split the discharge summaries into sections to avoid truncation and information loss. Prodigy's annotation output is already pre-tokenized and we used the pre-trained BERT-base-cased tokenizer for subword tokenization.

BERT Fine-Tuning For choosing the hyperparameters, a bert-base-cased model[8] was fine-tuned for maximally 15 epochs (early stopping after two epochs' patience) on the training set and evaluated on the development set using a grid search over learning rate values (1e-5, 2e-5, 3e-5, 4e-5, 5e-5) and batch size values (4, 8, 16). After selecting the hyperparameters, we trained a BERT model on 75% of the data (training and development combined) using the best-performing hyperparameters: 8 epochs, 3e-5 as the learning rate and 8 as the batch size.

Evaluation Details We evaluated on the held-out test set using the `nervaluate` package,[9] which is a Python implementation for evaluating NER models as defined in the SemEval 2013 - 9.1 task (Segura-Bedmar et al., 2013). We report the results following the type evaluation schema, which

[8] https://huggingface.co/google-bert/bert-base-cased

[9] https://github.com/MantisAI/nervaluate

requires some overlap between the system-tagged entity and the gold-standard annotation.

Model	P	R	F_1	Support
Llama-3.1-8B	0.08	0.40	0.13	1560
Llama-3.1-8B 3-shot	0.18	0.35	0.24	1560
Mistral-7B-v0.3	0.17	**0.47**	0.25	1560
Mistral-7B-v0.3 3-shot	0.05	0.30	0.09	1560
Qwen2.5-14B	**0.64**	0.42	**0.51**	1560
Qwen2.5-14B 3-shot	**0.64**	0.28	0.39	1560
Qwen2.5-72B*	0.48	**0.47**	0.48	1560

Table 5: Micro-averaged test results for each LLM showing precision (**P**), recall (**R**) and F_1-score ($\mathbf{F_1}$). *This is the 8-bit quantized version of this model. Values in **Bold** represent the highest performance for each metric among all tested LLMs.

Use of AI Assistants ChatGPT was partially used as an AI assistant for coding support.

Computing Environment The following packages were used for conducting the experiments:

- Transformers version 4.44.2[10]
- spacy version 3.7.5[11]
- Prodigy version 1.11.11[12]

The BERT experiments were run on a T4 GPU with 16GB. The LLMs were run on 2x NVIDIA RTX A6000 with 48GB each.

[10] https://huggingface.co/

[11] https://spacy.io/

[12] https://prodi.gy/

D Example Annotation

Figure 2 shows an example of how the discharge summaries were annotated.

Patient ID: 123456
Admission ID: 7890
Admission Date: 2022-03-15
Discharge Date: 2022-03-20
Chief Complaint: Chest pain

History of Present Illness:

The patient is a 64-year-old male presenting with acute onset chest pain radiating to the left arm. Pain began approximately 3 hours prior to admission and is described as a 7/10 in intensity. The patient also reports mild shortness of breath but denies nausea or vomiting. His daughter brought him to the hospital after noticing his discomfort. The patient notes that his daughter recently experienced a heart attack herself at the age of 40, which raises concern about a family history of early cardiovascular disease.

The patient admits he has not been consistently taking his prescribed medications, as he is skeptical about their effectiveness. He expresses doubts about the benefits of long-term medication, stating that he feels "fine most of the time" and is unsure that the medication makes a difference.

Family History:

- Father: Deceased at 70 due to a myocardial infarction.
- Mother: Deceased at 75 due to stroke.
- Daughter: Age 40, history of myocardial infarction one month prior.

Past Medical History:

- ...
- History of right foot amputation, partial (right great toe), due to diabetic complications

Medications on Admission:

- Metformin 500 mg PO BID (Non-adherent)
- Lisinopril 20 mg PO daily (Non-adherent)

Physical Exam:

- Vital Signs: BP 145/90 mmHg, HR 88 bpm, RR 18/min, Temp 98.6°F
- ...
- Extremities: Right foot with absent great toe, well-healed amputation scar, no signs of infection. No peripheral edema.

Assessment:

1. Acute coronary syndrome, rule out myocardial infarction
2. ...

Plan:

1. Initiate cardiac monitoring
2. ...
3. Start aspirin 81 mg PO daily and consider heparin infusion
4. Consult cardiology for further evaluation
5. Address patient's concerns regarding medication adherence; Schedule a follow-up appointment with primary care and a consultation with a pharmacist or healthcare educator to reinforce the importance of adherence.

Discharge Summary:

The patient was ruled out for myocardial infarction based on ... The patient and his daughter were provided educational materials and were encouraged to follow up in the cardiology clinic for further risk assessment, including possible genetic counseling.

Figure 2: A (generated) discharge summary with annotations based on the proposed schema.

E Example Prompts

Figure 3 shows an example prompt that was used with DSPy to extract the FCLT_PERSONNEL category. Note that the format is the same for the other categories; only the descriptions vary depending on the category that the model is supposed to extract.

Example Prompt

Given the fields `sentence`, produce the fields `extractions`.

—

Follow the following format.

Sentence: ${sentence}

Extractions: all mentions of hospital names, hospital units, labs, departments, facilities, consulting services/teams, floor and rooms, medical branches, outside doctors and medical personnel extracted from input sentence. Do not extract anything that is between [** **]. Respond with a single JSON object. JSON Schema: {"properties": {"health_fclt": {"items": {"type": "string"}, "title": "Health Fclt", "type": "array"}}, "required": ["health_fclt"], "title": "SentenceExtraction", "type": "object"}

—

Sentence:

Extractions: "health_fclt": []

Figure 3: The final prompt used by DSPy for extracting the FCLT_PERSONNEL category.

Investigating User Perspectives on Differentially Private Text Privatization

Stephen Meisenbacher, Alexandra Klymenko, Alexander Karpp, and Florian Matthes
Technical University of Munich
School of Computation, Information and Technology
Department of Computer Science
Garching, Germany
{stephen.meisenbacher,alexandra.klymenko,a.karpp,matthes}@tum.de

Abstract

Recent literature has seen a considerable uptick in *Differentially Private Natural Language Processing* (DP NLP). This includes DP text privatization, where potentially sensitive input texts are transformed under DP to achieve privatized output texts that ideally mask sensitive information *and* maintain original semantics. Despite continued work to address the open challenges in DP text privatization, there remains a scarcity of work addressing user perceptions of this technology, a crucial aspect which serves as the final barrier to practical adoption. In this work, we conduct a survey study with 721 laypersons around the globe, investigating how the factors of *scenario*, *data sensitivity*, *mechanism type*, and *reason for data collection* impact user preferences for text privatization. We learn that while all these factors play a role in influencing privacy decisions, users are highly sensitive to the utility and coherence of the private output texts. Our findings highlight the socio-technical factors that must be considered in the study of DP NLP, opening the door to further user-based investigations going forward.

1 Introduction

The pursuit of text privatization under the framework of Differential Privacy (DP) presents a promising, yet challenging task for researchers, who must balance the strong protections DP offers with the ability to retain meaningful utility from textual data (Klymenko et al., 2022). In recent years, numerous works at the intersection of data privacy and Natural Language Processing, better known as privacy-preserving NLP or PPNLP, have tackled this challenge in various methods and techniques leveraging DP for text privatization (Hu et al., 2024). These range from word replacement methods (Feyisetan et al., 2020), more advanced autoencoder-based methods (Igamberdiev and Habernal, 2023), and recent works leveraging LLMs for privatization (Utpala et al., 2023).

Addressing the technical challenges in realizing effective DP text privatization mechanisms has been at the forefront of researchers' goals in the recent literature. Often, researchers proposing new methods must not only prove that a mechanism satisfies DP, but they must also empirically demonstrate that the mechanism can provide some tangible privacy benefit while also producing private texts that are useful and coherent (Mattern et al., 2022b). Furthermore, operating in the domain of natural language introduces the complexities of syntactic hierarchy (Vu et al., 2024) and meaningful privacy budgets (Igamberdiev and Habernal, 2023), as well as clearly delineating the advantages of DP over traditional anonymization (Meisenbacher and Matthes, 2024b) and maintaining reproducibility, explainability, and comparability (Igamberdiev et al., 2022; Meisenbacher et al., 2024b).

Beyond these complexities, an under-explored aspect of DP in NLP remains measuring human perceptions of DP text privatization. Very few works have extended past the research sphere to engage everyday users in investigating their perspective on what effective DP text privatization actually means. A recent work by Weiss et al. (2024) opens the doors to this aspect, taking a *risk-based* approach in quantifying at which privacy budgets (or, the ε parameter) laypersons are comfortable in sharing their personal text data. Here, it is shown that users are influenced by the perceived risk of misuse of their data, as they are less likely to consent to sharing with higher stated risks.

Despite its important role in leading off the study of human perceptions of DP NLP, we see a number of limitations in the work proposed by Weiss et al. Firstly, the *risk perception* approach taken by this work is useful in simplifying data sharing scenarios to laypersons, yet it makes no direct connection to actual outputs of privatization mechanisms, thus largely ignoring the crucial factor of *language* in text privatization. Relatedly, the work only consid-

Proceedings of the Sixth Workshop on Privacy in Natural Language Processing, pages 86–105
April 4, 2025 ©2025 Association for Computational Linguistics

ers the *global* DP setup, which distances itself from tangible privatization outputs and abstracts the DP notion away from local users. Because of this, we gain little insight into user opinions and preferences of *local* privatization mechanisms, which comprise a large portion of the recent literature.

We build upon the previous research of Weiss et al. by focusing on these limitations, conducting a user study to investigate perceptions of text-to-text privatization in various data sharing scenarios. We frame our user study in the form of *vignettes*, allowing for richer scenarios in which the users are placed. In these vignettes, we explore the influence of several important factors in local DP text privatization, including mechanism type, privacy budget, sensitivity of scenario, and reason for data collection. The choice of tested mechanisms is guided by a literature review of recent DP NLP works.

Our survey with 721 users from around the world yields interesting insights and perspectives on DP text privatization. Above all, we find that the choice of privatization mechanism *does* matter, and users generally perceive mechanisms producing more coherent and natural outputs as preferable. If outputs are not so, users tend to choose *less* privacy in preference of "utility". Finally, we find that *sensitivity of scenario* and *reason for data collection* are important, but not of primary concern.

These findings provide a clear call to action for DP NLP researchers, namely to continue to study the perceptions of users, in order to align DP NLP research with real-world perspectives and needs. In this light, we make the following contributions:

1. We build upon previous work by investigating user perceptions of DP text privatization.
2. We are the first to employ a *vignette*-based user study in the context of text privatization.
3. We share the findings of our study, including statistically significant results leading to recommendations for future DP NLP research.

2 Related Work

Several recent works in DP NLP, although focusing on the technical aspect of the topic, point to the need for deeper consideration of the practical implications of DP text privatization. The work of Mattern et al. (2022b) critiques earlier word-level DP mechanisms, uncovering the issues of grammatical correctness and semantic coherence, a challenge more recent works have addressed (Weggenmann et al., 2022; Utpala et al., 2023; Meisenbacher and Matthes, 2024a). Specifically considering syntactics, Vu et al. (2024) demonstrate the importance of granularity, or syntactic hierarchy, especially in real-world data sharing scenarios. Quantifying and addressing these challenges becomes important to demonstrating the practical applicability of DP NLP (Meisenbacher and Matthes, 2024b), especially in light of more real-world challenges such as explainability and transparency (Klymenko et al., 2022; Igamberdiev and Habernal, 2023; Igamberdiev et al., 2024), as well as reproducibility and comparability (Igamberdiev et al., 2022; Meisenbacher et al., 2024b).

Particularly investigating the human aspect of text privatization, little work outside of Weiss et al. (2024) has been performed. However, beyond the field of NLP, usable privacy research has been considerably more active in exploring user perspectives on DP. Several works explore which communication methods are most effective in explaining DP to end users (Cummings et al., 2021; Franzen et al., 2022; Nanayakkara et al., 2023), which generally find that how DP is explained to users is important in fostering their understanding of the risks and implications. Karegar et al. (2022) find that high-level abstractions of DP may lead to misunderstandings or false expectations about DP, and Smart et al. (2022) conclude that sometimes explanations have little effect on users' willingness to share data. Interestingly, one work (Xiong et al., 2020) shows that local DP (LDP) concepts are more understandable than DP, and that in the LDP case, users exhibit more willingness to share data.

We are motivated by these previous works in the DP field, particularly to provide more clarity on user perceptions of DP NLP methods. In light of the importance found by these previous works on the *method* of investigating user perspectives, we focus in this work on showing direct *outputs* of LDP text privatization mechanisms to users, in the form of understandable *vignettes*, as employed by Nanayakkara et al. (2023) for DP. With these, we are able to analyze different factors in the context of DP text privatization, particularly those affecting user perceptions of text privatization outputs.

3 Experimental Design

We outline our experimental design, which consists of an initial literature review, followed by survey implementation, and finally, the survey conduction.

Mechanism Type	Syntactic Level	DP Definition	Sources
Word-level Noise Addition	Word	DP	(Weggenmann and Kerschbaum, 2018)
		MDP	(Fernandes et al., 2019; Xu et al., 2020)
		LDP	(Bollegala et al., 2023)
		MLDP	(Feyisetan et al., 2019, 2020; Lyu et al., 2020a; Xu et al., 2021a,b; Imola et al., 2022; Arnold et al., 2023a,b; Carvalho et al., 2023)
Binary Embeddings	Word	LDP	(Lyu et al., 2020b)
		MLDP	(Carvalho et al., 2021)
Exponential Mechanism-Based	Token	LDP	(Chen et al., 2023; Meisenbacher et al., 2024a)
	Word	UMLDP	(Yue et al., 2021)
	Sentence	DP	(Meehan et al., 2022)
Autoencoder-Based (AE)	Word	LDP	(Habernal, 2021; Plant et al., 2021; Krishna et al., 2021; Maheshwari et al., 2022)
		MLDP	(Feyisetan and Kasiviswanathan, 2021)
	Sentence	(ε, δ)-DP	(Bo et al., 2021)
		MLDP	(Du et al., 2023)
	Document	LRDP, (ε, δ)-DP	(Weggenmann et al., 2022)
		DP	(Beigi et al., 2019)
		LDP	(Igamberdiev and Habernal, 2023)
LLM-Based	Token	LDP	(Mattern et al., 2022a; Utpala et al., 2023)

Table 1: A selection of DP text privatization methods, resulting from our scoping literature review.

3.1 Literature Review

As our survey study is focused on presenting users with tangible outputs from DP text privatization mechanisms, our first step included an unstructured scoping literature review (Munn et al., 2018), with the goal of identifying available DP text privatization methods for inclusion in our survey. This review was largely aided by a recent survey (Hu et al., 2024), which we augmented with DP NLP papers published after this work. In particular, we excluded the methods denoted by Hu et al. as "Gradient Perturbation" methods, as well as those that involve DP vector perturbation in training or fine-tuning. In this way, we only include methods that result in private texts as a direct result of DP.

The results of our review are presented in Table 1, which delineates methods into five distinct mechanism types, the linguistic level on which the mechanism operates, and its DP notion. For the purposes of this work, we choose four representative methods, excluding the category of *Binary Embeddings* due to its inability to produce natural language outputs. The selection of the following four methods was performed to (1) represent a diversity in syntactic level, (2) focus solely on LDP, and (3) prioritize newer works:

- **Truncated Exponential Mechanism (TEM)** (Carvalho et al., 2023): word-level Metric LDP mechanism.
- **DP-MLM** (Meisenbacher et al., 2024a): token-level LDP mechanism leveraging masked language models.
- **DP-PROMPT** (Utpala et al., 2023): token-level LDP leveraging LLMs for paraphrasing.
- **DP-BART** (Igamberdiev and Habernal, 2023): document-level LDP mechanism leveraging the BART model (Lewis et al., 2020).

3.2 Survey Design

In order to learn about user perspectives on DP text privatization, we designed a survey study to answer the following research question:

> *What insights can be gained about the factors influencing user perception of differentially private text privatization?*

As previously mentioned, we chose to design our survey in the form of *vignettes* (Atzmüller and Steiner, 2010). Vignettes use short descriptions to prompt respondents to place themselves in a scenario and to respond accordingly. These scenarios allow for more realistic contexts, and they can be particularly effective for exploring sensitive topics (Auspurg and Hinz, 2014), such as privacy. Specifically, we employ the Factorial Survey Method (FSM), in which multiple factors, or dimensions, are varied and tested, allowing for an analysis of the causal relationship of these factors in influencing user responses (Auspurg and Hinz, 2014).

Our FSM model consists of four factors: *mechanism, privacy budget, reason for data collection,*

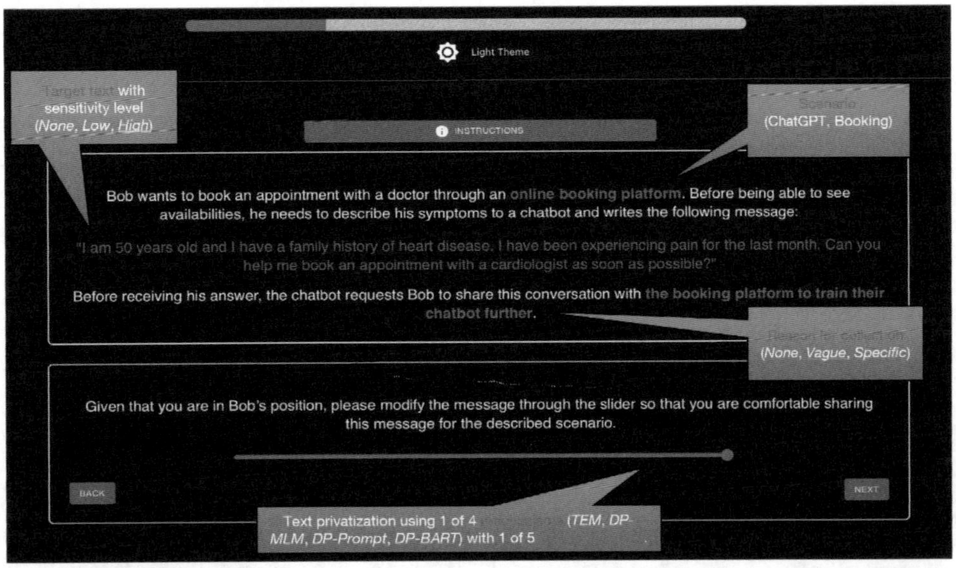

Figure 1: An example of a *vignette* on our survey platform. The annotations in the figure indicate the different *factors* of our FSM model, where underlined *treatments* are those depicted in the example. Participants were presented first with the original ($\varepsilon = \infty$) text, and then could proceed to use the slider to consider privatized counterparts.

Factor	Level	Treatment
Mechanism	Word	TEM
	Token	DP-MLM
	Document, AE	DP-BART
	Document, LLM	DP-PROMPT
Privacy Budget (ε)	TEM	$\varepsilon \in \{1.6, 2.4, 2.8, 3, \infty\}$
	DP-MLM	$\varepsilon \in \{20, 35, 50, 125, \infty\}$
	DP-PROMPT	$\varepsilon \in \{35, 45, 50, 65, \infty\}$
	DP-BART	$\varepsilon \in \{300, 400, 700, 1400, \infty\}$
Reason for data collection	None	No reason given
	Model Training	Vague reason given
	Privacy Protection	Specific reason given
Sensitivity of text	None	0 personal attributes
	Low	1 personal attribute
	High	2 personal and 1 sensitive attribute

Table 2: An overview of our FSM model's factors, levels, and treatments.

and *sensitivity of data*. In an FSM study, each factor contains a number of *levels*, which are realized in the survey by *treatments*. The factors, levels, and treatments are summarized in Table 2.

Vignette Creation. We sought to create vignettes that are both understandable and relatable to users, as well as representative of some plausibly sensitive data sharing scenario. The first step involved our research team brainstorming such scenarios, which resulted in eight distinct candidates. Each vignette was created with a similar structure: (1) introduction to the vignette, (2) presentation of the target text to be privatized, and (3) reason for data collection, explained below. In drafting the vignettes, we followed the best practices of Evans et al. (2015), namely to be clear and concise, use present tense, and keep a consistent structure across vignettes.

According to our FSM model, we then proceeded to draft different versions of the eight vignette scenarios, focusing on the two factors of *reason for data collection* and *sensitivity of data*. For the former, we included a text at the end of the vignette informing a user for which purpose the data was to be shared (see Table 2). To vary data sensitivity, we modified the text to be shared (i.e., privatized) with personal or sensitive attributes, as defined in Recitals 51 to 56 of the GDPR. Concretely, the *None* treatment contained no personal attributes, the *Low* treatment contained one personal attribute, and the *High* treatment contained two personal attributes and one sensitive attribute (e.g., medical condition). All eight vignette candidates can be found in Appendix A.

Our goal was to narrow the selection down to two scenarios for the survey study, primarily to keep the scope within reason. To accomplish this, we ran a committee vote in the form of a survey. In this survey, we asked respondents to rank each of the scenarios in terms of *relevance*, *plausibility*, and *understandability* for a data sharing scenario. The ranking was performed on a five-point Likert scale (*strongly disagree* to *strongly agree*). The committee consisted of 12 close research colleagues.

The top two scoring vignettes both involved a *health* scenario, one where a user is researching a medical condition with the help of ChatGPT, and the other where the user is interacting with an online booking platform chatbot to book a doctor's appointment. Although both vignettes operate in a similar sensitive domain, we decided to adhere to the committee vote without further adjustments.

With this, our study thus consisted of a vignette domain of 18 vignettes per mechanism (2 scenarios $\times$ 3 sensitivity levels $\times$ 3 collection reasons), resulting in an overall collection of 72 vignettes.

Mechanisms and Budgets. For each of the chosen mechanisms, we selected five privacy budgets (ε), the last of which was ∞, i.e., the original text. To ensure comparability between mechanisms, we decided to fix the remaining budgets based on the *average semantic similarity* between original and private text, given a mechanism and budget. We set four target similarities of $\{0.2, 0.4, 0.6, 0.8\}$, and proceeded to define an ε *range* for each mechanism, given roughly by the minimum and maximum values tested in the original papers, with 30 steps within this range. For each of these 30 values, we ran the mechanism 20 times on our two vignette target texts, and used a SENTENCE-TRANSFORMERS/ALL-MINILM-L6-V2 (Reimers and Gurevych, 2019) to compute the average cosine similarity. Then, the closest ε value to each of our targets was chosen, resulting in the values in Table 2. For the actual survey implementation (discussed next), the closest of the 20 texts to each target value was preserved; thus, the five texts used in each vignette are fixed. The privatized texts for each mechanism are provided in Appendix F.

Survey Platform Implementation. Due to the unique setup of our survey study, we decided that a custom web application would be best suited for our needs, rather than relying on existing online services. Most important was the facilitation of our ε *slider* functionality, where survey respondents could dynamically view the privatization of the target texts by switching between the five privacy budget values. For the application, we opted to use React[1] for the frontend and Node.js[2] for the backend. The flow of the survey was as follows:

1. *Introduction*: welcome / detailed instructions.
2. *Demographics*: information about gender, age, country, education, and occupation.
3. *IUIPC-10*: baseline questions about the respondent's general privacy opinion, using the Internet User Information Privacy Concerns Questionnaire (Malhotra et al., 2004), as utilized by Weiss et al. (2024).
4. *Vignettes*: as exemplified in Figure 1. We customized the vignette selection process to ensure that all vignettes were sampled equally.
5. *Open Feedback*: three free text fields asking for further comments on the survey.

The system architecture diagram of the survey web application can be found in Appendix G.

Participant Recruitment. We ran initial pilot tests with contacts in our personal network (n=41). The goal of these pilots was to estimate the total time of completion, as well as to identify and correct any ambiguities or technical issues. Before the pilots, we set an initial target goal that each unique vignette (72 in total) would be answered approximately 100 times each, for a total of 7200 responses needed. We set each survey to contain 10 vignettes; thus, our target sample size was 720.

The pilot tests identified no technical issues; however, improvements were made to the instructions to clarify to participants that text privatization would occur *locally*, and this process would not affect the quality of the response (i.e., from ChatGPT or the booking chatbot), as privatization in our context only affects the data *stored*. We measured an average completion time of around 10 minutes.

For the main study following the pilot tests, we used the Prolific[3] platform for recruitment. We did not limit participants by geographic region; however, we did require fluency in English and at least a high school diploma. We set the study for 680 total participants, paid £1.50 for survey completion (rate of £9/hr), marked by Prolific as a "good" wage. For the Prolific segment, it is important to note that two "attention checks" were inserted into the vignette portion, as required by the platform. Failure of these checks disqualified participants from compensation. In our survey, these checks took the form of normal vignettes, but with the explicit instruction to choose the slider value 3 (i.e., the middle value). One failed attention check was allowed, but two led to disqualification.

4 Results

We present the results of our user study, prefaced by our tested hypotheses and augmented by an analysis of our respondents' privacy preferences.

[1] https://react.dev/

[2] https://nodejs.org/

[3] https://www.prolific.com/

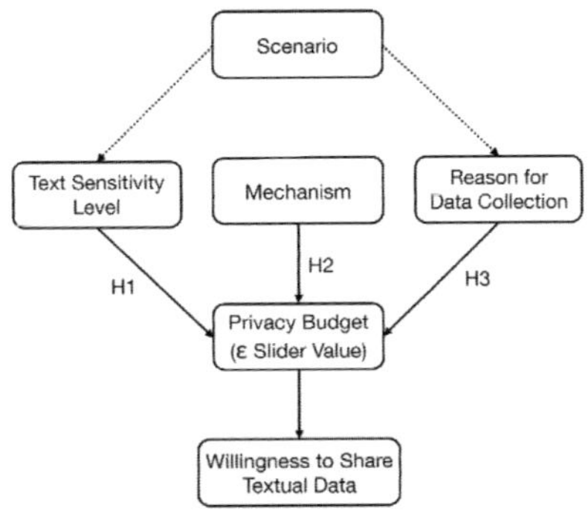

Figure 2: Our research model for the FSM study.

4.1 Hypotheses

To empirically measure the factors influencing user willingness to share textual data, particularly under local DP privatization, we construct a research model with three primary hypotheses, as follows:

H1: A higher sensitivity level in texts will result in a lower chosen privacy budget (ε), leading to increased preference of DP privatization.

H2: Mechanisms that lack linguistic and/or semantic preservation will lead to an increase in the chosen privacy budget.

H3: Providing a reason for data collection will increase the likelihood of users sharing their data under lower privacy regimes (higher ε), compared to not providing a reason.

We hypothesize that these factors of *data sensitivity* (H1), *mechanism* (H2), and *data collection reason* (H3) will impact a user's choice of privatization level (governed by ε), thereby influencing a user's willingness to share their textual data. Note that in the context of our work, we consider *generative* methods (i.e., DP-PROMPT and DP-BART) to preserve linguistics and semantics, and *non-generative* methods (i.e., DP-MLM and TEM) as lacking the ability to do so.

The research model is illustrated in Figure 2.

4.2 Participant Demographics

Our conducted survey consisted of 721 total respondents, including friends and family (n=41) and Prolific participants (n=680). Of these, 53.5% identified as female (n=386), 45.8% as male (n=330), and five respondents preferred not to answer. The survey participants were uniformly distributed across age ranges, including under 18 (n=2), 18-24 (n=151, 20.9%), 25-34 (n=321, 44.5%), 35-54 (n=193, 26.8%), and over 55 (n=54, 7.5%).

Category	$\overline{x}$ (σ)		
	Malhotra et al. (2004)	Groß (2021)	Our study
Control	5.67 (1.06)	5.87 (0.87)	6.09 (0.85)
Awareness	6.21 (0.87)	6.39 (0.65)	6.53 (0.67)
Collection	5.63 (1.09)	5.50 (1.09)	5.91 (1.16)
IUIPC-10	5.84 (1.01)	5.93 (0.67)	6.18 (0.66)

Table 3: Comparison of IUIPC-10 Results from two previous works and our observed sample. Values given represent average Likert scale scores (1-7), with standard deviations provided in parentheses.

The survey respondents were located in 41 different countries across six continents. The top-5 most frequent countries were South Africa (n=226, 31.3%), United Kingdom (n=132, 18.3%), Italy (n=46, 6.4%), United States (n=45, 6.2%), and Germany (n=39, 5.4%). Overall, the most respondents came from Europe (n=384, 53.3%), in addition to Africa (n=253, 35.1%), North America (n=55, 7.6%), Asia (n=16, 2.2%), South America (n=9, 1.2%), and Australia (n=4, 0.6%).

The largest group of respondents work in the industry (n=300, 41.6%), and the rest indicated being a student (n=123, 17.1%), unemployed (n=79, 6.5%), self-employed (n=50, 6.9%), in research (n=48, 6.7%), or "Other" (n=121, 16.8%). Nearly half of the respondents hold a Bachelor's degree (n=354, 49.1%), while others hold a Master's (n=147, 20.4%), High School or equivalent degree (n=127, 17.6%), apprenticeship (n=46, 6.4%), doctorate (n=27, 3.7%), or "Other" (n=20, 2.8%).

4.3 IUIPC Results

In Table 3, we present a comparative illustration of the observed IUIPC scores from our survey study, juxtaposed with results from previous works, including the original paper (Malhotra et al., 2004) and a more recent study (Groß, 2021). As can be seen, our study population self-reported as very privacy-conscious, scoring higher in each IUIPC-10 sub-scale than the referenced previous works. In addition to being a relevant basis for the ensuing analysis and discussion, these results imply a growing privacy awareness globally, which can be attributed to increasing attention paid to large-scale data processing, particularly related to modern AI. Most notably, the *Awareness* category received high scores, showing that knowledge of data collection and processing by third parties is a timely subject and is on people's minds. We refer the reader to Appendix D for a more in-depth analysis of the IUIPC results.

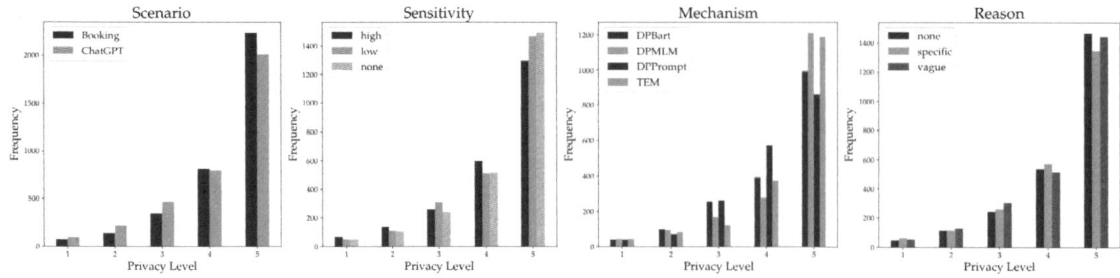

Figure 3: Raw frequency of privacy level responses (1-5) per each tested factor.

4.4 Analysis of Vignette Responses

The analysis of our survey study responses is centered on the influence of our chosen factors (i.e., those in our hypotheses) on the selection of privacy level for DP text privatization, indicated by the selected slider value in our vignettes. In the following, we perform statistical tests to determine the significance of these factors, as well as to support or refute our hypotheses.

4.4.1 Initial Testing

An initial review of the overall vignette responses revealed a very skewed distribution, with higher slider values (i.e., higher ε values) being chosen far more often. In particular, where slider value 5 corresponds to $\varepsilon = \infty$ and slider value 1 is the lowest chosen budget per mechanism, we observed the following out of 7210 responses: 5 (n=4260, 59.1%), 4 (n=1622, 22.5%), 3 (n=810, 11.2%), 2 (n=354, 4.9%), and 1 (n=164, 2.3%). As this clearly does not follow a normal distribution (shown in-depth in Appendix E), we opted to use non-parametric tests for our analysis, i.e., those that do not rely on assumptions about the data distribution.

4.5 Chi-squared Testing

We first examined the relationships between the dependent variable, or chosen privacy budget, with our four independent variables: *scenario*, *sensitivity*, *mechanism*, and (data collection) *reason*. Here, the privacy budget represents a categorical variable on a scale of 1 to 5 (slider values).

We chose to conduct Chi-squared tests to determine the influence of our independent variables on the chosen privacy budget value. In addition to our data being non-normally distributed, these tests were reasonable to conduct since they are well-suited to test relationships between *categorical* variables (as our variables are). Furthermore, we compare the observed frequencies of privacy choices to the expected frequencies under the null hypothesis that there exists no association between the independent and dependent variables.

The results of the Chi-squared tests are summarized as follows. The numbers in parentheses represent the *degrees of freedom*, determined by the number of variable combinations. For example, with four privacy budgets and four mechanisms, the degrees of freedom are calculated as $df = (5-1) \times (4-1) = 4 \times 3 = 12$.

- **Scenario**: $\chi^2(4) = 48.51, p < 0.001$. A significant relationship exists between the chosen privacy budget and the *scenario* (*Booking Chatbot* or *ChatGPT*), suggesting that the context matters in making privacy decisions.
- **Sensitivity**: $\chi^2(6) = 40.73$, $p < 0.001$. There is a significant association between the chosen privacy budget and *sensitivity*, showing that the perceived sensitivity of the text to be shared influences privacy selections.
- **Mechanism**: $\chi^2(12) = 263.45$, $p < 0.001$. There is a statistically significant relationship between the chosen privacy budget and *mechanism*, indicating that the mechanism used affects the values selected by participants.
- **Reason**: $\chi^2(6) = 19.08$, $p < 0.05$. A significant relationship was found between the chosen privacy budget and *reason*, indicating that the reason provided (specific, vague, or none) does affect the selected values.

4.6 Hypothesis Testing

As introduced in Section 4.1, we posit that *sensitivity* (H1), *mechanism* (H2), and *data collection reason* (H3) influence users' privacy choices in sharing their textual data. To test these hypotheses, we use a combination of Spearman's correlation (Spearman, 1904) and the Kruskal-Wallis H-test (Kruskal

	High	Low	None
High	1.0000	**0.0054**	**0.0000**
Low	**0.0054**	1.0000	0.1951
None	**0.0000**	0.1951	1.0000

(a) Sensitivity

	None	Specific	Vague
None	1.0000	**0.0250**	0.1971
Specific	**0.0250**	1.0000	1.0000
Vague	0.1971	1.0000	1.0000

(b) Reason

	DP-BART	DP-MLM	DP-Prompt	TEM
DP-BART	1.0000	**0.0000**	**0.0034**	**0.0000**
DP-MLM	**0.0000**	1.0000	**0.0000**	1.0000
DP-Prompt	**0.0034**	**0.0000**	1.0000	**0.0000**
TEM	**0.0000**	1.0000	**0.0000**	1.0000

(c) Mechanism

Table 4: Dunn's post-hoc test results. **Bolded** p-values indicate statistically significant results ($p < 0.05$).

and Wallis, 1952). The former allows us to analyze the correlation between the chosen privacy level and the factor in question (in the case of the ordinal *sensitivity* and *reason*), while the Kruskal-Wallis test informs us whether there exist any significant differences between the *treatments* within these factors (e.g., *High*, *Low*, *None* for *sensitivity*). Additionally, we calculate the η^2 effect size[4], which gives an indication of the strength of the association. Finally, we perform a post-hoc Dunn's test (Dunn, 1964) with Bonferroni correction[5], which extends the analysis to explain between *which* treatments there exist significant differences. The full Dunn's results are found in Table 4.

H1. We calculate the following values to test for significance regarding H1:

- **Spearman**: $\rho = -0.058, p < 0.001$
- **Kruskal-Wallis**: $H(2) = 24.83, p < 0.001$
- **Effect size** (η^2): 0.0034

Thus, we observe a statistically significant correlation between the chosen privacy budget and sensitivity level. However, the effect size indicates that this correlation is quite weak. Dunn's post-hoc test reveals a statistically significant difference between *High* and *None* sensitivity ($p < 0.001$), but no significant difference involving *Low*.

H2. We calculate the following values to test for significance regarding H2 (correlation not sensible here due to the categorical *mechanism* variable):

- **Kruskal-Wallis**: $H(3) = 146.31, p < 0.001$
- **Effect size** (η^2): 0.0203

We observe a significant difference in the selected privacy budget across our four selected mechanisms, supported by a *small to medium effect* ($0.01 \leq \eta^2 \leq 0.06$). Dunn's post hoc reveals significant differences between both TEM and DP-MLM with both DP-BART and DP-PROMPT (all with $p < 0.001$), showing a clear difference between generative and non-generative approaches. Additionally, a significant difference between DP-BART and DP-PROMPT was observed ($p < 0.01$).

H3. We calculate the following values to test for significance regarding H3:

- **Spearman**: $\rho = -0.030, p < 0.01$
- **Kruskal-Wallis**: $H(2) = 7.33, p < 0.05$
- **Effect size** (η^2): 0.0010

Although this indicates significance, the effect size implies that providing a reason has little influence on the choice of privacy level. However, Dunn's post-hoc test shows a significant difference between *specific* and *none* ($p < 0.05$), but not between *specific* and *vague* or *vague* and *none*.

5 Discussion

In light of the presented findings, we reflect on the lessons learned and discuss their implications.

What Matters with Text Privatization. Our statistical analyses demonstrate that the factors of *scenario*, *sensitivity*, *mechanism*, and *reason* all play statistically significant roles in influencing a user's choices for text privatization, as indicated by the chi-square tests. However, these factors are not equally impactful, as we learn that the choice of DP mechanism is most important in swaying user perceptions of privacy options. In this, we provide empirical evidence that when dealing with natural language, it is also crucial *how* text is privatized.

This above point is especially true in the case of text privatization with DP, where traditionally the ε is seen as an arbitrator between privacy and utility. The insights we gain from our user study imply that deciding privacy budgets in deployed systems may not be as simple as "more privacy needed, then lower ε" and vice versa; instead, one must take into account the methods and context in which privatization is to occur. While this potentially makes the task of DP text privatization more challenging, it also provides more criteria by which researchers and practitioners can justify their privacy budgets.

[4]Given by $H/(k-1)$, with k as the group size.

[5]Multiplying each p-value by the total number of tests.

Utility over Privacy? A very important finding regarding privatization preferences is manifested in the *appearance* of private output texts. As can be seen in Figure 3, users were much more confident in choosing lower privacy budgets with the generative approaches (DP-BART and DP-PROMPT), whereas TEM and DP-MLM received a significantly higher number of $\varepsilon = \infty$ choices. This suggests that when privatized texts are not as coherent or "natural" (as is in the case of word- or token-level, non-generative approaches), users tend to prefer coherence over privacy, a fact that seemingly contradicts the self-reported IUIPC privacy sentiments. Relating back to our choice of ε, these results point to a "tolerance" of at most 80% cosine similarity (slider 4) or more, whereas lower values received far less selections. Such results imply an "acceptability range" for text privatization, which we observe to be somewhere between 80-100% cosine similarity (this is of course specific to the chosen embedding model). In this, we learn that DP text privatization *must* generate reasonable output texts before it will be more widely accepted.

User Reasoning Patterns for Text Privatization. We analyzed and aggregated free-form survey feedback into four themes relating to privacy "reasoning patterns". In particular, participants provided insights into *why* they answered the way they did. For each pattern, we provide a representative quote.

- **The need to find a balance**: "*I tried to find the right balance between too much information and no information at all.*"
- **Depends on the use case**: "*I felt more comfortable sharing my data with the medical booking platform than with ChatGPT, since I did not like the aspect of my data potentially being used for training their model.*"
- **Coherence is key**: "*I chose the sentences which made the most sense written down. The other sentences on other points on the slider were not fully literate.*"
- **Personal information minimization**: "*The less information given, the better.*"

Such patterns provide researchers with important insights into the thought processes of laypersons when reasoning about text privatization. Although some of these points may be quite challenging to realize technically, they set a framework for human-acceptable DP text privatization.

A Roadmap for DP NLP Research. The findings we present give way to a series of important factors that must be considered going forward:

1. **DP NLP must be usable.** Focusing on text-to-text privatization with DP, we learn that well before other factors, the output of text privatization mechanisms must be coherent, correct, and readable; otherwise, perception of text privatization will be negative. Future work, therefore, would benefit from exploring what *usability* in DP text privatization means.
2. **DP NLP must consider context.** *Context* here refers to factors beyond the technical privatization procedures: for what scenario is textual data collected or shared, what type(s) of personal information may be contained in the data, and perhaps to a lesser degree, for what purpose the data is meant. These factors affect what type of mechanism is needed, and moreover, how much "privacy" is required.
3. **DP NLP must involve human studies.** Above all, our study teaches us that text privacy extends beyond technical challenges to the realm of *socio*-technical challenges, such as increasing general user awareness and *understanding* of how (DP) text privatization works and making clear what the implications of using such mechanisms are. Thus, we hold it crucial that further studies on *usable* DP NLP not only extend our work, but also focus on designing methods for fostering acceptance of this promising, yet challenging technology.

6 Conclusion

We conducted a survey study with 721 participants from six continents, investigating the influence of various factors on user perception of DP text privatization. Using a representative set of four DP mechanisms, we designed a series of vignettes to test for differences in the selection of text privatization level under a number of scenarios. We found that all tested factors play an important role in the context of text privatization, yet the factor of mechanism design is the most salient. In particular, mechanisms producing clearer and more natural outputs encourage users to choose higher privacy levels (lower ε budgets). Our findings reveal the importance of involving the general population in guiding the direction of DP NLP research, and we hope that our work motivates future studies on aligning DP NLP research and practice.

Acknowledgements

We would like to thank the anonymous reviewers for their feedback, as well as the committee and all survey participants for their valuable contributions. We also greatly appreciate Jian Kong and Timo Kühne for their assistance in survey deployment.

Limitations

The primary limitation of our work is inherent to conducting a general user study addressing a complex technical topic, such as DP text privatization. Although we focused on clear and understandable instructions for survey participants, we cannot be certain that all participants fully understood the task at hand. Indeed, in the feedback section, we received a number of comments with users expressing concern that they did not fully understand the task; while such comments were in the vast minority, this could still affect the calculation of our results. Nevertheless, we mitigated this threat to validity by selecting a large sample size, where each of the 72 vignettes was answered by at least 100 survey participants. We hope that future works will alleviate this challenge by working on standardized methods for communicating DP NLP topics.

Another clear limitation relates to the choice of four mechanisms that served as the basis for the vignettes we designed for the surveys. We did not perform any cleanup or post-processing of the privatized texts, often resulting in obvious grammatical errors (in the case of word-level privatization) or non-ASCII characters (in the case of the generative approaches), which could plausibly have biased the selection of slider values in the survey. While this was difficult to avoid, we argue that this enabled insights regarding different perceptions of different mechanism outputs, leading us to the conclusion that this factor is of utmost importance.

Finally, we caution that our survey sample may not be entirely representative in terms of the global population and language domains. The use of the Prolific platform limited our control over survey population, resulting in a particularly high number of respondents from South Africa, while less representation was had from North and South America and Asia. Furthermore, we perform no analyses regarding differences across regions, genders, professions, or educational backgrounds. Additionally, the primary focus was on texts related to the *medical* domain, as a result of the selected texts from our committee vote. Ideally, future studies could replicate our findings given different, more representative samples and broader text domains.

Ethics Statement

Our study was reviewed and approved by the ethics commission of the Technical University of Munich, with approval number 2024-86-NM-BA.

Particularly regarding the involvement of human subjects in our study, we affirm that participation was completely voluntary and compensated with a fair wage via the Prolific platform. Outside of the initial pilot study, no preference was given to any potential survey participant; this was conducted on a first-come-first-serve basis facilitated by Prolific. We ensured the well-being of our participants by creating an inviting and easy-to-navigate survey application, engaging (anonymously) with participants who had questions or concerns during the survey conduction, and not collecting or storing any personally identifiable information at any point.

As this work is centered on the timely and important topic of data privacy, we hope that its impact extends to both researchers working in the field of privacy (in NLP), as well as to end users who may increase their knowledge and awareness of current trends and issues in privacy research. In particular, we envision similar types of studies becoming more commonplace in privacy-preserving NLP research, and we hope that this work contributes positively to motivating such future works.

References

Stefan Arnold, Dilara Yesilbas, and Sven Weinzierl. 2023a. Driving context into text-to-text privatization. In *Proceedings of the 3rd Workshop on Trustworthy Natural Language Processing (TrustNLP 2023)*, pages 15–25, Toronto, Canada. Association for Computational Linguistics.

Stefan Arnold, Dilara Yesilbas, and Sven Weinzierl. 2023b. Guiding text-to-text privatization by syntax. In *Proceedings of the 3rd Workshop on Trustworthy Natural Language Processing (TrustNLP 2023)*, pages 151–162, Toronto, Canada. Association for Computational Linguistics.

Christiane Atzmüller and Peter M Steiner. 2010. Experimental vignette studies in survey research. *Methodology*.

Katrin Auspurg and Thomas Hinz. 2014. *Factorial survey experiments*, volume 175. SAGE Publications, Inc.

Ghazaleh Beigi, Kai Shu, Ruocheng Guo, Suhang Wang, and Huan Liu. 2019. Privacy preserving text representation learning. In *Proceedings of the 30th ACM Conference on Hypertext and Social Media*, HT '19, page 275–276, New York, NY, USA. Association for Computing Machinery.

Haohan Bo, Steven H. H. Ding, Benjamin C. M. Fung, and Farkhund Iqbal. 2021. ER-AE: Differentially private text generation for authorship anonymization. In *Proceedings of the 2021 Conference of the North American Chapter of the Association for Computational Linguistics: Human Language Technologies*, pages 3997–4007, Online. Association for Computational Linguistics.

Danushka Bollegala, Shuichi Otake, Tomoya Machide, and Ken-ichi Kawarabayashi. 2023. A neighbourhood-aware differential privacy mechanism for static word embeddings. In *Findings of the Association for Computational Linguistics: IJCNLP-AACL 2023 (Findings)*, pages 65–79, Nusa Dua, Bali. Association for Computational Linguistics.

Ricardo Silva Carvalho, Theodore Vasiloudis, and Oluwaseyi Feyisetan. 2021. BRR: Preserving privacy of text data efficiently on device. *Preprint*, arXiv:2107.07923.

Ricardo Silva Carvalho, Theodore Vasiloudis, Oluwaseyi Feyisetan, and Ke Wang. 2023. TEM: High utility metric differential privacy on text. In *Proceedings of the 2023 SIAM International Conference on Data Mining (SDM)*, pages 883–890. SIAM.

Sai Chen, Fengran Mo, Yanhao Wang, Cen Chen, Jian-Yun Nie, Chengyu Wang, and Jamie Cui. 2023. A customized text sanitization mechanism with differential privacy. In *Findings of the Association for Computational Linguistics: ACL 2023*, pages 5747–5758, Toronto, Canada. Association for Computational Linguistics.

Rachel Cummings, Gabriel Kaptchuk, and Elissa M. Redmiles. 2021. "I need a better description": An investigation into user expectations for differential privacy. In *Proceedings of the 2021 ACM SIGSAC Conference on Computer and Communications Security*, CCS '21, page 3037–3052, New York, NY, USA. Association for Computing Machinery.

Minxin Du, Xiang Yue, Sherman S. M. Chow, and Huan Sun. 2023. Sanitizing sentence embeddings (and labels) for local differential privacy. In *Proceedings of the ACM Web Conference 2023*, WWW '23, page 2349–2359, New York, NY, USA. Association for Computing Machinery.

Olive Jean Dunn. 1964. Multiple comparisons using rank sums. *Technometrics*, 6(3):241–252.

Spencer C. Evans, Michael C. Roberts, Jared W. Keeley, Jennifer B. Blossom, Christina M. Amaro, Andrea M. Garcia, Cathleen Odar Stough, Kimberly S. Canter, Rebeca Robles, and Geoffrey M. Reed. 2015. Vignette methodologies for studying clinicians' decision-making: Validity, utility, and application in icd-11 field studies. *International Journal of Clinical and Health Psychology*, 15(2):160–170.

Natasha Fernandes, Mark Dras, and Annabelle McIver. 2019. Generalised differential privacy for text document processing. In *Principles of Security and Trust: 8th International Conference, POST 2019, Held as Part of the European Joint Conferences on Theory and Practice of Software, ETAPS 2019, Prague, Czech Republic, April 6–11, 2019, Proceedings 8*, pages 123–148. Springer International Publishing.

Oluwaseyi Feyisetan, Borja Balle, Thomas Drake, and Tom Diethe. 2020. Privacy- and utility-preserving textual analysis via calibrated multivariate perturbations. In *Proceedings of the 13th International Conference on Web Search and Data Mining*, WSDM '20, page 178–186, New York, NY, USA. Association for Computing Machinery.

Oluwaseyi Feyisetan, Tom Diethe, and Thomas Drake. 2019. Leveraging hierarchical representations for preserving privacy and utility in text. In *2019 IEEE International Conference on Data Mining (ICDM)*, pages 210–219.

Oluwaseyi Feyisetan and Shiva Kasiviswanathan. 2021. Private release of text embedding vectors. In *Proceedings of the First Workshop on Trustworthy Natural Language Processing*, pages 15–27, Online. Association for Computational Linguistics.

Daniel Franzen, Saskia Nuñez von Voigt, Peter Sörries, Florian Tschorsch, and Claudia Müller-Birn. 2022. Am i private and if so, how many? communicating privacy guarantees of differential privacy with risk communication formats. In *Proceedings of the 2022 ACM SIGSAC Conference on Computer and Communications Security*, CCS '22, page 1125–1139, New York, NY, USA. Association for Computing Machinery.

Thomas Groß. 2021. Validity and reliability of the scale internet users' information privacy concerns (iuipc). *Proceedings on Privacy Enhancing Technologies*.

Ivan Habernal. 2021. When differential privacy meets NLP: The devil is in the detail. In *Proceedings of the 2021 Conference on Empirical Methods in Natural Language Processing*, pages 1522–1528, Online and Punta Cana, Dominican Republic. Association for Computational Linguistics.

Lijie Hu, Ivan Habernal, Lei Shen, and Di Wang. 2024. Differentially private natural language models: Recent advances and future directions. In *Findings of the Association for Computational Linguistics: EACL 2024*, pages 478–499, St. Julian's, Malta. Association for Computational Linguistics.

Timour Igamberdiev, Thomas Arnold, and Ivan Habernal. 2022. DP-rewrite: Towards reproducibility and transparency in differentially private text rewriting. In *Proceedings of the 29th International Conference on Computational Linguistics*, pages 2927–2933, Gyeongju, Republic of Korea. International Committee on Computational Linguistics.

Timour Igamberdiev and Ivan Habernal. 2023. DP-BART for privatized text rewriting under local differential privacy. In *Findings of the Association for Computational Linguistics: ACL 2023*, pages 13914–13934, Toronto, Canada. Association for Computational Linguistics.

Timour Igamberdiev, Doan Nam Long Vu, Felix Kuennecke, Zhuo Yu, Jannik Holmer, and Ivan Habernal. 2024. DP-NMT: Scalable differentially private machine translation. In *Proceedings of the 18th Conference of the European Chapter of the Association for Computational Linguistics: System Demonstrations*, pages 94–105, St. Julians, Malta. Association for Computational Linguistics.

Jacob Imola, Shiva Kasiviswanathan, Stephen White, Abhinav Aggarwal, and Nathanael Teissier. 2022. Balancing utility and scalability in metric differential privacy. In *The 38th Conference on Uncertainty in Artificial Intelligence*.

Farzaneh Karegar, Ala Sarah Alaqra, and Simone Fischer-Hübner. 2022. Exploring User-Suitable metaphors for differentially private data analyses. In *Eighteenth Symposium on Usable Privacy and Security (SOUPS 2022)*, pages 175–193, Boston, MA. USENIX Association.

Oleksandra Klymenko, Stephen Meisenbacher, and Florian Matthes. 2022. Differential privacy in natural language processing: The story so far. In *Proceedings of the Fourth Workshop on Privacy in Natural Language Processing*, pages 1–11, Seattle, United States. Association for Computational Linguistics.

Satyapriya Krishna, Rahul Gupta, and Christophe Dupuy. 2021. ADePT: Auto-encoder based differentially private text transformation. In *Proceedings of the 16th Conference of the European Chapter of the Association for Computational Linguistics: Main Volume*, pages 2435–2439, Online. Association for Computational Linguistics.

William H Kruskal and W Allen Wallis. 1952. Use of ranks in one-criterion variance analysis. *Journal of the American statistical Association*, 47(260):583–621.

Mike Lewis, Yinhan Liu, Naman Goyal, Marjan Ghazvininejad, Abdelrahman Mohamed, Omer Levy, Veselin Stoyanov, and Luke Zettlemoyer. 2020. BART: Denoising sequence-to-sequence pre-training for natural language generation, translation, and comprehension. In *Proceedings of the 58th Annual Meeting of the Association for Computational Linguistics*, pages 7871–7880, Online. Association for Computational Linguistics.

Lingjuan Lyu, Xuanli He, and Yitong Li. 2020a. Differentially private representation for NLP: Formal guarantee and an empirical study on privacy and fairness. In *Findings of the Association for Computational Linguistics: EMNLP 2020*, pages 2355–2365, Online. Association for Computational Linguistics.

Lingjuan Lyu, Yitong Li, Xuanli He, and Tong Xiao. 2020b. Towards differentially private text representations. In *Proceedings of the 43rd International ACM SIGIR Conference on Research and Development in Information Retrieval*, SIGIR '20, page 1813–1816, New York, NY, USA. Association for Computing Machinery.

Gaurav Maheshwari, Pascal Denis, Mikaela Keller, and Aurélien Bellet. 2022. Fair NLP models with differentially private text encoders. In *Findings of the Association for Computational Linguistics: EMNLP 2022*, pages 6913–6930, Abu Dhabi, United Arab Emirates. Association for Computational Linguistics.

Naresh K Malhotra, Sung S Kim, and James Agarwal. 2004. Internet users' information privacy concerns (iuipc): The construct, the scale, and a causal model. *Information systems research*, 15(4):336–355.

Justus Mattern, Zhijing Jin, Benjamin Weggenmann, Bernhard Schoelkopf, and Mrinmaya Sachan. 2022a. Differentially private language models for secure data sharing. In *Proceedings of the 2022 Conference on Empirical Methods in Natural Language Processing*, pages 4860–4873, Abu Dhabi, United Arab Emirates. Association for Computational Linguistics.

Justus Mattern, Benjamin Weggenmann, and Florian Kerschbaum. 2022b. The limits of word level differential privacy. In *Findings of the Association for Computational Linguistics: NAACL 2022*, pages 867–881, Seattle, United States. Association for Computational Linguistics.

Casey Meehan, Khalil Mrini, and Kamalika Chaudhuri. 2022. Sentence-level privacy for document embeddings. In *Proceedings of the 60th Annual Meeting of the Association for Computational Linguistics (Volume 1: Long Papers)*, pages 3367–3380, Dublin, Ireland. Association for Computational Linguistics.

Stephen Meisenbacher, Maulik Chevli, Juraj Vladika, and Florian Matthes. 2024a. DP-MLM: Differentially private text rewriting using masked language models. In *Findings of the Association for Computational Linguistics: ACL 2024*, pages 9314–9328, Bangkok, Thailand. Association for Computational Linguistics.

Stephen Meisenbacher and Florian Matthes. 2024a. Just rewrite it again: A post-processing method for enhanced semantic similarity and privacy preservation of differentially private rewritten text. In *Proceedings of the 19th International Conference on Availability, Reliability and Security*, ARES '24, New York, NY, USA. Association for Computing Machinery.

Stephen Meisenbacher and Florian Matthes. 2024b. Thinking outside of the differential privacy box: A case study in text privatization with language model prompting. In *Proceedings of the 2024 Conference on Empirical Methods in Natural Language Processing*, pages 5656–5665, Miami, Florida, USA. Association for Computational Linguistics.

Stephen Meisenbacher, Nihildev Nandakumar, Alexandra Klymenko, and Florian Matthes. 2024b. A comparative analysis of word-level metric differential privacy: Benchmarking the privacy-utility trade-off. In *Proceedings of the 2024 Joint International Conference on Computational Linguistics, Language Resources and Evaluation (LREC-COLING 2024)*, pages 174–185, Torino, Italia. ELRA and ICCL.

Zachary Munn, Micah DJ Peters, Cindy Stern, Catalin Tufanaru, Alexa McArthur, and Edoardo Aromataris. 2018. Systematic review or scoping review? guidance for authors when choosing between a systematic or scoping review approach. *BMC medical research methodology*, 18:1–7.

Priyanka Nanayakkara, Mary Anne Smart, Rachel Cummings, Gabriel Kaptchuk, and Elissa M. Redmiles. 2023. What are the chances? explaining the epsilon parameter in differential privacy. In *Proceedings of the 32nd USENIX Conference on Security Symposium*, SEC '23, USA. USENIX Association.

Richard Plant, Dimitra Gkatzia, and Valerio Giuffrida. 2021. CAPE: Context-aware private embeddings for private language learning. In *Proceedings of the 2021 Conference on Empirical Methods in Natural Language Processing*, pages 7970–7978, Online and Punta Cana, Dominican Republic. Association for Computational Linguistics.

Nils Reimers and Iryna Gurevych. 2019. Sentence-BERT: Sentence embeddings using Siamese BERT-networks. In *Proceedings of the 2019 Conference on Empirical Methods in Natural Language Processing and the 9th International Joint Conference on Natural Language Processing (EMNLP-IJCNLP)*, pages 3982–3992, Hong Kong, China. Association for Computational Linguistics.

Samuel Sanford Shapiro and Martin B Wilk. 1965. An analysis of variance test for normality (complete samples). *Biometrika*, 52(3-4):591–611.

Mary Anne Smart, Dhruv Sood, and Kristen Vaccaro. 2022. Understanding risks of privacy theater with differential privacy. *Proc. ACM Hum.-Comput. Interact.*, 6(CSCW2).

C Spearman. 1904. The proof and measurement of association between two things. *The American Journal of Psychology*, 15(1):72–101.

Saiteja Utpala, Sara Hooker, and Pin-Yu Chen. 2023. Locally differentially private document generation using zero shot prompting. In *Findings of the Association for Computational Linguistics: EMNLP 2023*, pages 8442–8457, Singapore. Association for Computational Linguistics.

Doan Nam Long Vu, Timour Igamberdiev, and Ivan Habernal. 2024. Granularity is crucial when applying differential privacy to text: An investigation for neural machine translation. In *Findings of the Association for Computational Linguistics: EMNLP 2024*, pages 507–527, Miami, Florida, USA. Association for Computational Linguistics.

Benjamin Weggenmann and Florian Kerschbaum. 2018. SynTF: Synthetic and differentially private term frequency vectors for privacy-preserving text mining. In *The 41st International ACM SIGIR Conference on Research & Development in Information Retrieval*, pages 305–314.

Benjamin Weggenmann, Valentin Rublack, Michael Andrejczuk, Justus Mattern, and Florian Kerschbaum. 2022. DP-VAE: Human-readable text anonymization for online reviews with differentially private variational autoencoders. In *Proceedings of the ACM Web Conference 2022*, WWW '22, page 721–731, New York, NY, USA. Association for Computing Machinery.

Christopher Weiss, Frauke Kreuter, and Ivan Habernal. 2024. To share or not to share: What risks would laypeople accept to give sensitive data to differentially-private NLP systems? In *Proceedings of the 2024 Joint International Conference on Computational Linguistics, Language Resources and Evaluation (LREC-COLING 2024)*, pages 16331–16342, Torino, Italia. ELRA and ICCL.

Aiping Xiong, Tianhao Wang, Ninghui Li, and Somesh Jha. 2020. Towards effective differential privacy communication for users' data sharing decision and comprehension. In *2020 IEEE Symposium on Security and Privacy (SP)*, pages 392–410. IEEE.

Nan Xu, Oluwaseyi Feyisetan, Abhinav Aggarwal, Zekun Xu, and Nathanael Teissier. 2021a. Density-aware differentially private textual perturbations using truncated gumbel noise. In *The International FLAIRS Conference Proceedings*, volume 34.

Zekun Xu, Abhinav Aggarwal, Oluwaseyi Feyisetan, and Nathanael Teissier. 2020. A differentially private text perturbation method using regularized mahalanobis metric. In *Proceedings of the Second Workshop on Privacy in NLP*, pages 7–17, Online. Association for Computational Linguistics.

Zekun Xu, Abhinav Aggarwal, Oluwaseyi Feyisetan, and Nathanael Teissier. 2021b. On a utilitarian approach to privacy preserving text generation. In *Proceedings of the Third Workshop on Privacy in Natural Language Processing*, pages 11–20, Online. Association for Computational Linguistics.

Xiang Yue, Minxin Du, Tianhao Wang, Yaliang Li, Huan Sun, and Sherman S. M. Chow. 2021. Differential privacy for text analytics via natural text sanitization. In *Findings of the Association for Computational Linguistics: ACL-IJCNLP 2021*, pages 3853–3866, Online. Association for Computational Linguistics.

A Sensitive Data Sharing Scenarios – Committee Vote

Thank you for taking the time to participate in this survey.

Background: we are well on our way in a study investigating user perceptions of (text) data sharing. Specifically, we aim to study the effect of Differential Privacy (DP) rewriting mechanisms, more particularly the effect of the privacy parameter (epsilon).

For the research, we have opted to conduct a vignette study, in which users will be prompted to place themselves into a provided scenario, thereafter answering to what extent they are comfortable sharing their text data given different levels of text privatization.

In the administered survey, we plan on presenting two overarching vignettes (with varying parameters, but not important here). To start, we have drafted a number of such vignettes, with the goal of narrowing down to the two most **relevant, plausible, and understandable** scenarios. For this, we need your help!

Please answer the following questions to the best of your ability. By doing so, you are helping to advance our study. Welcome to the committee :)

Candidate Vignettes

For each of the following candidates, you will be asked how well the scenario depicts a "sensitive" data sharing scenario. As introduced, we are searching for the best vignettes in terms of:

- **Relevance**: this is a timely and relevant scenario, and it is a scenario which indeed involves some sensitive or private information.
- **Plausibility**: this is something which you can imagine actually taking place in the real world. It does not have to be exactly so.
- **Understandability**: the scenario makes sense to you – there are no major ambiguities as to what is going on.

For each question, you will first be presented with a textual description of the scenario. There are three levels of "sensitive information", corresponding to three versions of the vignette, so it is important to view the scenarios as a whole. You will then be asked to judge how well this scenario overall fits the above criteria.

Candidate 1a

Bob is researching his health condition with ChatGPT, and he types the following message to the chatbot:

a) **Highly Sensitive Information**: "I was diagnosed with a lung cancer last week and I'm feeling overwhelmed. I'll be treated at IsarHealth in Munich starting June 1st. Can you tell me some information about treatments and potential side effects?"

b) **Low Sensitive Information**: "I have a significant medical treatment in Munich coming up. How can I best prepare for this upcoming challenge?"

c) **No Sensitive Information**: "I have an important new chapter in my life starting soon that will last for a long time. How can I best prepare for this?"

Before receiving his answer, ChatGPT requests Bob to share this conversation with OpenAI.

Question: This scenario depicts a relevant, plausible, and understandable data sharing scenario.
[Response options from 1 (strongly disagree) to 5 (strongly agree)]

Candidate 1b

Bob is researching his financial situation with ChatGPT, and he types the following message to the chatbot:

a) **Highly Sensitive Information**: "Due to my recent cancer treatment, I've had to take on a significant amount of debt, and I'm struggling to manage my finances. My monthly income is $4,000, and my expenses have increased to $3,500. I need a detailed plan to help me manage my finances and get out of debt."

b) **Low Sensitive Information**: "I've recently taken on more financial responsibilities and my expenses have increased significantly. I earn $4,000 a month and need advice on budgeting and managing my finances effectively."

c) **No Sensitive Information**: "I'm looking to improve my financial management skills. What are some effective budgeting strategies I can use?"

Before receiving his answer, ChatGPT requests Bob to share this conversation with OpenAI.

Question: This scenario depicts a relevant, plausible, and understandable data sharing scenario.
[Response options from 1 (strongly disagree) to 5 (strongly agree)]

Candidate 1c

Bob is researching his career transition with ChatGPT, and he types the following message to the chatbot:

a) **Highly Sensitive Information**: "I was unexpectedly laid off from my job at Autotable last month due to my affiliation with the rightwing party BrW. I'm really anxious about finding new employment in the current economic situation. I have a background in marketing and have been applying to several positions but haven't had any luck yet. Can you help me create a job search plan and provide tips on coping with this stress?"

b) **Low Sensitive Information**: "I'm currently searching for a new job in the marketing field and could use some advice on creating a strong job search strategy and managing the stress that comes with it."

c) **No Sensitive Information**: "I'm planning to change careers and would like some guidance on how to effectively search for jobs and prepare for this transition."

Before receiving his answer, ChatGPT requests Bob to share this conversation with OpenAI.

Question: This scenario depicts a relevant, plausible, and understandable data sharing scenario.
[Response options from 1 (strongly disagree) to 5 (strongly agree)]

Candidate 2a

Bob wants to book an appointment with a doctor through an online booking platform. Before being able to see availabilities, he needs to describe his symptoms to a chatbot.

a) **Highly Sensitive Information**: "I am 50 years old and I have a family history of heart disease. I have been experiencing pain for the last month. Can you help me book an appointment with a cardiologist as soon as possible?"

b) **Low Sensitive Information**: "I am not feeling well in my chest. I'd like to book an appointment with a doctor to get it checked out."

c) **No Sensitive Information**: "I'm not feeling well and need to see a doctor. Can you help me find an available appointment?"

Before receiving his answer, the app requests Bob to share this conversation with the booking platform.

Question: This scenario depicts a relevant, plausible, and understandable data sharing scenario.
[Response options from 1 (strongly disagree) to 5 (strongly agree)]

Candidate 2b

Bob is registering on an online forum for a support group. Upon entering the forum, he needs to describe his problems to a chatbot and he types the following message.

a) **Highly Sensitive Information**: "I am 22 years old and I have been struggling with depression and anxiety for the past year. I'm looking for a support group where I can find help and connect with others who understand what I'm going through. Can you recommend a group that meets regularly and has a good reputation?"

b) **Low Sensitive Information**: "I've been dealing with some health challenges and am interested in joining a support group. Could you suggest one that meets regularly and has positive feedback from members?"

c) **No Sensitive Information**: "I'm looking to join a support group to connect with others and find some help. Can anyone recommend a good one?"

Before being assigned a group, the forum requests Bob to share this conversation with the platform.

Question: This scenario depicts a relevant, plausible, and understandable data sharing scenario.
[Response options from 1 (strongly disagree) to 5 (strongly agree)]

Candidate 3a

Sam is seeking legal advice in a forum.

a) **Highly Sensitive Information**: "I am currently going through a divorce with my partner. There are complicated issues regarding the division of assets. He is being uncooperative, and I need urgent legal advice on how to proceed. Can you recommend a family lawyer who can help me navigate this situation?"

b) **Low Sensitive Information**: "I'm dealing with some family legal issues and need advice on finding a good lawyer specializing in family law. Can anyone recommend a reliable legal advisor?"

c) **No Sensitive Information**: "I'm looking for recommendations for a good lawyer. Can anyone suggest where to start?"

Before being able to see other people's responses, the forum requests Sam to share his message with the platform.

Question: This scenario depicts a relevant, plausible, and understandable data sharing scenario.
[Response options from 1 (strongly disagree) to 5 (strongly agree)]

Candidate 4a

Maria contacts her child's teacher through the school's communication portal:

a) **Highly Sensitive Information**: "Hello, I'm concerned about my son Hongdi's recent grades. Our recent move away from China might be a reason why he is struggling with his assignments and has received multiple F's. Can we set up a meeting to discuss how we can support his learning at home?"

b) **Low Sensitive Information**: "Hello, I'm concerned about my son Hongdi's recent grades. He seems to be struggling. Can we set up a meeting to discuss how we can support his learning at home?"

c) **No Sensitive Information**: "Hello, I'm concerned about my child's recent performance in school. Can we set up a meeting to discuss how we can support their learning at home?"

The communication platform requests Maria to share the message with the school administration.

Question: This scenario depicts a relevant, plausible, and understandable data sharing scenario.
[Response options from 1 (strongly disagree) to 5 (strongly agree)]

Candidate 5a

Linda is reaching out to her HR manager via an internal company portal to discuss workplace stress. Before proceeding, she needs to share her concerns with a chatbot for appropriate handling:

a) **Highly Sensitive Information**: "Hi, I've been feeling anxiety with my workload in the project BlueUrban lately. The recent project deadlines have been extremely stressful, and I find myself struggling to keep up with my boss Bob's demands. Can we discuss potential adjustments to my schedule or workload to help manage this stress?"

b) **Low Sensitive Information**: "Hi, I want to talk to someone regarding my workload and the recent deadlines in the project BlueUrban. I'm finding it difficult to keep up. Can we discuss possible adjustments to my schedule or workload?"

c) **No Sensitive Information**: "Hi, I'm finding my current workload quite challenging. Can we discuss possible adjustments to help manage it better?"

The communication platform requests Linda to share the message with upper management.

Question: This scenario depicts a relevant, plausible, and understandable data sharing scenario.
[Response options from 1 (strongly disagree) to 5 (strongly agree)]

Thank you!

B Selected Scenarios for the Survey Study

Scenario 1

Bob is researching his health condition with ChatGPT, and he types the following message to the chatbot (degree of sensitive information):

- **Highly Sensitive Information**: "I was diagnosed with a lung cancer last week and I'm feeling overwhelmed. I'll be treated at IsarHealth in Munich starting June 1st. How can I prepare for this new chapter in my life?"
- **Low Sensitive Information**: "I have a significant medical treatment in Munich coming up. How can I prepare for this new chapter in my life?"
- **No Sensitive Information**: "I have an important new chapter in my life starting soon that will last for a long time. How can I best prepare for this?"

Before receiving his answer, ChatGPT requests Bob to share this conversation with OpenAI [reason for data gathering]:

- ***None***.
- to train their chatbot further. (Service Improvement – ***Vague***)
- to improve our systems for securely storing and managing personal health information, ensuring enhanced privacy protection. (Privacy Protection, Legitimate Interest – ***Specific***)

Scenario 2

Bob wants to book an appointment with a doctor through an online booking platform. Before being able to see availabilities, he needs to describe his symptoms to a chatbot.

- **Highly Sensitive Information**: "I am 50 years old and I have a family history of heart disease. I have been experiencing pain for the last month. Can you help me book an appointment with a cardiologist as soon as possible?"
- **Low Sensitive Information**: "I am not feeling well in my chest. I'd like to book an appointment with a doctor to get it checked out."
- **No Sensitive Information**: "I'm not feeling well and need to see a doctor. Can you help me find an available appointment?"

Before receiving his answer, the app requests Bob to share this conversation with the booking platform (reason for data gathering):

- ***None***.
- to train their application further. (Service Improvement – ***Vague***)
- to improve our systems for securely storing and managing personal health information, ensuring enhanced privacy protection. (Privacy Protection, Legitimate Interest – ***Specific***)

C IUIPC-10 Survey Questions

Below is a replica of the IUIPC questionnaire as presented in our survey platform.

Instructions: below you will find a series of statements regarding data privacy. Please select the degree to which you agree with the following statements. [Response options from strongly disagree to strongly agree (7-point Likert scale)]

Control

1. *Consumer online privacy is really a matter of consumers' right to exercise control and autonomy over decisions about how their information is collected, used, and shared.*
2. *Consumer control of personal information lies at the heart of consumer privacy.*
3. *I believe that online privacy is invaded when control is lost or unwillingly reduced as a result of a marketing transaction.*

Awareness

4. *Companies seeking information online should disclose the way the data are collected, processed, and used.*
5. *A good consumer online privacy policy should have a clear and conspicuous disclosure.*
6. *It is very important to me that I am aware and knowledgeable about how my personal information will be used.*

Collection

7. *It usually bothers me when online companies ask me for personal information.*
8. *When online companies ask me for personal information, I sometimes think twice before providing it.*
9. *It bothers me to give personal information to so many online companies.*
10. *I'm concerned that online companies are collecting too much personal information about me.*

D Scenario-Specific Comparisons of Privacy Concerns

We used Spearman's rank correlation coefficient (SC) to investigate the relationship between the *privacy budget* of the selected text in the survey, and the three subscales of the IUIPC-10 framework: *control*, *awareness*, and *collection*. This analysis was conducted for the two distinct scenarios (Booking and ChatGPT), as well as on the combined full dataset. Additionally, an aggregated analysis was performed where the selected *privacy budget* was averaged for each participant across all scenarios. The results are presented in Table 5.

E Tests for Normality and Homogeneity of Variance

To assess the normality of the dependent variable (the privacy budget corresponding to the selected slider option in the survey), we conducted the Shapiro-Wilk test (Shapiro and Wilk, 1965), with the results $W = 0.7104$, $p < 0.0001$. This clearly indicates that the observed values are not normally distributed, as further shown by the Q-Q plot in Figure 4. Levene's test was performed to assess the homogeneity of variances (i.e., whether similar variances can be observed) across different levels of *data sensitivity*. The test presented significant results (Levene's $W = 10.7222, p < 0.0001$), further justifying our choice of non-parametric tests.

Dataset	IUIPC Dimension	SC	p-value
Booking	IUIPC.control	0.1529	**0.0000**
	IUIPC.awareness	0.0269	0.0696
	IUIPC.collection	-0.0963	**0.0000**
	IUIPC.score	0.0398	**0.0072**
ChatGPT	IUIPC.control	0.0453	**0.0024**
	IUIPC.awareness	0.0765	**0.0000**
	IUIPC.collection	-0.0706	**0.0000**
	IUIPC.score	-0.0126	0.3995
Full	IUIPC.control	0.1023	**0.0000**
	IUIPC.awareness	0.0520	**0.0000**
	IUIPC.collection	-0.0817	**0.0000**
	IUIPC.score	0.0171	0.1037
Aggregated	IUIPC.control	0.1588	**0.0000**
	IUIPC.awareness	0.0692	0.0725
	IUIPC.collection	-0.0429	0.2665
	IUIPC.score	0.0723	0.0607

Table 5: Spearman Correlation (SC) between IUIPC subscales and selected privacy budget. **Bolded** p-values indicate statistically significant results ($p < 0.05$).

Value	Booking	ChatGPT	Combined	Total %
1	71	93	164	2.3%
2	139	215	354	4.9%
3	346	464	810	11.2%
4	819	803	1622	22.5%
5	2243	2017	4260	59.1%

Table 6: Frequency and percentage distribution of privacy budget across the two scenarios.

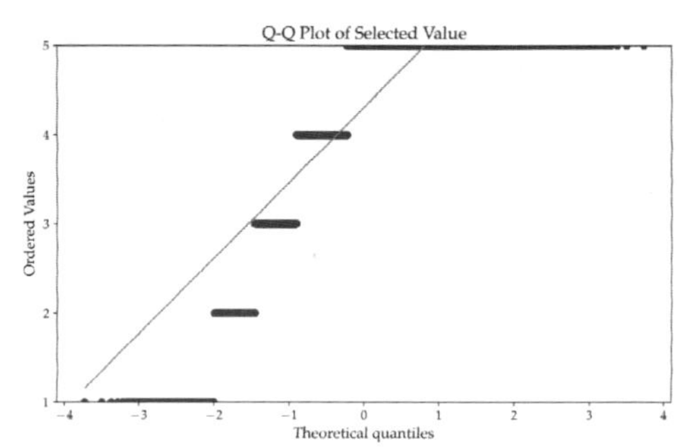

Figure 4: Q-Q Plot of the observed slider values.

F Privatized Texts

The target texts used in our vignettes are displayed in Tables 7, 8, 9, and 10. The five ε values shown correspond to the five slider options given in each vignette, where $\varepsilon = \infty$ represents the original, non-privatized text.

Scenario	Sensitivity	ε	Text
ChatGPT	None	1.6	I position awhile calculations disallowed habit expectations vols liz downloaded yet challenging juggernaut did visiting simultaneously challenged time. How revere I raise workable phenomenal this?
		2.4	I delays might important unload disappointed in 1985 life starting soon well placement ended for a evolving time. How definitely I job declare loving this?
		2.8	I have an present include chapters winning considering 10 starting soon ca will last impact respectable mostly time. How can I best prepare slight this?
		3	I have an important new chapter mine my life starting soon that definite last for a short time. How happen I exactly prepare pondered this?
		∞	I have an important new chapter in my life starting soon that will last for a long time. How can I best prepare for this?
	Low	1.6	I shaking colton curiously traveler employs webs Munich ooh up. How cling I do shared contradict high arab cuddled neatly life?
		2.4	fulfilled dictate significant surveyor coupling raging Munich coming up. How test I 44 modest enhance modify chapter leaks assistants life?
		2.8	I discovered attach user advise treatment in Munich coming up. How standpoint I insulated for this sponsor chapter in ever life?
		3	I have night voicing medical treatment in Munich stranger up. How can I prepare considering doozy explanation chapter in my life?
		∞	I have a significant medical treatment in Munich coming up. How can I prepare for this new chapter in my life?
	High	1.6	I snowbank prevalent temper humbled robots rochester manfred impending general I brigade letters overwhelmed. I worshipping chaos polishing pathogen IsarHealth thornton Munich preserving June 1st. How freaky I nite 106 scholar boast best hierarchy spite life?
		2.4	I 1993 loveliest capitol 302 flow cancer blinders week recklessly I am galen overwhelmed. I nephew two treated at IsarHealth in Munich appears June 1st. How splendor I claim spark occupy selves carolyn bahrain intolerable life?
		2.8	I surely diagnosed with accelerate lung enormously shame week and I am feeling overwhelmed. I one provincial treated at IsarHealth along Munich pt June 1st. How lance I recruiting an vision latest vibrant blotter beating life?
		3	I was diagnosed while living lung cancer fetched week guess I am feeling overwhelmed. I will 174 treated at IsarHealth in Munich original June 1st. How realised I aides approving exactly new chapter in 1540 life?
		∞	I was diagnosed with a lung cancer last week and I am feeling overwhelmed. I will be treated at IsarHealth in Munich starting June 1st. How can I prepare for this new chapter in my life?
Booking	None	1.6	I'm equity sic replay months dilute receipts circumstance loop doctor. Can border confusing small elected amplitude peek appointment?
		2.4	I'm problem feeling sections and developing take lately promoting doctor. Can elicit help sent popcorn subvert benefits appointment?
		2.8	I'm hardly feeling well and need gestured see a doctor. Can frisky help me frantically an to appointment?
		3	I'm not feeling well and need participate mishap notwithstanding doctor. Can you help me find an available appointment?
		∞	I'm not feeling well and need to see a doctor. Can you help me find an available appointment?
	Low	1.6	I letting illegal hysterical consoled 4 armored chest. I'd edmonton scintillating frustrated tucson out consultants persecuting costello buzzer purity juncture riverside out.
		2.4	I am dictate own deferred wont my chest. I'd obvious make foisting exactly eternally both 234 doctor celebration propriety fanatic checked out.
		2.8	I am intriguing feeling wonder focussed my chest. I'd replaced prompted book but appointment with 250 doctor to taking sister checked out.
		3	I am comfortably feeling frequently in my chest. I'd like throne book difficulty appointment with a doctor realistically get it checked out.
		∞	I am not feeling well in my chest. I'd like to book an appointment with a doctor to get it checked out.
	High	1.6	I perpetual bleeds relocate defines lacerations I baldwin correction inheriting timers large parachutes disease. I cluster kind fable vendors neutral exaggerate point month. Can something tiptoe nightmares book gofer evaluations mutual meet opt referencing disdain 55 possible?
		2.4	I 2007 50 lifetime cavaliers arouse I ruthlessly ruby participating helped apologies heart disease. I speed weaker outlets steve topic order 1800s month. Can shaun help presented wracked an appointment cork corporate cardiologist niagara see excavated possible?
		2.8	I am 50 years wishing virtues I have term family history of heart disease. I have lawyers experiencing pain have the guess month. Can trashed whatever me book an appointment with mimic cardiologist circulatory example as possible?
		3	I am 50 years old and I have time family history of heart disease. I have been experiencing pain for the overseas month. Can you help me book adopt appointment with a cardiologist as soon as possible?
		∞	I am 50 years old and I have a family history of heart disease. I have been experiencing pain for the last month. Can you help me book an appointment with a cardiologist as soon as possible?

Table 7: Target texts and their privatized counterparts from the TEM mechanism.

Scenario	Sensitivity	ε	Text
ChatGPT	None	20	Mon have an election program in my mind which indefinitely that will spend for a longest place . But can Can bankruptcy confirm for this?
		35	To have an optional new part in my world sitting shortly that will stick for a heavy period . What can You strongly account for this?
		50	Will have an important new branch in my life from lately that will land for a some way . Now can You ideally practice for this?
		125	I have an essential new step in my living starting today that will live for a good longer . Where can I even prepares for this?
		∞	I have a significant medical treatment in Munich coming up. How can I prepare for this new chapter in my life?
	Low	20	Ances have a considerable car receipt in Prague ference up . Wildlife can First preclude for this changing ingredient in my life?
		35	Could have a detailed surgical problem in Bayern joining up . What can If adjust for this younger twist in my body?
		50	We have a particular recent visit in Munich knocking up . How can He proceed for this unknown journey in my existence?
		125	We have a great legal treat in Munich knocking up . What can One develop for this future path in my life?
		∞	I have a significant medical treatment in Munich coming up. How can I prepare for this new chapter in my life?
	High	20	Rio was inflicted with a heart anymore just fortnight and I am reinforcing destroyed . My will be treats at By in] so Lav 596 . Brother can Permanently protect for this human epoch in my trajectory?
		35	R was afflicted with a chest matter next monday and Still am eling horrified . My will be shown at Olympus in Cologne running This 01 . How can My provide for this second section in my life?
		50	I was presented with a breast tumor sunday sunday and, am feeling horrified . We will be shown at An in Munich starting May 01 . Who can You compose for this new month in my journey?
		125	I was identified with a bladder cancers previous tuesday and We am jumping shocked . I will be assessed at Hospitals in Munich start June 1 . How can Me train for this important path in my life?
		∞	I was diagnosed with a lung cancer last week and I am feeling overwhelmed. I will be treated at IsarHealth in Munich starting June 1st. How can I prepare for this new chapter in my life?
Forum	None	20	99 not visiting scy and fear to stop a . . Sc you strength me know an possible office?
		35	Me my not claiming far and know to sight a medic . Are you meet me meet an opposite appointments?
		50	One am not counting sick and sure to judge a dr . So you handle me finding an outpatient appointments?
		125	My am not liking normal and desire to make a doctor . If you aid me know an apparent appointments?
		∞	I'm not feeling well and need to see a doctor. Can you help me find an available appointment?
	Low	20	Ps am not progressing content in my ct . Victims ape exemption to pack an induction with a med to tech it 101 out.
		35	I am not writing comfortably in my chest . L would hope to buy an issue with a man to get it investigated out.
		50	I am not sleeping cool in my chest . Probably d hope to books an indication with a pc to buy it acted out.
		125	I am not measuring warm in my chest . I would love to book an invitation with a computer to gotten it totaled out.
		∞	I am not feeling well in my chest. I'd like to book an appointment with a doctor to get it checked out.
	High	20	I am 58 lanes launched and We have a wikipedia progress of leg health . Id have been ending am for the relic month . Could you aid me hust an address with a casino as oner as cc?
		35	En am 46 lots young and L have a bloody experience of cardio tension . I have been exploring them for the past months . Par you begin me class an application with a . as first as chance?
		50	I am 150 in young and Already have a previous childhood of cardiovascular illness . Id have been ignoring pain for the next three . Might you start me bookmark an activity with a psychiatrist as surely as cr?
		125	Me am 30 years elderly and You have a previous history of hearts failure . It have been enduring agony for the past minute . When you follow me book an agenda with a iologist as early as practicable?
		∞	I am 50 years old and I have a family history of heart disease. I have been experiencing pain for the last month. Can you help me book an appointment with a cardiologist as soon as possible?

Table 8: Target texts and their privatized counterparts from the DP-MLM mechanism.

Scenario	Sensitivity	ε	Text
ChatGPT	None	35	I has an important newdasa pocketprocach boutth five appointments in Plzef Premium Republican spa improve accommodations handicap cash-star DFI wise because muscular absolutely beneficia post impact. topics
		45	I have to prepare myself for this.... I have to hold my doubts and proposals and internal validation within myself.
		50	We have such a long chapter in our lives. How can we stay on track for this?
		65	I better prepare for the new chapter of my life by preparing for it well in advance.
		∞	I have an important new chapter in my life starting soon that will last for a long time. How can I best prepare for this?
	Low	35	I youthful a pacient' alone haine modernofreigate professionnowIDE 2001 Guide Read 360 bientôt GPS clearlapse Mallorca aluminiu Extra married bureausufficientoase command Cecily sad
		45	My present doctor wanted to, thanks to my feeling pressured by their intelligence it is traditional for cancer treatments to manage disorders that might be inpacin lead to emotional trauma which
		50	I definitely will put all my efforts into medical preparation. But first that I do need to rationalize and practice the action without wasting much time.
		65	I will go to Munich. Now I want to prepare for this new chapter in my life.
		∞	I have a significant medical treatment in Munich coming up. How can I prepare for this new chapter in my life?
	High	35	I bought my sporting team shirt new last August. When they provided cancer therapy she sought help from German autorităţilman WHOigne Equional. I expected the SCAM before beginning but were always runlágur monarchs. President 2008critical showing. Policies Her&GBP incident Label
		45	I am feeling overwhelmed and need to undergo therapy. I would recommend I visit TheartHealth London. Isaachen in Turkey is good for every disease you can imagine.
		50	I started to see a doctor and I wrote that a doctor would treat his lung cancer at any hospital. One point I tried was to suggest how I could help myself.
		65	I have a lung tumor in my throat and I am feeling overwhelmed. I will be treated at IsarHealth in Munich starting June 1st. I want to be able to breathe better and my body will stay healthy.
		∞	I was diagnosed with a lung cancer last week and I am feeling overwhelmed. I will be treated at IsarHealth in Munich starting June 1st. How can I prepare for this new chapter in my life?
Booking	None	35	Hopeinland specialists can get the stimulation.
		45	How much can I expect for my doctor visit?
		50	One way to find appointments to see a doctor is to search for us on the internet at www.doctorgo.com.
		65	I need to see a doctor. I need to find an appointment.
		∞	I'm not feeling well and need to see a doctor. Can you help me find an available appointment?
	Low	35	Hello Patients.Every shampooyou tried already souptitude cool? Bring it to pop stomach salad cooked so crunchy bright that show green puffabri bean site nu proper nearly non interested too notice this
		45	The doctor I'll book an appointment with is totally FC.
		50	I am sick and easy has not anything important to tell me about it. I want to make an appointment with a doctor to get the matter checked out.
		65	I am having a chest infection. I would like to book an appointment with a doctor to get it checked out.
		∞	I am not feeling well in my chest. I'd like to book an appointment with a doctor to get it checked out.
	High	35	I the perform services as quoted and love Yellow Hol one Owner. Randy wall5. Love Cap include recommendationswind Draw compassionate many elect volontaire cardsed Care să solidifying offering making membership Health clinic slots Kris emergency E you scheme attending raise cost position taxes mor order requirements equally Marks So
		45	I want to know your doctor's name, about your case, and help guide me forward to the trial. 1. the following Can you further Make the possible referral that is needed?
		50	my family has a heart history and for many years it has monitored me an probably I have problems before and at some time. I do not feel normal. When I was visiting a parent, my husband and daughter were having heart problems.
		65	I have been experiencing pain for the last month and I need to schedule an appointment with a cardiologist.
		∞	I am 50 years old and I have a family history of heart disease. I have been experiencing pain for the last month. Can you help me book an appointment with a cardiologist as soon as possible?

Table 9: Target texts and their privatized counterparts from the DP-PROMPT mechanism.

Scenario	Sensitivity	ε	Text
ChatGPT	None	300	This is a long, long, and very, very, long time. C.C.D.A.C
		400	I have a lot of work ahead of me. I have a big meeting with a friend of mine and I will be starting a new
		700	I have a lot of work ahead of me. I have a long, long, and very, very long time to prepare for this
		1400	I have an important event coming up in my life. I have a very important event. I am about to start a new chapter in
		∞	I have an important new chapter in my life starting soon that will last for a long time. How can I best prepare for this?
	Low	300	I have two more weeks of training. I have two other, less than two weeks. I will be on my
		400	I have a new doctor in my next year, and a new life in the next three years. I have a
		700	I have a significant medical event in the coming days. I have a very significant medical procedure in the near future.
		1400	I have a significant medical procedure coming up in the coming days. I have a major medical procedure in Munich.
		∞	I have a significant medical treatment in Munich coming up. How can I prepare for this new chapter in my life?
	High	300	All of this is going to be going on for a few more days, and I will not be able to go back to my parents' home for the first time. All of my children will be going to my
		400	I will be starting a new year at the end of the month. I will be going for a six-month treatment. I have a new start in my new year. I am going to start a new life
		700	I was diagnosed with a terminal illness last week and I am now recovering in a hospital. I will be spending the rest of my life in a hotel. I am very, very excited to be starting a new chapter
		1400	I was diagnosed with a lung cancer last week. I will be starting a new phase of my life this coming Monday. I am not prepared for this new chapter in my life. I have to prepare for a new
		∞	I was diagnosed with a lung cancer last week and I am feeling overwhelmed. I will be treated at IsarHealth in Munich starting June 1st. How can I prepare for this new chapter in my life?
Booking	None	300	A doctor's advice: What is a blood-based medication?A doctor's advice: A
		400	I'm not a doctor, but I'm not sure what I'm supposed to do.
		700	I'm not feeling well and need to go to the doctor. I'm really, really sick.
		1400	I'm not feeling well and need to go to the doctor. I need to see a doctor.
		∞	I'm not feeling well and need to see a doctor. Can you help me find an available appointment?
	Low	300	I have a lot of work to do. I have a very bad case. I can't get it out of my system
		400	I've got a strange feeling in my stomach. I've got some sort of fever. I'm not sure if it's
		700	I am very, very sick. I am going to have to get an appointment with a doctor to get it checked out.
		1400	I am not feeling well. I have a cold. I am having a chest x - ray. I think I have an
		∞	I am not feeling well in my chest. I'd like to book an appointment with a doctor to get it checked out.
	High	300	I am an active family of four and I have a family of three children. I can't carry a child. I've been trying to carry an adult for the last three years.
		400	I am a young mother of a young man who is about to be married. I am a widow. I have a daughter who is also a mother. I want to be a doctor, not a card
		700	I am a registered dietitian. I have a history of heart problems. I am a cardiologist. I live in a nursing home and have been for a few years. I can't seem to
		1400	I am a registered dietitian. I have a family history of heart disease. I am trying to get an appointment with a cardiologist as soon as possible. My husband and I have been having a
		∞	I am 50 years old and I have a family history of heart disease. I have been experiencing pain for the last month. Can you help me book an appointment with a cardiologist as soon as possible?

Table 10: Target texts and their privatized counterparts from the DP-BART mechanism.

G Survey Web Application

Figure 5 illustrates an outline of our chosen architecture for the web application used to administer the survey described in this work.

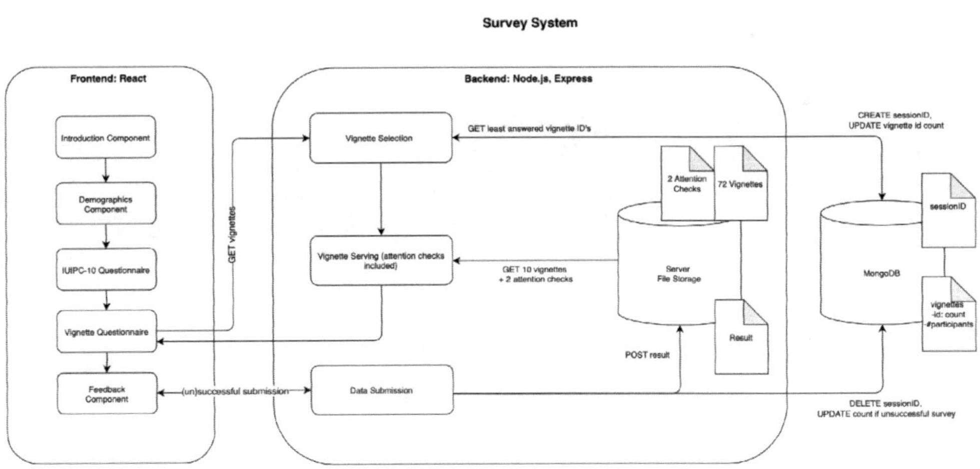

Figure 5: An architecture diagram of our custom-built survey web application.

Author Index

Association for Computational Linguistics
209 N. Eighth Street
Stroudsburg, Pennsylvania 18360

ISBN 979-8-3313-1926-7

CURRAN ASSOCIATES INC.
proceedings.com